Amateurs and Professionals in Post-War British Sport

Editors

ADRIAN SMITH

University of Southampton New College

DILWYN PORTER

University College Worcester

FRANK CASS
LONDON • PORTLAND, OR

First published in 2000 in Great Britain by
FRANK CASS PUBLISHERS
Newbury House, 900 Eastern Avenue, London IG2 7HH

and in the United States of America by
FRANK CASS PUBLISHERS
c/o ISBS, 5804 N.E. Hassalo Street
Portland, OR 97213-3644

Website www.frankcass.com

British Library Cataloguing in Publication Data

Amateurs and professionals in post war British sport. –
(British politics and society)
1. Professional sports – Great Britain – History – 20th
century 2. Athletes – Great Britain
I. Smith, Adrian II. Porter, Dilwyn, 1947–
796'.042'0941

ISBN 0 7146 5086 2 (cloth)
ISBN 0 7146 8127 X (paper)
ISSN 1467-1441

Library of Congress Cataloging-in-Publication Data:

Amateurs and professionals in post-war British sport / editors, Adrian
Smith, Dilwyn Porter.
     p. cm. – (British politics and society, ISSN 1467-1441)
Includes bibliographical references and index.
ISBN 0-7146-5086-2 (cloth) – ISBN 0-7146-8127-X (pbk.)
1. Sports–Great Britain–History–20th century. I. Smith, Adrian,
1952– II. Porter, Dilwyn, 1947– III. Series.
GV605 .A54 2000
796'.0941'09045-dc21   00-055579

This group of studies first appeared in a special issue of Contemporary British History,
ISSN 1361-9462, Vol.14, No.2 (Summer 2000) published by Frank Cass and Co. Ltd.

Printed in Great Britain by
Antony Rowe Ltd., Chippenham, Wiltshire.

Contents

Introduction

DILWYN PORTER and ADRIAN SMITH

Historians, even social historians, were once inclined to consign any consideration of sport to the margins. A few, like Asa Briggs, did grasp the extent to which it preoccupied the British public and empathised accordingly. 'To many Englishmen', Briggs observed in the mid-1950s, 'football is not an element in national culture but life itself.'[1] But, in general, historians have only recently begun to acknowledge the important part that sport often played in people's lives, not to mention its wider economic, social and political significance. A.J.P. Taylor's *English History 1914–1945*, published in 1965, though it incorporated a chapter promisingly entitled 'Half Time', devoted only one of its 650 or so pages to sport, squeezed in alongside the cinema and the *palais de danse* as one of the popular entertainments of the period. Kenneth Morgan's *The People's Peace*, covering the period from 1945 to 1989, published a quarter of a century later, was similarly reticent on the subject.[2] In works such as these, the inquisitive lay reader, seeking enlightenment from these magisterial sources, finds an account of the recent past that barely acknowledges a world in which it is not uncommon to read the back page of a newspaper first. It is now something of a shock to open Arthur Marwick's contribution to the *Pelican Social History of Britain* series, first published in 1982, and to discover just one paragraph concerned with sport.[3] This is, in itself, an indication of the extent to which historians have come to embrace this aspect of past experience over the last 20 years.

Ross McKibbin's *Classes and Cultures: England 1918–1951*, with its chapter on 'The Sporting Life' acknowledging sport as 'one of the most powerful of England's civil cultures', is indicative of the way in which attitudes have changed.[4] In part this developing trend reflects the emergence of the History of Sport as a significant sub-division of academic labour. Encouraged by ground-breaking work in Australia and the US, pioneers such as Tony Mason, J.A. Mangan, Richard Holt and Wray Vamplew set up a base from which a small army of graduate researchers has advanced into territory that historians were once content to leave to the gentlemanly chronicler of past sporting triumphs and the anoraked statistician. Their work in the 1970s and 1980s helped to establish the History of Sport as a 'vibrant and productive subject for scholarly research', meriting the serious attention of graduate researchers and undergraduate students.[5] But, in a wider sense their most important contribution to historiography, as Martin Polley has suggested, has been to embed sport in an appropriate economic, social and political context. This has enabled historians to make connections and to nail once and for all the idea that sport 'has nothing to do with anything else'.[6] 'The point,' as one historian of English football has observed, '... is not to describe football matches but to study what football meant and why it mattered.'[7]

The essays in this collection, focusing on various aspects of amateurism and professionalism in British sport since 1945, reflect this tendency. Definitions of 'amateur' and 'professional', though legalistic in form, were rooted in lived experience, contingent on class and status, and subject to change over time. An amateur was expected to participate for the love of the game, whereas a professional received some form of remuneration, but in practice it was rather more complicated. Definitions were often blurred and there was variation from one sport to another. Referring in 1960 to the contentious issue of the payment of travelling and subsistence expenses to amateurs, the Wolfenden Committee noted a lack of uniformity, acknowledging that each governing body might 'draw its arbitrary line where it believes that the best interests of its sport require that it should be drawn'. This led to confusion, as Tony Pawson, distinguished amateur cricketer, footballer and fly-fisherman, argued a few years later. 'Amateur rules', it seemed, varied like detergents, 'from the whiter than white of fencing to the Brand X of tennis, with its registered players – or paid amateurs'.[8] Neither was it easy to distinguish between an amateur and a professional by the manner in which they competed. As David Miller of *The Daily Telegraph*, observed recently: 'Many of the most sportsmanlike competitors I have known have been professionals, and some of the worst have been amateurs.'[9] National Hunt jockey John

Francome's refusal to ride once he had equalled the number of winners ridden by the injured Peter Scudamore in 1982, thus denying himself the professional jockeys' championship, comes to mind here.

Definitions of amateur and professional status generally dated from the nineteenth century when gentlemen with the leisure, money and inclination to pursue their sporting interests were confronted by a challenge from below. The Amateur Athletic Club, predecessor of the Amateur Athletic Association, found it necessary in 1866 to deny membership to 'mechanics', 'artisans' and 'labourers'. Such measures, later matched, for example, in rowing, helped to ensure that opportunities for overturning the existing social order in sporting competition were limited. The subsequent development of sport as business, however, in which the achievement of success was a commercial necessity, made it increasingly difficult to sustain social exclusion in this form. It encouraged entrepreneurs who sought profit and prestige from sport to tap reserves of working-class talent, raising the possibility that the apparently effortless superiority of the gentleman might evaporate as mechanics, artisans and labourers, selected for their proficiency at sport and paid accordingly, applied themselves to their work. From the perspective of the late twentieth century, the source of an athlete's income might seem of little importance: 'If a competitor is preparing full time to compete in the Olympic Games, it is irrelevant…whether he or she is supported by wealthy parents, self-interested college, government grant or commercial sponsorship.'[10] But, in the nineteenth century, and on into the mid-twentieth, such distinctions remained crucial in that they helped to maintain a pre-existing set of social relations. Regulation separating the amateur from the professional, evidenced in its most extreme form after rugby's great schism in 1895, often served to preclude or circumscribe class competition in sport. And, where invidious comparison with the artisan professional remained a possibility, the prestige of the gentleman amateur was shored up by snobbery and social convention. When 'Plum' Warner of the Marylebone Cricket Club (MCC) remarked that Jack Hobbs, Surrey and England professional, played cricket 'like an amateur', it was no doubt intended as a compliment.

'Sport,' as Martin Polley has argued, 'is not passive; it co-exists with its society, and, for post-war Britain, it is an important component of that society.'[11] Changes in society have impacted on sport and those who participate in it as competitors, administrators and spectators. During the period under consideration here the apparatus of regulation and convention sustaining the distinction between amateur and professional began to crumble. The status attached to amateurism, derived from deeply-rooted ideas relating to the innate superiority of those who could afford, if they chose, to play the game for its own sake, was subjected increasingly to critical scrutiny. In the late 1950s and early 1960s, as 'the Establishment' came under attack from those who sought to modernise Britain and its institutions, the idea that the gentlemanly amateur should outrank the paid professional, one of the most conspicuous buttresses of an outmoded class system, became unfashionable. The non-specialist 'amateur', whether a Foreign Office mandarin, a captain of industry or the leader of an under-performing side in cricket's County Championship, was deemed to be a factor in Britain's fall from Great Power status. There was, in short, a reaction against being officered 'by birth and breeding' and recognition that 'modern professional management' was an essential prerequisite of sustainable economic growth.[12] In these circumstances regulations and conventions relating to amateurism and professionalism in sport dating from the nineteenth century were drawn into political discourse. Where they could no longer be sustained their abandonment, as Harold Wilson grasped, was symbolic of the kind of change that was necessary if Britain was going to match the performance of its more dynamic competitors. 'In a country…which has now begun to take cricket seriously enough for even the MCC to abolish the distinction between Gentlemen and Players, we are still prepared to allow too much of British industry, on which alone we depend to prevent this country becoming a second-class power, to be officered from the pages of *Debrett*.'[13] By the end of the 1960s there were some clear indications that attitudes had changed. Informed by a triumphant executive that his commercial television company had secured the rights to cover the 1968 Olympics, Lew Grade is said to have responded: 'That's amateurs, isn't it? We don't want amateurs. Get professionals.'[14]

The first two essays in this collection examine the resilience of the amateur ideal as it came under pressure in the post-war period. In association football, the most commercialised of British sports, the technical supremacy of the professional had been established by the start of the twentieth century. Though there was nothing to prevent an amateur competing alongside and against professionals few were capable of making the grade at the highest level.[15] Competition, with the notable exception of the Football Association (FA) Challenge Cup, was organised on different levels, with amateurs and professionals playing in segregated leagues. Dilwyn Porter examines the meteoric rise and fall of Pegasus Football Club, a true-blue amateur team drawing its playing strength from the old universities, in its period context. Pegasus was more than an exotic throwback to an earlier period when the gentleman amateur had predominated, to the days when C.B. Fry and other Corinthian heroes had been able to take on the professionals and win. For the club's founder and principal moving spirit, Harold Thompson, as well as for Stanley Rous at the FA, Pegasus represented an attempt to counter what were perceived to be negative images emanating from an over-commercialised professional game and the cynical 'shamateurism' then prevailing in the senior amateur leagues. Despite achieving spectacular and unexpected success in the early 1950s the Pegasus project was abandoned in 1963, by which time even Thompson had come to realise that it was neither practical nor desirable to maintain the nineteenth century distinction between amateur and professional.

Stephen Wagg's essay examines the tradition of amateur captaincy in English county cricket in the 20 years or so before the distinction between gentlemen and players was cast aside in 1963. What emerges here is the tenacity with which those who ran the first class game clung to the idea that there were officers and gentlemen to be found who were equipped to lead teams comprising mainly professionals, whatever their own sometimes embarrassingly manifest technical deficiencies with bat and ball. There is, it seems, a danger in assuming that progress towards the happy day in 1963 when Lords embraced modernisation was either steady or inevitable. Significant milestones along the way, such as Leicestershire's appointment of a professional captain in 1935, transpire, on close examination, to have been dictated by expediency rather than any heartfelt desire to ride with the tide of social change. County clubs that appeared to be in the vanguard of modernisation, like Warwickshire, having appointed a professional, Tom Dollery, to lead the side in 1948, later retreated from this position, appointing an amateur, M.J.K. Smith, to the captaincy in 1957. Where professionals led it was often by default. 'It would be a mistake,' as one left-wing newspaper observed in 1953, 'to underestimate the Old School Tie.' Traditionalists had not taken kindly to Len Hutton, the first professional to lead England, and the test selectors still retained 'the power to ruin everything by appointing an amateur as captain'.[16] Reform, when it came, was prompted by an intense crisis as the game hovered on the edge of a financial abyss from which it was subsequently rescued by commercial sponsorship. In the meantime a good deal of port and Stilton was consumed by the commissioned officers of the county game in the comfort of their well-appointed dressing rooms.

It is evident that changes in British society generally modified the nature of amateurism in both soccer and cricket. By the 1950s, for example, many amateur captains were receiving salaries from county clubs for services rendered in various administrative capacities. Thus the form, if not the substance, was preserved. Professionalism was similarly subject to modification, as Ray Physick and Richard Holt demonstrate in their account of relations between the tournament golfer and the Professional Golfers Association (PGA) between 1945 and 1975. As tournament golf became more commercialised, sustaining a new generation of star players who could earn a good living without enduring a lifetime of subservience to an established club and its committee, the PGA, founded in 1901 to represent the interests of the run-of-the-mill club pro, was found wanting. Tournament golfers, such as Henry Cotton and Dai Rees, became increasingly critical of the PGA from the mid-1950s, in effect distancing themselves and their colleagues from the idea of the professional golfer as a skilled artisan employed to provide a specialist service to club members. Thereafter, as the flow of money derived from media coverage and commercial sponsorship of tournaments increased year by year, the pressures on the PGA multiplied. The Association survived but in a drastically modified form, its two 'divisions' after 1976 representing an explicit acknowledgement of the way in which the structure of the profession had changed over the previous 20 years or so.

Martin Polley traces the changing face of post-war British athletics. Here again is an ageing group of well-intentioned if misguided middle- and upper-class volunteers endeavouring to defend a set of obsolescent values. Such values, however laudable in their day, were embodied in a set of rules and regulations which increasingly lacked credibility, and generated great resentment whenever the authorities attempted to enforce them. It is hard to feel sympathy for the senior officials of the Amateur Athletic Association (AAA) when as a body they were largely self-selecting and shamelessly enjoyed the perks and privileges of their position. Athletes like Gordon Pirie and Derek Ibbotson were sporting meritocrats, eager to exploit their natural talent to achieve success on the track and secure recognition off it. They took their sport seriously – witness the severity of their training schedules. 'Varsity runners' like Roger Bannister, Chris Chataway and Chris Brasher shared a similar determination to break records and win medals. They trained hard, witness their outstanding achievements between 1954 and 1956. Nevertheless, that very success was seen as justifying the amateur/public school assumption that guts and 'character' were the secret of successful middle-distance running. Bannister, Chataway and Brasher were establishment heroes, for all the latter's subsequent railings at the reluctance of the AAA to reform. Denied privileged upbringings, Pirie and Ibbotson demonstrated an ambition and lack of deference which within a generation would be taken for granted. Yet in the late 1950s and early 1960s such behaviour was still seen as presumptuous and as an unashamedly working-class challenge to what within the closed world of British athletics constituted the established order. Polley demonstrates how the first athletes familiar to a television audience laid the foundation for Alan Pascoe, David Hemery, Lynn Davies and other Olympians to challenge the authority of the sport's ruling bodies. The 1970s witnessed significant shifts in attitude, not least with reference to the status and position of women athletes in Britain, but the key changes were invariably a response to global developments, most notably the 1981 acceptance of payment for performance. The arrival of professional athletics coincided with another golden era in British middle-distance running: Steve Ovett, Seb Coe and Steve Cram readily acknowledged their debt to the single-minded pioneers of an earlier generation.

As Ross McKibbin argued in relation to the period before 1950, horse-racing was a sport that 'successfully and consciously bridged England's rural past and its urban-industrial present'.[17] Wray Vamplew's study of the contemporary professional jockey suggests that this bridge remains in place, even in a largely post-industrial, suburban era. Some aspects of the occupational culture which professional jockeys inhabit are clearly long established and dictated by the technical requirements of the sport. The flat-racing jockey of the late twentieth century may not resort to the crude purgative prescribed for Fred Archer a hundred years earlier but he remains tied to a regime which ensures that weight is maintained at an unnaturally low level. This means that eating disorders remain a significant occupational hazard, not to mention the still considerable risk of being injured during a race. Professional jockeys, Vamplew concludes, are 'extraordinary sportspersons' yet, in their relationship with both the owners of racehorses and those who administer the sport, they have only recently gained the respect that is their due. It remains surprising, even shocking, to discover that the likes of Willie Carson and Eddie Hide were addressed by their surnames and required to stand to attention by the stewards at York as recently as 1982. Yet the occupational culture of the professional jockey has been significantly modified, partly through the collective efforts of jockeys themselves, partly through the emergence of millionaire superstars such as Frankie Dettori.

In 1995 rugby union upstaged the centenary celebrations of rugby league by declaring the game open. In the southern hemisphere Australia, New Zealand and South Africa took the Murdoch dollar and effortlessly entered the professional era. At all levels of the game the demands of the national squad were seen as paramount, with leading players centrally contracted. In Europe the old order prevailed, and current internationals were still expected to honour their club contracts. This tension was most evident in England, a nation desperate for World Cup success but handicapped by fundamental differences between the senior sides and the governing body. The Rugby Football Union (RFU) was itself deeply split between corporate modernisers and the guardians of the grassroots – amateur – game. Twickenham's critics saw the RFU's moratorium on professionalism as the root cause of British rugby's five-year failure to secure success both on and off the pitch: the vacuum created during the 1995–96 season was speedily filled by entrepreneurs, not all of whom had the capital and/or knowledge of the game to ensure the long-term survival of their chosen team. The top English clubs' eagerness to maximise television revenue and corporate sponsorship put added pressure upon the RFU to break with the other Home Nations and negotiate a separate television deal with Sky. The resulting mayhem did little to enhance club rugby's chances of becoming a mass spectator sport. The professional game may boast faster, fitter and more skilful players, but off the field commercial viability remains as elusive as ever. In the final essay Adrian Smith traces the bemusing and turbulent history of English rugby union in the 1990s. This long and complex story ends with the disappointment of Wales 1999, when once again a southern hemisphere team lifted the World Cup. Yet, despite the England team failing to progress beyond the quarter-final, the RFU and the elite clubs entered the twenty-first century still showing no sign of agreement on the future structure and direction of the game.

The sight of English rugby selling its soul for £87.5 million was one of the less edifying examples of post-war British sport warmly embracing television. The first three decades of mass TV audiences witnessed an exponential growth in the coverage of sport, but the arrival of satellite television and a further two terrestrial channels offered even the most esoteric of athletic pursuits its 15 minutes of fame. Throughout much of the twentieth century broadcasters, sponsors and advertisers enjoyed varying degrees of influence over genuinely global sports, most especially football, but in the 1990s they began seriously calling the shots. The speed with which rugby union embraced professionalism – in Britain at appalling cost in terms of the game's image and reputation – highlighted the degree to which major sports had become dependent upon sponsorship and the sale of broadcasting rights. Only at the end of the decade did sports executives begin to appreciate just how much satellite television needed premium events in order to recruit fresh subscribers, let alone retain high-spending advertisers. The ITV stations and Channel 4 were similarly dependent on advertising revenue, while a beleaguered post-Birt BBC boosted its sports budget in order to justify retention of the licence fee. At the same time a growing number of governing bodies recognised that unilateral multi-million pound deals with Sky offered only short-term advantage if their sport no longer enjoyed maximum exposure. Thus, both cricket and rugby union looked to terrestrial television as the most effective means of reviving their appeal among non-specialist sports fans.

The symbiotic relationship between sport and television has become a key element of life in Britain at the start of the twentieth-first century, which no social commentator would be so short-sighted as to ignore. Just as elsewhere in the world, sport has become a powerful and all-pervasive force – witness the eagerness with which politicians in the 1990s discovered the Premiership. The football phenomenon is unprecedented, but Premier League players are by no means unique in discovering that global recognition and super salaries have their price. For the professional sports person forever in the public eye, one regrettable incident and a reputation can be destroyed or severely damaged: the rewards can be enormous, both financially and in terms of personal satisfaction and achievement, but the pressures have never been greater.

NOTES

1. Asa Briggs, 'Football and Culture', *Encounter*, 16 Jan. 1955, p.69.
2. A.J.P. Taylor, *English History 1914–1945* (Oxford: OUP, 1965), p.313; Kenneth O. Morgan, *The People's Peace: British History 1945–1989* (Oxford: OUP, 1990), pp.257–8. There are other fleeting references to sport in Morgan's book but only where it impinges on politics.
3. Arthur Marwick, *British Society since 1945* (Harmondsworth: Penguin Books, 1982), p.156.
4. Ross McKibbin, *Classes and Cultures: England 1918–1951* (Oxford: OUP, 1998), pp.332–85.
5. Matthew Taylor, 'Football archives and the historian', *Business Archives*, Vol.78 (November 1978), p.1.
6. See Martin Polley, *Moving the Goalposts: a History of Sport and Society Since 1945* (London: Routledge: 1998), pp.4–5.
7. Nicholas Fishwick, *English Football and Society, 1910–1950* (Manchester: MUP, 1989), pp.xi–xii.
8. *Sport and the Community: The Report of the Wolfenden Committee on Sport* (London: Central Council of Physical Recreation, 1960), pp.66–7; Tony Pawson, 'Sweeping under the carpet', *The Observer*, 8 Dec. 1963.
9. David Miller, 'Professionalism and the Olympic Ideal', in David Welch (ed.), *The Daily Telegraph Century of Sport* (London: Macmillan, 1998), pp.130–31.
10. Miller, 'Professionalism'.
11. Polley, *Moving the Goalposts*, p.6.
12. John Vaizey, 'The Public Schools', in Hugh Thomas (ed.), *The Establishment* (London: Anthony Blond, 1959), p.21; *Attitudes in British Management: A PEP Report* (Harmondsworth: Penguin Books, 1966), pp. 60–62. See also the analysis of 'the amateur ideal' in Anthony Sampson, *Anatomy of Britain* (London: Hodder and Stoughton, 1962), pp.631–2. Jeremy Paxman has remarked on 'the mountains of literature chronicling the decline of Britain in the twentieth century [which] deal with the inadequacies of the amateur British civil service'; Jeremy Paxman, *Friends in High Places: Who Runs Britain?* (Harmondsworth: Penguin Books, 1991), p.133.
13. Speech at the Royal Albert Hall, 5 Apr. 1964, in *The New Britain: Labour's Plan outlined by Harold Wilson* (Harmondsworth: Penguin Books, 1964), pp.131–2.
14. Philip Purser, obituary for Bill Ward, *The Guardian*, 26 Oct. 1999.
15. For the recollections of an amateur who played First Division football for Charlton Athletic see Tony Pawson, 'All-rounder who has done it all', *The Observer*, 19 Dec. 1999.
16. *The Daily Worker*, 1 Jan, 1953.
17. McKibbin, *Classes and Cultures*, p.353.

Amateur Football in England, 1948–63: The Pegasus Phenomenon

DILWYN PORTER

As a soccer romance the story of Pegasus FC takes some beating. Founded in May 1948, and taking the field for the first time in December, the combined Oxford and Cambridge Universities side rapidly established itself as a major power in English amateur football. Only three years after it had been formed Pegasus were playing at Wembley in the final of the Football Association's [FA] Amateur Cup in front of 100,000 people, an attendance record for an amateur football match. Winners of the Amateur Cup in 1951, and again in 1953, they were widely admired for their intelligent application of the fluent 'push and run' style favoured by Arthur Rowe's successful Tottenham Hotspur side of the same era. Though the peaks of achievement scaled between 1948 and 1953 were not reached again there is no doubt that Pegasus left a significant mark. For Geoffrey Green, football correspondent of *The Times*, Pegasus was one of the outstanding clubs of the 1950s, as important in its own sphere as Real Madrid or Manchester United in theirs.[1]

Yet it was not simply a matter of how well Pegasus played the game. The club also attracted support and goodwill on account of its true-blue amateurism, its successes warming the hearts of those who had mourned the passing of the famous Corinthians and the 'spirit' with which they had been associated. Pegasus, as Green recalled, was seen as the heir to this tradition and its players 'were openly spoken of as the new Corinthians'. It is not easy to discern exactly what contemporary references to the Corinthian spirit implied beyond playing the game for its own sake in a manner which reflected creditably on gentlemen who had enjoyed the benefits of a good school and one or other of the ancient universities. But it is clear that a degree of aristocratic swagger was expected, with an emphasis on attack rather than defence. Writing of R.E. ('Tip') Foster, a celebrated Corinthian of the early 1900s, C.B. Fry observed that 'his feet had, as it were, the Oxford accent'.[2] This touch of class, it seemed, was what had distinguished the Corinthians from their professional counterparts. Edward Grayson, the most sympathetic twentieth-century chronicler of the old Corinthians, noted the 'intelligent nonchalance' of their football. 'In their tailored shirts and well-cut shorts,' he added, 'they brought a quality and culture to the game which, since their leisure and talents were dimmed by the First World War, Pegasus alone have recaptured.'[3]

It would be an injustice, however, to regard Pegasus as simply a late flowering of the Corinthian spirit, a throwback to an era of elite amateurism when sport 'had not only to be played in good spirit, it had to be played with style'.[4] Interviews with former players, along with Ken Shearwood's intimate history of the club, leave the impression that they simply sought enjoyment from playing in congenial company at the highest level of the amateur game, giving little thought to the glory that was Corinth.[5] Though H.W. ('Tommy') Thompson of St John's College, Oxford, the club's founder, was not uninfluenced by such considerations, Pegasus is best understood in its more immediate historical setting as a phenomenon of the 1940s and 1950s. 'Comparisons between Pegasus and the Corinthians are rather too obvious and might be misleading,' Roland Allen observed in *The Sunday Times* after their first Amateur Cup triumph. 'Pegasus have to create their own history in a different sort of football world.'[6] In raising the profile of the game at the old universities, where it had lived long in the shadow of rugby union, Pegasus struck an important blow against the anti-soccer prejudice that had come to prevail amongst England's middle classes. Soccer was 'a gentleman's game played by hooligans': thus ran the conventional wisdom. By promoting amateurism in its traditional form, Pegasus supplied an antidote to those aspects of professionalism that were said to be bringing soccer into disrepute. Any success it achieved sent out the message that soccer was a game at which both Oxbridge undergraduates and working-class heroes could excel. All this carried weight with the FA's secretary, Stanley Rous, who had had been obliged to switch to rugby while

2

teaching at Watford Grammar School in the 1920s. In short, Pegasus was assigned an educational role. It was expected to lead by example, stiffening the resolve of those schools that had hitherto resisted the drift to rugby. And if, along the way, Pegasus was able to achieve a moral victory or two in the FA's long-running campaign against 'shamateurism', so much the better. The intention here is to set Corinthian rhetoric aside and locate this account of Pegasus, its rise to prominence and its subsequent decline, in an appropriate mid twentieth-century context.

Beginnings

Though Oxford and Cambridge were inclined to disagree as to when and where the idea of a joint universities side had first been floated it seems clear that Thompson was canvassing support in the spring of 1948. A number of Oxford-based Pegasus players remembered a journey with the university team to Birmingham as being of particular significance: 'The suggestion [was] … made by Dr H.W. Thompson as our train left Banbury and discussed by the players thoroughly.'[7] Contact with Cambridge was established and a meeting 'to discuss the formation of a joint Oxford and Cambridge Universities Association Football Club' was held in London in May 1948. This meeting, attended by Thompson, John Tanner and Denis Saunders from Oxford, by Douglas Insole and G.H.G. Doggart from Cambridge, and by three representatives from the Corinthian-Casuals club, appears to have achieved everything for which Thompson could have hoped. Insole proposed that a joint club be formed and it was agreed that membership was open to all members of both Oxford University (OUAFC) and Cambridge University (CUAFC) clubs on payment of 2/6d (12½p). The suggestion that the new club should be named 'Pegasus', the winged horse of Greek mythology representing an amalgam of the 'Centaurs' (Oxford) and the 'Falcons' (Cambridge), was carried unanimously and a constitution, previously drafted by Thompson, was 'provisionally accepted'. This included the so-called 'one year rule', designed primarily to protect the interests of Corinthian-Casuals, the anticipated final destination of most Oxford and Cambridge players. The intended effect of the rule was to restrict the pool from which Pegasus could select to players at university and those in their first year after university. Thompson agreed to act as honorary secretary and treasurer until such time as officers were formally elected.[8]

There seems no doubt as to who was in the driving-seat at this stage. Thompson, an Oxford blue in 1928–29 and the Oxford University representative on the FA's Council, was setting the pace. By the start of July arrangements were in hand for the first formal meeting of the new club to take place in London in October. With this achieved Thompson set about organising support for a bid to secure entry on favourable terms into the high-profile Amateur Cup competition in 1948–49. This required the approval of the FA's Amateur Cup Committee, due to meet at the end of May, and the full FA Council five weeks later. Thompson anticipated 'a lot of opposition' at this stage and nothing could be taken for granted. It was necessary, therefore, to articulate in some detail the reasons why Pegasus had come into existence and what its promoters hoped to achieve. This was set out in a memorandum sent out to all members of the Amateur Cup Committee early in May and elaborated in subsequent correspondence.[9]

In making the case for Pegasus Thompson had to tread carefully. He was seeking entry to the competition for a club which, at the time of application, did not exist. It was thus necessary to acknowledge that 'special sanction of the Committee would be required'. This posed less of a problem than the idea that Pegasus should be exempt from the qualifying stages of the competition. With a team mainly comprising undergraduate students Pegasus would not be in a position to play any matches before the start of term in October, thus precluding participation in the early qualifying rounds. This, however, was not the only complication. Both OUAFC and CUAFC were anxious to keep their squads together for the varsity match, traditionally played in the first week of December. Thus they were unwilling to release players to assist Pegasus in the fourth and final qualifying round due to be completed in late November. In these circumstances Thompson had little option but to ask 'for as much exemption as possible, i.e. until the first round proper in January'. As one member of the committee pointed out, this raised an awkward question because it breached the principle 'that exemption should be looked upon primarily as a reward for meritorious performance in the Amateur Cup in the previous season'.[10] It soon became clear that it would not be possible to meet Thompson's requirements in full without bruising a few toes.

4

In this situation it made sense to have a 'least-worst' option in reserve. Prompted by Andrew Ralston, secretary of the Isthmian League, who argued that opposition would be minimised by a strategic concession, Thompson indicated that he was open to the 'less satisfactory possibility' of exemption to the fourth qualifying round. This was on the understanding that Pegasus would be permitted to postpone its cup debut until after the Oxford–Cambridge match. It was not likely, he argued, that opponents would object 'since without being presumptuous, it is felt that the first match played in the Competition by the new Club would prove a definite attraction'.[11] Writing to Rous before the meeting Thompson predicted a clear majority in favour of allowing Pegasus to enter but observed that opinion on the committee was equally divided as to exemption, 'with a few members inclined to favour some exemption if certain conditions were fulfilled'. The final outcome – exemption to the fourth qualifying round with permission to postpone the tie – was probably as much as Thompson had come to expect. Even so it caused 'a certain amount of murmuring' in senior amateur circles.[12]

Thompson had lobbied resourcefully to achieve this result, deploying arguments that would be sympathetically received at FA headquarters. In his memorandum he reminded committee members of the debt which the modern game owed to pioneers at Oxford and Cambridge and to their Corinthian successors. Noting that 'the revival of the Corinthian F.C. in its old form is the ardent wish often expressed by many people of widely different connection', Thompson admitted that such a possibility 'has obviously been in the minds of the members of the new Club'. He elaborated this point in reply to a correspondent who had written to him lamenting the demise of the old Corinthians, the club having merged with the less illustrious Casuals in 1939. 'Of course our ultimate object is just what you say, namely the revival of the Corinthians, but we shall have to step very slowly and carefully, and I do not yet know how well it will go.' Implicit in this line of thought was the idea that the Corinthian-Casuals, bottom of the Isthmian League in 1947–48, had proved less than satisfactory as standard-bearers of the old tradition. 'I am glad that you have raised the point that the Corinthian-Casuals Club has disgraced itself,' he wrote privately to Harry Huband of the London Football Association, 'for with that we frankly agree.' But he recognised the importance of retaining goodwill and the advantage of being able to assure potential critics that the Casuals had agreed 'to give the Pegasus Club whole-hearted *support*'.[13]

Though it was necessary to focus on the business of securing entry and exemption Thompson did not allow the minutiae of Amateur Cup rules and regulations to obscure the wider issues which had prompted his initiative. Allusions to the old Corinthians helped to ease the way but Thompson also indicated in his memorandum that the new club was intended to address more immediate concerns. 'It is now everywhere agreed', he wrote, that 'such a step would provide an enormous impetus to further improvement at the Universities' while helping 'to maintain a proper balance between Association and Rugby Football'. He was convinced that the new club represented 'a welcome step for Amateur Football as a whole'. Though the exemption was not quite what Thompson would have wished, a foothold had been secured in what was then the premier competition for senior amateur clubs, a remarkable achievement as Pegasus had yet to kick a ball in anger. To many of those who wished the new club well, especially former Corinthians, the FA was simply showing a proper regard for the old universities, seeing in Pegasus 'a real possibility of raising the standard of amateur football generally'.[14]

The Varsity Influence

'If this can be termed the century of the Common Man,' Rous observed, 'then Soccer, of all sports, is surely his game.'[15] In some ways it was surprising that Thompson's arguments, based on the premise that the state of the game in the old universities was important, should have prevailed. Why should anyone have believed, in the immediate aftermath of 'the people's war', that amateur football as a whole would benefit from the advent of Pegasus? It was, after all, a game played predominantly by working-class men. With Ernie Bevin at the Foreign Office and the pits in public ownership, it was bucking a trend to look to the dreaming spires for inspiration. No one could deny that the universities, along with the public schools, had been a formative influence but this had declined with the development of professionalism and the recognition that soccer, at its highest levels, was big business. Previewing the Varsity Match in 1949, Geoffrey Green reminded readers of *The Field* 'that amateur football in general and the University match in particular now, alas, take a diminished place within the vast framework of a game that has become the free trade of nations'. There was also a question or two to be asked about what football at Oxford and Cambridge had to offer. Even its best friends acknowledged that standards had fallen in the inter-war period when varsity soccer, always 'famed for its square shoulder charge, became to its detriment a slogging match and nothing else'.[16] The Corinthians, representing the best of university and public school old boys football, had a thin time in the FA Cup and it had become increasingly apparent 'that the attraction of professional football could not be equalled by a purely amateur collection of players, however skilful and enthusiastic'.[17]

But it would be a mistake to underestimate the extent of varsity and public school influence at the FA and in the organisation of English football generally. It may have diminished but it was still considerable in the late 1940s. Representatives from Oxford and Cambridge Universities, along with one from the public schools, sat on the FA Council, alongside those from the various county associations. The Amateur Football Alliance (AFA), existing largely to protect the interests of public and grammar school old boys teams, was granted a similar privilege. In this sense Pegasus was exceptionally well-connected in that both Thompson (Oxford) and Graham Doggart (Cambridge), its first treasurer, were members of Council, as was the Rev. K.R.G. Hunt (AFA), its first president. It seems unlikely that any other club, amateur or professional, could have boasted that three of its officials had achieved this status at Lancaster Gate. In relation to the amateur game and football in the schools the Corinthian element more than punched its weight. When a sub-committee was set up in 1946 to consider the contentious issue of 'broken time' payments to compensate amateur footballers for wages lost when called upon to play in international matches, its members included both Hunt and Thompson. Three years later a key report on the state of the game in public and secondary schools was drafted by a sub-committee chaired by the indefatigable Thompson which included both Doggart and Major Stewart (Public Schools).

It was thus hardly surprising that a view of amateurism derived from the Corinthian experience should have retained its purchase on the English game at large. Rous was certainly aware that a 'purist' view of amateurism prevailed that was out of line with the rest of the football world.[18] The proliferation of amateur competitions, especially in and around London, which looked to ancient Greece for a title was indicative here. Founders of the Isthmian League, the oldest of these competitions, in 1905, had hoped 'to revive the ideals of the ancient Greek Olympics before they became, as they did, commercialised and debased'. Their aim had been to create 'a genuinely amateur football league, in which competition should be clean and keen, and in which trophies and individual prizes should have no place'.[19] By the late 1940s they had inspired imitation in the shape of the Athenian, Spartan and Corinthian Leagues. The classical connection died hard. As late as 1962 the compiler of 'Club Notes' in Barnet's programme found himself explaining that the Mithras Cup, a new floodlit competition, had been named after 'the God of Heavenly Light, an enemy of the powers of darkness and evil, and protector of the righteous in this world'.[20] Harry Huband, elected to council in 1907 and still going strong in the late 1940s, was the FA's honorary treasurer, and a member of the Amateur Cup Committee that approved Thompson's application on behalf of Pegasus. He had devoted his life in football to the maintenance of 'Isthmian standards'. What this meant was keeping the professional and the amateur player apart while remaining ever vigilant against unauthorised payments and any other practices which might corrupt those who were supposed to play the game for its own sake. 'Every shamateur', it was said, 'knows what it means to be up against Mr Huband on Commissions of Inquiry.'[21]

Amateur football in England was a divided house. Those who ran the game were mainly, though not exclusively, middle class: those who played it were mainly, though not exclusively, working class. In these circumstances it was not surprising that difficulties should arise. At minor level some clubs formed leagues outside the jurisdiction of their county associations, regarding the required affiliation fee as 'an unfair levy on working class boys who wanted a game of football'.[22] It also seems that some of the 'indiscipline' that worried administrators of the amateur game in the inter-war years was simply a product of a class culture they did not understand. 'Thus physicality, strong language and disrespect for fussy, often middle-class officials [the referees] jarred with the Corinthian standards of the football authorities.'[23] A similar explanation might be advanced to explain the antipathy of the FA towards 'shamateurism', where class differences were again important. In 1928, the year that the FA broke with FIFA (Fédération Internationale de Football Association) over its more relaxed attitude

8

to broken-time payments, 341 amateur players in County Durham were suspended following an investigation into clandestine professionalism. The county association, however, sprang to the defence of its senior amateur clubs, arguing that out-of-touch officials at the FA had wilfully misinterpreted the local convention of paying flat-rate expenses, or 'tea money'.[24] Thereafter the FA's bureaucracy engaged in a prolonged and largely unsuccessful rearguard action against 'shamateurism' in its many and various manifestations. It was, of course, perfectly legitimate that the FA should seek to ensure that clubs entering amateur competitions kicked off on equal terms but its efforts in this direction generated a lot of red tape and good deal of resentment.

The minutes of the FA's Exemption Committee for the late 1940s suggest that the ruling body took this aspect of football administration very seriously. The amateur, whether he liked it or not, was to be saved from the corrupting influence of money. Any ex-professional wishing to undertake even the humblest administrative role at the lower levels of the game was required individually to seek exemption from Rule 37, which precluded service 'on the Council of this Association, or on the Committee of any Association, League or Club'.

> MOORE, A., formerly a professional player for Gainsborough Trinity and Scunthorpe United F.C. for permission to serve on the Committee of Scunthorpe and District Intermediate League and Scunthorpe Sea Cadets.

Thus ran the record in relation to one, not untypical, application for exemption. This particular request, like most others, was granted but the procedure, which enabled the FA to vet all applicants, was hardly designed to encourage the ex-professional to take an active interest. The decisions of the Consultative Committee, which dealt with routine business between meetings of Council, are even more strongly indicative of the desire to safeguard a purist view of amateurism. Clubs wishing to make presentations to players, for example, were required to seek special permission.

> BROMLEY F.C. – An application from Bromley F.C. for permission to make a wedding present of a clock to their player, F. Noakes, was refused.

LEYTONSTONE F.C. – Permission was given to the club to make a presentation, to the value of £10, to the player, I.E. Nicholls, on the occasion of his wedding.

These apparently contradictory decisions, ratified at successive meetings of the FA Council, suggest that the committee weighed each case very carefully. Undoubtedly, the requirement to ask permission was often honoured in the breach but any club wishing to make a public presentation would have been unwise to risk censure. Walthamstow Avenue, a major force in London amateur football and inclined to sail rather close to the wind, were fined five guineas in 1948 for playing two players in a cup-tie after presenting them 'with gifts of some value'. The fine itself was trivial: more serious was the warning to the players concerned 'that any further lapse on their part might result in their being declared professionals'.[25]

The Amateur Cup Committee was especially vigilant in protecting the status of its competition. When it discovered in January 1947 that a Walton and Hersham player, then serving in the forces, had previously been attached to the Scottish junior club, Blantyre Celtic, as a semi-professional, the committee went to great lengths to track him down, before suspending him for the rest of the season. No effort was spared to bring the miscreant to book and his embarrassment was no doubt compounded when the FA invited his Commanding Officer to attend the disciplinary hearing. Clubs that entered the Amateur Cup in good faith but subsequently took on professionals to play in league matches were 'struck out of the competition'. Bridport and Oswestry Town in 1948, and Ilkeston Town in 1949, suffered this indignity.[26] It was possible for professionals to seek permission to revert to amateur status but, even when reinstated, many senior competitions remained closed to them. The Isthmian, Athenian, Spartan and Corinthian Leagues would not allow their clubs to field 'permit' players.[27] But, for all the FA's efforts to keep the professional at a distance from the amateur, to eliminate 'boot money' payments and to discourage the 'poaching' of players by clubs offering employment outside football, little was achieved. Though the Corinthian flame burned bright on the FA Council and amongst the county associations the first tentative advocates of an open game were making themselves heard. The editor of the short-lived *Amateur Sport* was prepared to admit 'some feeling for the talented amateur footballer of modest means who has no wish to become a professional, who enjoys the game, but is not averse to a little pocket money'.[28] In many ways this simply represented an acceptance of what had come to pass.

By the late 1940s, as Shearwood suggests, there were three types of footballer at senior level: 'the professional; the school, university and old-boy type of player; and the working-class amateur, the "shamateur", imitating the professional with varying results, and often given some form of remuneration'.[29] It was for Pegasus, unblemished by either professionalism or 'shamateurism', to prove that 'the school, university and old-boy type' still had an important place in the modern game. The main purpose of Thompson's initiative, as Rous understood, was not a Corinthian revival as such, but to raise the profile of soccer at Oxford and Cambridge, thereby 'encouraging Association Football in the schools, since so many of the masters were apt to take a lead from the universities'.[30] The advent of Pegasus addressed a number of issues that had been causing the FA increasing concern. Here was an opportunity to modify the 'pools and Woodbines' image, derived from professional football, which minor public schools and socially ambitious grammar schools found so off-putting. Given the influence exercised by Thompson and his allies at Lancaster Gate, along with their capacity for setting the agenda as far as the amateur game was concerned, it was not surprising that the obstacles that stood in the path of the newly-formed club were so quickly overcome.

Seizing the Moment

It was also a question of seizing the moment. If ever there was a time when university football was well placed to make an impact it was in the immediate post-war years. In his memorandum to the Amateur Cup Committee Thompson argued that varsity soccer, having plumbed the depths, had improved from about 1935. After the war an influx of mature undergraduates taking up their places after military service widened the pool of available talent. At the same time both OUAFC and CUAFC turned increasingly to grammar school educated undergraduates, compensating for the shortfall in ex-public school players. Green, himself a Cambridge blue in the late 1920s, noted that the years since 1945 had seen 'a marked revival in the skills of the game'. Outstanding university players were once again attracting the

11

attention of the amateur international selectors. Moreover, some of the players available to Pegasus in its early years had benefited from previous experience with professional clubs. John Tanner appeared in Huddersfield Town's first team in 1948–49; Roy Sutcliffe, Ralph Cowan and Gordon McKinna had all played as juniors for Manchester United. Improvements in technique were also attributed to coaches from the professional game employed by the varsity clubs. The efforts of Frank Soo (Stoke City and Luton Town) at Cambridge in the immediate post-war years were matched by Len Goulden (West Ham and Chelsea) and Laurie Scott (Arsenal) at Oxford. It says much for the strength of university soccer at this time that the Oxford side of 1947–48, coached by Scott and including three amateur international caps, was defeated 2–0 by Cambridge in the annual varsity match.[31]

For the new club the single most important achievement in its first season was the victory achieved at Enfield on its first appearance in the Amateur Cup in December 1948. As Shearwood wrote later, this was 'the most important cup-tie Pegasus ever played'. Although Pegasus had been drawn at home they were obliged to concede ground advantage to their opponents who argued that they had been inconvenienced by having to postpone the tie until after the Varsity Match. Defeat would have consigned Pegasus to the first qualifying round for the following season, jeopardising the club's existence. Victory meant entry to the first round proper, played in January, thus securing the status necessary if Pegasus was to have any chance of achieving the objectives for which it had been established. Having disposed of Enfield, Pegasus went on to play four consecutive home ties at the Iffley Road ground in Oxford, each match attracting a larger attendance than the one before. A crowd of around 12,000 witnessed the quarter-final on 25 February when Pegasus were beaten 4–3 by Bromley. Shearwood's recollections of this match suggest that distinctive features of the Pegasus style were already in evidence. 'We tended to push the ball about more and keep it on the ground. They tended to use the long ball, sweeping it out to their wingers or thumping it up the middle.'[32] In reaching the last eight of the most important senior amateur competition Pegasus achieved more in its first season than the most ardent advocates of the university game had thought possible. There was even some consolation in defeat. 'By their splendid display against Bromley, one of the two strongest amateur clubs in the country, they have put University soccer right on the map.'[33]

It could not be doubted that the Amateur Cup provided an excellent showcase for what the new club had to offer. Pegasus emerged at a time when football had never been more popular as a spectator sport. English Football League attendances, reaching an all-time peak at 41 million in 1948–49, reflected popular enthusiasm for a form of entertainment, simultaneously communal and escapist, that caught the post-war mood.[34] But it was not only the professional game that was thriving: the amateur game, especially at senior level, had never attracted so much interest. Pegasus had an early taste of this when arrangements had to be made for around a hundred coaches conveying Bromley supporters to the quarter-final tie at Oxford. A survey of *English Life and Leisure*, published in 1951, noted that in High Wycombe, almost one in five, about 7,000 out of a population of 40,000, would be watching amateur football on a Saturday afternoon. Around 5,000 of these were likely to be at Loakes Park, home of Wycombe Wanderers, then an Isthmian League side, with others scattered along the touchlines at minor matches, such as those played by local works teams.[35] It might be argued that Wycombe was untypical, that its relative isolation from the counter-attractions of the professional game ensured that the local favourites were unusually well placed to benefit from the post-war attendance boom. But, even where a senior amateur club was surrounded by professionals, not to mention other amateur clubs of a comparable standing, it was still possible to attract a more than respectable home gate. Leytonstone, in East London, with Leyton Orient, West Ham and Tottenham Hotspur a mere bus ride away, and senior amateur rivals like Walthamstow Avenue and Leyton just down the road, were averaging around 5,000 in the late 1940s.[36] The FA's decision to stage the final of the Amateur Cup at Wembley was quickly justified by an attendance of 93,000 for the Bromley–Romford final in 1949, and 88,000 a year later for Willington–Bishop Auckland, especially remarkable when the long journey for both sets of supporters is considered. There was every reason to believe that success in the Amateur Cup would put university football 'on the map'. A Wembley final, with the trophy presented by a distinguished public figure, was an event of national importance indicating that amateur football mattered. It was part of the FA's strategy to persuade grammar and public schools to stick with soccer. A schools conference was organised to coincide with the first Wembley final in 1949 and it was customary thereafter to supply schoolmasters who attended with complimentary tickets.[37]

13

If Pegasus was to play a part in this initiative it was essential to maintain the impressive momentum of its first season. Almost immediately it became necessary to revisit the principles on which the club had been established and, in particular, the rule that Pegasus could draw only on players currently resident at the universities or in their first year after leaving. The wisdom of retaining this rule was first questioned at an extraordinary general meeting in April 1949 but it was a deathbed intervention by the club's president, the Rev. K.R.G. Hunt, which proved decisive in putting the issue on the agenda. Hunt was anxious lest the Corinthian renaissance should falter. 'He wants me to say', his wife wrote, 'that the rule of qualification for only one year after "going down" should be altered at once, otherwise the club will die a natural death in a very few years.' The arguments for framing the rule so as to achieve greater continuity were discussed by the committee at the end of April and again in June. Though Graham Doggart defended the original provision, arguing that Pegasus should remain 'essentially a University rather than an ex-University organisation', he was in a minority. It was not yet clear, however, how the interests of Pegasus could be secured without damaging the Corinthian-Casuals, whose representatives asked for assurances that their club 'would be specifically protected in any change of rules that might be made'. A further meeting in September was required before the committee agreed a form of words to put before the membership at the annual general meeting in December. 'All members' would be eligible to play for the club, though the selectors would 'choose primarily those players who are either resident at university or who went down the previous season'. A clarifying statement regarding selection policy was added to the effect that Corinthian-Casuals should have first claim on those players, members of both clubs, who had been down from university for more than one year. Arguably, the element of protection that the Casuals sought had been significantly reduced by the introduction of the word 'primarily' into the revised one-year rule in that it implied recognition of circumstances in which these principles would not apply. It was further weakened when the general meeting adopted an amendment reflecting the majority view 'that players should be free to play for either the Corinthian-Casuals or Pegasus according to their personal wishes'. This element of player power, consistent with the idea that the true amateur should be free to choose his team, was embodied in a club rule that stated: 'The final decision rests with the player himself.'[38]

The one-year rule and exactly what it meant caused much friction over the years. As modified it enabled Thompson, who had come to regard it as a difficulty, to retain a core of experienced players well beyond the end of their undergraduate days. The importance of the change was widely recognised. By the early 1950s, university footballers were significantly younger on average than those who had formed the first Pegasus side, nearly all of whom had seen war service. 'It was felt', noted Pangloss of *The News Chronicle*, on the occasion of the 1951 semi-final, 'that without the steadying influence of one or two matured players the Club would find it hard to live up to the reputation established for them by their founder player members.' This justified the inclusion of five members of the 1948 side in the semi-final line-up.[39] Within the club there was tension between Cambridge-based players, who were inclined to adhere to the one-year principle as they graduated from CUAFC via Pegasus to Corinthian-Casuals, and Oxford-based players who tended to look primarily to the new club. This was, perhaps, a reflection of Thompson's greater influence at Oxford and the adoption of Iffley Road as a home ground. There was also a developing tension between Pegasus and Corinthian-Casuals. While Pegasus were exempt from the early qualifying rounds the Casuals were obliged to compete 'with sides like Ward Street Old Boys, Aspatria Spartans and Parliament Street Methodist – well-run and enthusiastic clubs, no doubt, but little known to the general public'.[40] With media attention focused on Pegasus and its dramatic cup run, the Casuals ground out another disappointing season in the Isthmian League, finishing eleventh out of fourteen in 1948–49 and slipping back to thirteenth the following season. It was understandable that varsity soccer types whose first loyalty was to the Casuals should begin to feel that the success enjoyed by the newcomers was gained partly at their expense.

And there could be no doubt that Pegasus was moving onwards and upwards. In its second season, 1949–50, progress in the Amateur Cup was halted in the second round by Walthamstow Avenue, knowingly referred to by Shearwood as a 'semi-professional side', but there was some compensation in that Pegasus won its first trophy, the Oxfordshire Senior Cup.[41] Having thus consolidated, Pegasus went on to win the Amateur Cup in 1950–51, triumphing 2–1 over Bishop Auckland, and enhancing the profile of the university-educated amateur footballer in just the way that Thompson and his supporters at the FA had envisaged when the club had been founded three years earlier. Its performance was widely commended in the quality press. 'The football by which Pegasus won was essentially in the modern style – almost continental – and no doubt their coach, Victor Buckingham from the Spurs, had a lot to do with that.'[42] Thompson had mapped out the road to Wembley before the start of the season when he had informed playing members that Pegasus should have first claim on their services for Amateur Cup matches. More specifically, he had reminded 'senior players' that they should not deny themselves the attractive possibility of playing for Pegasus at the later stages of the competition by appearing for Corinthian-Casuals in the qualifying rounds.[43] It was an important practical detail but Casuals players and officials were offended by the implication that their cup ambitions were of no account. When the Pegasus committee met at Oxford in November 1950, prior to the start of the 1950–51 Amateur Cup campaign, no representative from either CUAFC or Corinthian-Casuals was present. As the season went on, progress to Wembley was accompanied by indications that the minority group of Pegasus members was becoming increasingly disaffected. These surfaced dramatically when an article by Insole was published in *Light Blue*, a Cambridge magazine, just before the semi-final in March. Insole attributed 'the split that now exists' to the abandonment of the original one-year rule. Pegasus was no longer representative of football at the universities and its selection policy had 'cut across' the interests of Corinthian-Casuals who might otherwise have benefited from an influx of talented ex-university players. 'The attraction and glamour of Pegasus left the club', he argued, 'when it became just another club, and ceased to be a varsity team.'[44]

With the Amateur Cup won Thompson was able to deal with the unhappy minority from a position of strength. In June 1951, less than two months after the final, he arranged a meeting on his home territory at St John's, Oxford, summoning only members of the committee, the university club secretaries and the eleven who had played at Wembley. With Insole and most of those who shared his views thus excluded the honorary secretary berated the enemy within and outlined plans for the club's future in terms that could only have further antagonised the disaffected. There were pragmatic arguments to justify the way in which the club had been run since the one-year rule had been modified. Tanner had summarised them in the form of a reply to Insole, indicating that the circumstances in which Pegasus was now placed precluded a return to the original arrangements. 'The good undergraduate player will still continue to find his place in the Pegasus side but the club will not flourish without a stiffening of maturer players.'[45] Thompson, addressing the meeting, followed the same line but was less circumspect in tone, locating his remarks in the context of the hopes that had been raised by the club's recent success.

> An enormous number of letters had been received congratulating the Club on its Amateur Cup victory, and expressing the hope that it would go on with even greater strength. These had come from Amateur and Professional Clubs, from schools and masters, from past Oxford and Cambridge men, and very many others.[46]

Although Thompson's vanity may have been a factor, these letters seem to have reinforced his sense of the club's wider obligation 'to stimulate interest in Association Football at the Universities and to provide an example of the best Amateur spirit'. It was important that the new club should not 'fail in its responsibility to the country and to the game', even though the practical steps that were necessary to achieve this might cause offence at Cambridge and amongst the Casuals. With the cup secured Thompson was in a mood to burn bridges, accusing Doggart, who had recently become president of Corinthian-Casuals, of seeking repeatedly 'to limit our success by opposing the playing of a few senior players'. At the same time he denounced members who conspired against the interests of the club. 'There had been deliberate attempts to unsettle our players, to coerce them, to say unpleasant things about them because they were loyal to us, and so on.' Doggart protested but Thompson proved irresistible, securing approval for his proposal that what was left of the one-year rule should be set aside. The Pegasus committee endorsed this decision when it met the following day and instructed Thompson 'to proceed with arrangements for next season on the assumption that all members of the Club would be eligible to play'.[47]

Pegasus in Decline

Thus, by the start of 1951–52 season, the conditions that were to shape the subsequent history of the club were in place. With the one-year rule virtually abandoned the availability of key experienced players was ensured. They provided the foundation on which to build the side that reached the semi-final in 1952 and won the Amateur Cup for a second time in 1953. Those who put Corinthian-Casuals first retreated in the face of Thompson's onslaught, Doggart resigning as treasurer for reasons of ill-health in November 1951. It was no doubt especially satisfying for Thompson that Pegasus should have defeated an improving Casuals side, albeit in a rather dour encounter, on its way to the 1953 final. 'Those who expected academic Soccer were disappointed,' observed Norman Ackland in *The Daily Telegraph*; 'so too were those who came in quest of thrills.'[48] The show that Pegasus put on in the final, defeating unfashionable Harwich and Parkeston by 6–0, more than compensated. 'Pegasus showed the arts and graces that one has come to expect from only a handful of professional sides,' wrote Alan Ross in *The Observer*. 'It was the most civilised, polished football and it could not but have given the capacity crowd of 100,000, wherever their hearts lay, great pleasure.'[49] The Pegasus club was perfectly poised to continue in its role as the representative of all that was best in the university and old boys game. For a while yet, a friendly match with Pegasus, 'the household word in Amateur soccer', remained an eagerly anticipated event. 'Wherever they appear they are always a great attraction.'[50] It was also clear that Thompson was firmly in control of the club's destiny. This was to prove something of a mixed blessing. On the one hand, his commitment to the cause was self-evident and his organisational drive second-to-none. On the other, he seems to have been a rather touchy, authoritarian figure, accustomed to getting his own way and as likely to make enemies as friends. There is some justice in Brian Glanville's recent assessment of him as 'at once the founder and the ultimate destroyer of the Pegasus club'.[51]

Though Pegasus did not win the Amateur Cup again, or even reach the final, it remained a significant force in the mid 1950s. The side was good enough to make the last eight in 1953–54 and 1954–55 but thereafter failed to advance beyond the second round. Defeat in the first round in 1961–62 consigned Pegasus to the fourth qualifying round for the following season when Windsor and Eton beat them at home. It was some time, however, before decline took on the appearance of inevitability. A number of outstanding players appeared for Pegasus in this period, including goalkeeper Mike Pinner, who played for a string of Football League clubs and gained a record number of amateur international caps; John Harding, a full-back who later captained the England amateur side; and Martyn King, who went

18

on to make over two hundred appearances as a professional with Colchester United. Meanwhile Denis Saunders, who had played in the club's first season and was to play in its last, continued to perform with distinction in midfield. With players living in Oxford, Cambridge, London and elsewhere it was rare for Pegasus to train together but in other respects the team was well prepared. The annual winter tour, undertaken just after Christmas, was especially important in bringing the squad together for a few days before the first round proper of the Amateur Cup. Pegasus, in its own way, prepared very thoroughly for cup-ties. Thompson anticipated Don Revie in supplying players with dossiers assessing the strengths and weaknesses of the opposition before important matches. In February 1955, with Wycombe Wanderers in prospect, this included details of the notorious slope at Loakes Park. 'Pinner ought to be very careful in throwing the ball, for it will not carry up the hill at either end, and firm clearances will be much safer.'[52]

Even before the 1953 Amateur Cup triumph Thompson was predicting difficulties ahead. The current university teams, he suggested, contained 'few resident players of the quality we need'. He also recognised that it might be difficult to retain senior players, especially those living in the North: 'It is a real self-sacrifice for them to travel so far south every week, and not all may feel that the claims of our cause are so great as to justify it.' Though Thompson was unduly pessimistic about immediate prospects he had identified the two problems that were to undermine the club's playing strength in the late 1950s and early 1960s. By 1957, when Pegasus were coached by Arthur Rowe, the ability to hold on to key players had become critical. What Rowe called the 'new team' had the potential to 'quite possibly emulate the deeds of the old XI' but only if 'certain matured, ex-varsity players can be retained'.[53] By the end of season 1959–60 Rowe's successor, Trevor Churchill, was getting a little desperate:

> What a pity the Club cannot cut loose from the young hopefuls and play an experienced team. I fear we shall not repeat the Amateur Cup wins until this happens... Young players coming to University seem to me to be highly over-rated and in many cases lacking the qualities and moral fibre which a club of the character of Pegasus demands.[54]

For a few years after 1953 those who ran the club sheltered behind the idea that it was passing through a 'transitional' phase but it became apparent that this could not go on indefinitely. Writing to members in June 1957, Thompson noted that the FA had once again granted exemption until the first round proper of the Amateur Cup, 'but it has been made very clear to us that this is the last time on which any such concession will be made unless there is a marked improvement in our performances'.[55] Pegasus did just enough to put off this evil day for five more years but it was skating on thin ice. Some measure of the extent to which Thompson's confidence was eroding in this period is evident in his response to the 'tempting' suggestion that Pegasus should join the Isthmian League in 1958. Replying to Charles King, the Bromley secretary, who had made the approach, Thompson cited the problems he would have in raising sides in the period before Christmas, a sure indication of unwillingness to modify his original conception of the club. He concluded by indicating that he was uncertain as to 'making ends meet financially, since we might not get a regular gate here in the face of competition from Headington United and Oxford City'.[56] This was, no doubt, prudent but it suggested that Pegasus which, only five years before, had attracted a capacity crowd to Wembley, were in significant retreat.

Throughout its period of gradual decline from the high peak of the early 1950s Pegasus continued to fulfil its responsibilities to amateur football in general and to the schools and universities. The club took its 'missionary work' very seriously. While funds permitted there was room for generosity towards amateur clubs less well situated than themselves. After a match at Leyton, in March 1953, Pegasus was praised for returning part of its share of a disappointing gate to the home club. The visitors, it was reported, believed that the 'Lilywhites' needed the money more than they did.[57] Some matches, such as a fixture arranged later the same year to resuscitate Croydon Amateurs, were entirely at Pegasus's expense. Both OUAFC and CUAFC benefited from direct grants and from significant contributions towards the costs of ground maintenance. Pegasus regularly ran up expenses by playing matches against various university and school sides though Rowe was more than a little sceptical as to whether such fixtures helped players to maintain a competitive edge. 'This is why', he explained to Tanner, 'I urged the players so strongly to go out and whack the Schools XI at Cambridge.'[58] At the same time the club made substantial donations to organisations such as the AFA, the Middlesex

Grammar Schools Football Association, the Central Council of Physical Recreation and the National Association of Boys Clubs. Thompson, writing in 1955, confirmed that such activities were part of the club's *raison d'être*. 'For our cup victories, for the way we have behaved both on and off the field, and for the Club's moral help to the game through matches and financial help to deserving causes, we are respected everywhere, and all those who wish the game well are looking to us to continue the work we have begun.'[59] But doubts were now emerging regarding the club's ability to meet these expectations.

Given its unique character Pegasus was a difficult club to run. With its playing strength widely scattered and individual members subject to competing loyalties, not to mention the time-consuming business of arranging friendly matches against quality opposition, the club's honorary officials were severely stretched. Thompson, who resigned as secretary in 1954, taking up the position of chairman, proved a difficult act to follow, not least because he was unable to resist the temptation to interfere in day-to-day affairs. 'I have attempted to keep things running smoothly in the face of continual upsets from Tommy,' explained Ben Brown on his resignation as secretary in 1957. It struck him as no coincidence that two treasurers had 'felt obliged to give up their official positions with the Club in similar circumstances'. It was quite an achievement to have alienated Brown, a veteran of both Wembley finals. Tanner, who served as secretary in difficult circumstances a little later, also discovered that working with Thompson could be frustrating, especially when he showed little inclination to honour a new working agreement with Corinthian-Casuals, arrived at after some awkward negotiations in November 1960. 'Once, exasperated beyond measure by Thompson's obduracy, Tanner hit him.'[60] Whatever debt the club owed him, and it was huge, it seems likely that Thompson's impact was almost entirely negative by this stage. Members of early Pegasus sides, especially ex-servicemen, could take Thompson or leave him. The younger, less experienced players of later years were more likely to regard him as a disconcerting, even intimidating figure. They simply left him. Writing to the club president, Harvey Chadder, in December 1959, Thompson observed gloomily:

> We seem...to have reached a very serious stage. No less than seven of the present undergraduates, nearly all of whom would have qualified for our first team, have left us for the Casuals or

elsewhere. The reasons for this are largely not our fault, but I cannot see the Club going on for long in this way.

He went on to indicate his intention to resign as chairman adding, without a discernible trace of irony, that he intended to delay the announcement so as not to cause disquiet amongst the players.[61]

By the early 1960s Pegasus was struggling to hang onto its place amongst the elite of senior amateur football. It was noted with regret at the AFA, which had come to regard Pegasus as ambassadors for 'real amateur soccer', that 'full strength sides have not been fielded as they were in the early days'.[62] The club's precarious status was increasingly at odds with its wider aims. Those who looked to Pegasus to spearhead a Corinthian revival were disappointed as the apparently effortless superiority of Wembley 1953 faded into distant memory. From 1956, when they reached the Amateur Cup final, the Casuals seemed better equipped than Pegasus to carry the Corinthian banner. 'In their hyphenated title', wrote Green, 'there still lives on the memory, the spirit, and the glory that once was Corinth.'[63] The Casuals had been helped by the inclination of CUAFC players to comply with the original one-year rule. Seven of the side that reached Wembley had been at Cambridge. 'One couldn't help speculating', observed Shearwood, 'how strong we'd have been with their services.'[64] This reversal of fortunes was significant. When Pegasus officials met their Casuals counterparts in 1960 with a view to settling outstanding differences they were in a relatively weak position. This was reflected in an agreement that gave the Casuals first call on senior players who had been down from Oxbridge for more than a year.

Pegasus and the Amateur Game in the Early 1960s

By the end of 1960 Pegasus was in deep trouble. Writing in the previously sympathetic *Sunday Times* at the time of the Pegasus-Casuals agreement, Glanville had been unsparing in his analysis. Reluctance to contemplate league football, restricting Pegasus to 'a tepid series of friendlies', had made it difficult to retain players of quality. Moreover, as players struggled in vain to recapture former glories, it became difficult to keep up appropriate standards of behaviour. 'The vigour of their appeals to the referee this season has, on occasion, I am told, been reminiscent of a desperate Third Division side.' Though it was unfair to criticise on the basis of hearsay, these strictures were difficult to refute. Tanner's reply, rehearsing the same arguments for not playing before Christmas that Thompson had used in 1948, suggested that Pegasus was incapable of changing to secure its survival. A few months later he warned Thompson privately that 'unless something is done very soon the club will drift straight onto the rocks'.[65] By March 1963, when the committee decided to put Pegasus into 'cold storage', it was clear that the level of success likely to be achieved on the field no longer justified the voluntary effort required to keep the club ticking over. As Brown observed, 'there was now no one who was prepared to run the Club in the face of apathy and defections.' Thompson, now club president, had contributed to this situation by undermining the new relationship with Corinthian-Casuals, prompting the long-suffering Tanner to resign as secretary.[66]

Starved of success Pegasus were less able to assist the schools and amateur football generally. One of the reasons that the club survived for as long as it did was that it engaged the loyal support of those, like Denis Saunders, for whom it was 'a crusade'.[67] Pegasus members who were masters at soccer-playing public schools were especially inclined to this view. By playing attractive football in the right spirit Pegasus would help to counteract the negative influence of the professional game on middle-class opinion. 'The example they have set by their standard of play and behaviour on the field – no complaining to the referee; no handshakes or war-whoops when they score – has made a deep impression,' it was observed in 1951. At the same time, it was claimed, the shift from soccer to rugby in grammar and public schools had been 'completely arrested'.[68] If this was so it was a temporary phenomenon, though it does seem that the rate at which public and grammar schools were switching to rugby may have slowed a little. A survey undertaken by the FA towards the end of the 1950s found that 23 had changed to rugby since the war and that a further 55 had introduced rugby alongside soccer. Movement in the other direction was negligible. No school had changed from rugby to soccer and only seven rugby-playing schools had incorporated soccer into the syllabus. 'The significance of the trend must be taken seriously,' Rous urged. What worried headmasters was 'the standard of behaviour in senior professional and amateur matches' and, more vaguely, 'the flouting of moral obligations'. Their anxieties in this respect could only have been sharpened by sensational coverage in the popular press, much of it

23

focused on alleged corruption. Any example that Pegasus may have set by spurning the 'war-whoop' has to be seen in this wider context.[69]

After the Amateur Cup final in 1951 an unnamed FA official was heard to say: 'What a magnificent game, and how refreshing that a truly amateur team has won the Amateur Cup after so many years.'[70] As this suggested, the Pegasus role model had a limited impact on 'shamateurism'. FA commissions descended on a number of clubs in the 1950s handing out fines and suspensions and occasionally depriving players of their amateur status. The team manager at Eastbourne, for example, was one of three club officials suspended *sine die* in 1954 after admitting broken time payments to players. They had been paid 'in round sums which were later entered in the Expenses Book as odd amounts in order to avoid suspicion'.[71] But, for the most part, such practices went unpunished for want of firm evidence. The FA Council, after 'a lengthy and enlivened discussion' in September 1952, concluded 'that it was difficult to take action in these matters unless real evidence was made available'. Those anxious to nail Walthamstow Avenue were frustrated in 1953 when it was reported that 'the Petty Cash vouchers and receipts for payments made during last season had been accidentally destroyed'.[72] By the early 1960s, some influential voices were calling for radical reform. Tony Pawson, former Pegasus player and England amateur international, was among them, contributing to a minority opinion in the Central Council of Physical Recreation's report on *Sport and the Community*, published in 1960. The time had now come, he urged, 'to abolish the formal distinction between amateur and professional, and to allow any participant, if he needs or wishes it, to be paid as a player, without stigma, reproach or differentiation'.[73] It was in this context that the FA decided in 1963 to address the whole question of 'shamateurism'.

A joint meeting of the Amateur Cup Committee and the Amateur International Committee having established that there was 'a prima facie case for an investigation of alleged payments to amateur players', it was decided to set up a special sub-committee to recommend an appropriate course of action. This met between March and October and presented its report to the FA Council in December 1963.[74] For Thompson, the work of this sub-committee, of which he was a member, coincided with the period when Pegasus was closing down. A statement issued by Thompson and Brown, explaining that Pegasus would no longer play competitive football, was released in July, generating some controversy. Not surprisingly, Thompson's current preoccupations were much in evidence: he was convinced that the deteriorating moral climate in senior amateur football had created conditions in which Pegasus could no longer function. 'Illegal payments are widespread and amateur football is a misnomer', they complained; 'even undergraduates have been attracted by such incentives.' It was clear, the statement concluded, that what was now required was 'an entirely different approach to amateurism'.[75] If Thompson was seeking to distract attention from his own shortcomings by blaming 'shamateurism' for the club's demise, the tactic backfired. John Dewar, chairman of Tooting and Mitcham, affronted by the suggestion that clubs like his colluded with the 'shamateur', responded vigorously. 'We attract and hold our players', he explained disingenuously, 'by offering them first-class facilities with the opportunity to tour abroad in style.' James Aitken, in *The Observer*, sided with Tooting, dismissing the Pegasus statement as 'the tactics of a drowning man'.[76]

But, though Thompson was embittered by what had happened to Pegasus, he also learned from the experience. This was evident in his relations with the Amateur Status sub-committee which, in its final recommendations, advocated a series of measures designed to curb 'shamateurism' in its various forms. Club officials and players were warned that they would be subject to unlimited suspension if they were found to have made or accepted payments in excess of those allowed to cover out-of-pocket expenses. Inducements to move from one club to another, financial or otherwise, were to be dealt with in the same way. Restrictions on movement during the season were to be introduced in order to curtail the unauthorised transfer market, along with a residence qualification limiting the amateur player's choice of club to within 50 miles of his normal place of residence or business. These provisions, though adopted by the FA in December 1963, were advanced without confidence and received without enthusiasm. The sub-committee acknowledged that, despite its best efforts, 'shamateurism' was likely to continue. 'While there existed officials prepared to make payments to a player in cash or in kind and players prepared to receive such payments there was always the likelihood of illegal payments being made and received.' And, as many perceived, there was an irony in seeking to safeguard the amateur by restricting his liberty. 'Football would become a strange business', noted J.L.

Manning in *The Daily Mail*, 'if professionals have more freedom of movement than amateurs.' The views of Alan King, Hounslow Town's secretary, represented majority opinion amongst London's senior amateur clubs: 'They'll run into a lot of trouble trying to enforce these new rules.'[77] It was, at best, an unsatisfactory compromise but had allowed the advocates of 'true-blue amateurism ... to make their last fighting stand'.[78]

Though he signed the report Thompson was in no doubt that it offered too little and had come too late. Having read an early draft in May 1963 he wrote to Denis Follows, who had replaced Rous as secretary of the FA, distancing himself from its conclusions. Thompson asked that his name be removed from the list of those endorsing the report and enclosed a paragraph embodying his minority position.

> In my view the proposed changes of rule...are entirely inadequate to deal with the present state of illegal payments in Amateur Football and they are unlikely to have any appreciable effect. I feel that the situation has been allowed to degenerate so far, and the social trends today are of such a kind, that steps should be taken to examine the detailed consequences of removing the distinction between Amateur and Professional players. I believe that to remove this distinction is the only honest solution.[79]

Thompson was persuaded to let his initial endorsement of the report stand but immediately regretted allowing 'sentiment to overcome my proper conviction' and made his position clear in a letter to council members.[80] He later elaborated his views in an article for *The Times*, its appearance coinciding with the first round proper of the Amateur Cup. As the FA could not hope to enforce its new regulations it was 'more appropriate to have done with it now, and call them all footballers'.[81] Though it was another ten years before the FA took this radical step Thompson was echoing sentiments that were, by the early 1960s, widely held amongst the senior clubs. 'If the FA were to take a vote among people connected with the amateur game', claimed Charles King of Bromley, '999 out of every thousand would be in favour of calling all players footballers.'[82] Given all that Pegasus had represented Thompson's high-profile conversion was courageous and highly significant. It was an indication that this aspect of the game's modernisation could not be long delayed.

ACKNOWLEDGEMENTS

The author wishes to thank Gordon McKinna, who allowed him access to the records of Pegasus AFC, and was helpful in many other ways. John Harding and Tony Pawson gave generously of their time to share memories of their playing days with Pegasus and of amateur football generally. Thanks are also due to David Barber at the Football Association, Dave Twydell and Daniel Porter.

NOTES

1. Geoffrey Green, *Soccer in the Fifties* (London: Ian Allen, 1974) p.37.
2. C.B. Fry, *Life Worth Living: Some Phases of an Englishman* (London: Pavilion Books, 1986) p.271.
3. Edward Grayson, *Corinthians & Cricketers* (London: Naldrett Press, 1957) p.27.
4. Richard Holt, *Sport and the British: A Modern History* (Oxford: OUP, 1989), pp.99–100.
5. Gordon McKinna interviewed 7 Jul. 1999; John Harding interviewed 9 Jul. 1999; Tony Pawson interviewed 27 Oct. 1999; also Ken Shearwood, *Pegasus* (Oxford: Oxford Illustrated Press, 1975). For a brief history and complete playing record see Dave Twydell, *Defunct F.C.* (Harewood: author, n.d.) pp.164–217.
6. *The Sunday Times,* 22 Apr. 1951.
7. Courtesy of G.H. McKinna, Pegasus F.C.Papers, (hereafter Peg.), 6, document headed *Pegasus: Reply to a Criticism*, n.d; see also Peg., 1, Thompson to W.E. Greenland, 25 Aug. 1948 (copy); and Peg., 5, Denis Saunders to John Tanner, 10 Dec. 1959. This version is endorsed by Shearwood, *Pegasus*, pp.11–12.
8. Peg., 1, Notes of meeting held at the East India and Sports Club, 2 May 1948; also in Twydell, *Defunct F.A.*, pp.168–69. The suggestion that the club be named 'Pegasus' originated with Thompson's wife, a distinguished classical scholar; see Grayson, *Corinthians and Cricketers*, pp.174–5.
9. Peg.,1, Memorandum on the Pegasus AFC, n.d. [May 1948].
10. Peg., 1, Stanley Brown (Kent County FA) to Thompson, 24 May 1948.
11. Peg., 1, Andrew Ralston to Thompson, 5 May 1948; Memorandum (May 1948).
12. Peg., 1, Thompson to Rous, 19 May 1948 (copy); see also *Amateur Sport*, 14 May 1949.
13. Peg, 1, Pegasus Memorandum, (May 1948); Thompson to Claud Godefroy, 15 May 1948 (copy); Thompson to Harry Huband, 24 May 1948 (copy).
14. A.G. Doggart, 'The Pegasus Experiment: an attempt to establish the spirit of the Corinthians', *The Field*, 7 Jan. 1950, p.23.
15. *The Football Association Year Book 1951–52* (London: Naldrett Press, 1952), introduction.
16. Geoffrey Green, 'The Universities at Tottenham', *The Field*, 3 Dec. 1949., p.817. Rous, who refereed some varsity matches between the wars, was equally unimpressed. See Sir Stanley Rous, *Football Worlds: A Lifetime in Sport* (London: Faber & Faber, 1978), pp.31–2.
17. 'The Corinthians', *The Football Association Year Book 1948–49* (London: Naldrett Press, 1949), pp.91–4.
18. Rous, *Football Worlds*, pp.122–3.

19. 'The Story of the Isthmian League', *The Football Association Year Book 1950–51* (London: Naldrett Press, 1951), pp.98–100.
20. Match programme, Barnet v Barking, Mithras Floodlit Cup, 20 November 1960.
21. 'Profile: H.J. Huband', *FA Year Book 1950–51*, pp.16–17.
22. Robert Barltrop, *Bright Summer-Dark Autumn: growing up in North East London between the wars* (Walthamstow: London Borough of Waltham Forest, 1986), p.15.
23. Nicholas Fishwick, *English Football and Society, 1910–1950* (Manchester: MUP, 1989), p.21.
24. Tony Mason, 'Football', in Tony Mason (ed.), *Sport in Britain: A Social History* (Cambridge: CUP, 1989), p.148. See also Harry Pearson, *The Far Corner: A Mazy Dribble through North-East Football* (London: Warner Books, 1994), pp.216–21.
25. The Football Association Archives [hereafter FAA], Lancaster Gate, London: *Minutes 1946–47*, Council 14 Oct. 1946, 18(a); *Minutes 1949–50*, Council, 29 Apr. 1949, 65; 2 Jul. 1949, 9; *Minutes 1948–49*, Council, 3 Jul. 1948, 4(f).
26. FAA, *Minutes 1946–47*, Council 10 Feb. 1946, 46(a), 11 Apr. 1946, 62; *Minutes 1948–49*, Council, 11 Oct. 1948, 25(a); *Minutes 1949–50*, Council 12 Dec. 1949, 11.
27. *Amateur Sport*, 19 November 1949.
28. 'It can be hard to stay strictly amateur', *Amateur Sport*, 18 Jun. 1949.
29. Shearwood, *Pegasus*, p.39.
30. Rous, *Football Worlds*, p.32.
31. Green, 'Universities at Tottenham', p.817; Colin Weir, *The History of Oxford University Association Football Club 1872–1998* (Harefield: Yore Publications, 1998), pp.73–4.
32. Shearwood, *Pegasus*, pp.27–8, 33. For fixtures and attendances in 1948–49 see Twydell, *Defunct F.C.*, pp.188–9.
33. *The Daily Telegraph*, 27 Feb. 1949.
34. See Neil Wrigglesworth, *The Evolution of English Sport* (London: Frank Cass, 1996), pp.131–2.
35. B. Seebohm Rowntree and G.R. Lavers, *English Life and Leisure: A Social Study* (London: Longman, 1951), p.398. For attendances generally see Dave Russell, *Football and the English: A Social History of Association Football in England, 1863–1995* (Preston: Carnegie Publishing, 1997), pp.131–3.
36. *Amateur Sport*, 19 Feb. 1949.
37. FAA, *Minutes 1957–58*, Council, 2 May 1958, Memorandum on Schools and Association Football.
38. Peg.1, C.Mary Hunt to Thompson, 28 Apr. 1949; committee minutes, 30 Apr., 16 Jun., 17 Sept. 1949; AGM minutes, 3 Dec. 1949.
39. Arsenal FC match programme, FA Amateur Cup semi-final, Pegasus v Hendon, 17 Mar. 1951.
40. *Amateur Sport*, 7 Sept. 1949.
41. Shearwood, *Pegasus*, p.51.
42. *The Sunday Times*, 22 Apr. 1951.
43. Peg.1, Thompson to John (?), n.d. (copy), [June/July 1950]; notice issued by Thompson, n.d. [June/July 1950].
44. For the complete text of Insole's article see Shearwood, *Pegasus*, pp.74–7.
45. Peg., 6, document headed 'Pegasus: Reply to a Criticism', n.d. [April/May 1951].
46. Peg., 1, notes on a meeting held at St John's College, Oxford, 16 Jun. 1951.
47. Peg., 1, committee minutes, 17 Jun. 1951.

48. *The Daily Telegraph*, 9 Feb. 1953.
49. *The Observer*, 12 Apr. 1953.
50. Match programme, Maidstone United v Edgware Town, Corinthian League, 22 Oct. 1955.
51. Brian Glanville, *Football Memories* (London: Virgin, 1999), p.129.
52. Peg., 2, Thompson's report on Southall, 4 Mar. 1953; Peg., 3, report by Thompson and Brown on Wycombe Wanderers, 15 Feb. 1955.
53. Peg.,2, draft letter from Thompson, probably to members of the Pegasus committee, dated 5 Feb. 1953; Peg., 4, Arthur Rowe to Tanner, 17 Jul. 1957.
54. Peg.,6, Pegasus AFC Coaching Report 1959–60.
55. Peg.,4, Memorandum by Thompson headed 'Pegasus Football Club', 26 Jun. 1957.
56. Peg., 5, Thompson to King, 15 Mar. 1958 (copy).
57. *Walthamstow Guardian*, 20 Mar. 1953.
58. Peg., 4, Rowe to Tanner, 17 Jul. 1957.
59. Peg.,3, document headed 'Pegasus Football Club'; for the list of donations etc drawn up by Thompson, Brown and Weinstein in November 1955 to assist the club in its negotiations with Inland Revenue; see also Thompson's memorandum headed 'Important', Sept. 1955.
60. Glanville, *Football Memories*, p.129.
61. Peg., 5, Thompson to Harvey Chadder, 27 Dec. 1959 (copy).
62. Peg., 6, Greenland to Thompson, 11 Mar. 1960.
63. *The Times*, 7 Apr. 1956.
64. Shearwood, *Pegasus*, pp.177–8.
65. For Glanville's comments and Tanner's response see *The Sunday Times*, 6 and 20 November 1960; also Peg., 7, Tanner to Thompson, 24 Apr. 1961 (copy).
66. Peg.,7, committee minutes, 9 Mar. 1963; also in Twydell, *Defunct F.A.*, pp.177–8.
67. Peg., 5, Saunders to Tanner, 10 Dec. 1959.
68. 'Pangloss' in the Arsenal F.C. match programme, Pegasus v. Hendon, 17 Mar. 1951.
69. FAA, *Minutes 1957–58*, Council 2 May 1958, Memorandum on Schools and Association Football; for the influence of the press see Russell, *Football and the English*, pp.140–41.
70. Royal Society, London, Sir Harold Thompson Papers, (hereafter Thom.), E.371, undated draft of Thompson's article for *The Times*, 11 Jan. 1964. This sentence did not appear in the published version.
71. For examples of commission reports see FAA, *Minutes 1949–50*, Council 13 Feb.; 28 Apr. 1950, re Grays Athletic; *Minutes 1951–52*, Council 17 Sept., 17 Dec. 1951, re Chingford Town; *Minutes 1953–54*, Council 13 Dec. 1954, re Eastbourne.
72. FAA, *Minutes 1952–53*, Council 29 Sept. 1952, report of conference of chairmen and secretaries; *Minutes 1953–54*, Council 1 Jul. 1953, consultative committee decisions.
73. *Sport and the Community: the Report of the Wolfenden Committee on Sport*, (London: Central Council of Physical Recreation, 1960), pp.68–9; Pawson interviewed, 27 Oct. 1999.
74. FAA, *Minutes 1962–63*, Council 28 Jan. 1963, 51(b), for the genesis of this sub-committee; *Minutes 1963–64*, Council 2 Dec. 1963, for its report.
75. *Oxford Mail*, 20 Jul. 1963.
76. 'Pegasus v Tooting', *The Observer*, 21 Jul. 1963.
77. *The Daily Mail*, 3 Dec. 1963.

78. *The Times*, 3 Dec. 1963; see also Pawson's article, 'Sweeping Under the Carpet', *The Observer*, 8 Dec. 1963.
79. Thom., E.369, Thompson to Denis Follows, 28 May 1963 (copy).
80. Thom., E.369, Thompson to Denis Follows, 11 November 1963 (copy).
81. 'Competition Under a Cloud', *The Times*, 11 Jan. 1964.
82. *Evening News* (London), 3 Dec. 1963.

'Time Gentlemen Please':
The Decline of Amateur Captaincy
in English County Cricket

STEPHEN WAGG

[For Colonel Nicholson] the total output of a few men unused to manual labour was negligible, while the extra effort that would be made under the supervision of efficient officers was immense.

Pierre Boule, *The Bridge on the River Kwai*[1]

Even for some of the more conservative members of the cricket public it remains a source of some dismay that on the scorecards issued to spectators on English county grounds before 1963, the initials of amateur cricketers preceded their names, while those of professionals came after. It is part of English cricket lore that the following announcement was made before a Middlesex game at Lords in the late 1950s: 'Ladies and gentlemen, there is a correction to your scorecards. For F.J. Titmus, read Titmus F.J.'[2] The real significance of this still widely-told story is that a social distinction taken largely for granted in the 1920s and 1930s had, for many observers, come to look faintly ridiculous two decades on. This new perception was in part a function of the fact that in cricket, unlike other English sports, amateurs and professionals had always played together. Status distinctions, therefore, defined face-to-face relationships and not separate social worlds.

This essay is about the steady erosion of the social divide separating amateurs and professionals at English county cricket clubs in the two decades following the Second World War and, more specifically, about the decline of the long-held principle that team captains at these clubs should hold amateur status. Given the social circumstances of English county cricket after 1946 the resilience of this principle was quite

31

remarkable. Indeed, it was never comprehensively rejected by club committees or by those who administered the game. It simply disappeared from view with the abolition of the distinction between 'gentlemen' and 'players' in 1963.

Gentlemen and Players

By the end of the nineteenth century the distinction between the amateur and the professional was firmly established in English cricket, as was the tradition of amateur captaincy. The early professionals were usually hired by gentlemen to play for their teams or by the Marylebone Cricket Club (MCC) as practice bowlers, the first of these being taken on in 1825. From the outset, amateurs tended to be batsmen while professionals were bowlers, and their relationship, effectively that of masters and men, was defined partly through accommodation, partly through struggle. The first Gentlemen versus Players match, organised by the MCC in 1806, assumed a degree of peaceful coexistence, but repeated attempts after the 1820s to restrict the delivery actions of bowlers suggested otherwise. Cricket's County Championship, founded in 1873, followed a period in which county sides had competed against fully commercialised teams of travelling professionals; its emergence as the major domestic competition represented a victory for the MCC, with its roots in the landed classes, over the professional touring elevens.[3] It was always the hope of progressives within the MCC, however, that amateurs and professionals would play together in integrated teams. This was how the first county sides, some of which were actually captained by professionals, had been constituted.[4] But, by the turn of the century, for a professional to captain a county side had become unthinkable. This reflected a greater concern to define and enforce amateur–professional distinctions after the 1870s as the amateur elite reasserted its old authority over the professionals. Professionals were required to address amateurs as 'Mister' or 'Sir'; in reply, they were addressed only by their surnames. A breach of etiquette by a 'pro' could mean dismissal. By 1900 these relationships were well entrenched, with amateurs and professionals allocated different changing rooms and walking onto the field of play through different gates. At mealtimes they ate from separate tables. A photograph of a Derbyshire eleven of the late nineteenth century shows the amateur captain standing a yard apart

32

from his colleagues. In 1904, Lancashire, the new county champions, were photographed in separate amateur and professional groupings.[5] The inherent leadership qualities of the gentleman amateur were often fiercely asserted. 'Few professional cricketers (it is a well-known fact) make good captains,' observed A.G. Steel, former Lancashire and England captain, in 1904. 'Amateurs', he continued, 'have always made, and always will make, the best captains; and this is only natural. An educated mind, with a logical power of reasoning, will always treat every subject better than one comparatively untaught.'[6]

After the First World War, however, it became increasingly difficult for counties to act in accordance with this view. Not only were fewer amateur players available than before 1914; there were fewer amateur players of the requisite quality. Of those now appointed to county captaincies, some had business commitments that restricted their availability and others had little experience. In these circumstances, the amateur county captain became more reliant than ever on his professionals and, particularly, on the 'senior pro', who deputised in his absence, gave advice when needed and, on his behalf, performed the duties of sergeant-major in relation to the other professionals. The changing relationship between amateur captain and professional was also influenced by the role of cricket in the popular culture of the inter-war years. Extensive newspaper and radio coverage conferred hero status on a number of professional players. This created difficulties for proponents of the amateur–professional divide and its attendant ethos: heroes, after all, should not be subordinates. Besides, some professionals plainly expressed in their cricket the traits so frequently ascribed to amateurs. The best example here was Jack Hobbs, the son of a college groundsman, who first played for Surrey in 1904 and within ten years was regarded as the best batsman in the world. The grace of his batting led Pelham Warner, Middlesex captain between 1908 and 1920, to claim him as a token member of the game's social elite: Hobbs, he said, was 'a professional who played just like an amateur'.[7]

The relative dearth of suitable amateur candidates to captain England after 1918 created problems for the MCC and, in particular, for those imperialists – notably Lord Harris, Lord Hawke and Warner – who believed that the right type of leadership was essential if the game was to fulfil its 'civilising mission'. Both at home and overseas the lower orders could be bonded to the imperial elite through 'the republic of the playground'.[8] In 1925, prompted by Cecil ('Ciss')

Parkinson of Lancashire, who had argued that England should 'look to a pro' if no amateur captain reached the required playing standard, Lord Hawke remarked infamously to the annual general meeting of the Yorkshire County Cricket Club:

> Pray God, no professional shall ever captain England. I love and admire them all but we have always had an amateur skipper and when the day comes when we shall have no more amateurs captaining England it will be a thousand pities.

It seems possible, as his biographer suggests, that Hawke was merely reasserting the conventional wisdom of his class in a clumsy fashion or that he was simply lamenting the possibility of no amateur being deemed good enough to captain the English team. But the reactions to his speech indicated that amateur captaincy had become contested terrain with professionals, through the popular press, now granted a voice in the ensuing debate. An autocrat, unused to the vagaries of modern publicity, Hawke discovered that he had unwittingly provoked a public outcry.[9] Surrey captain Percy Fender spoke in *The Daily Herald* of a 'gratuitous insult to the main body of professional cricketers' which, readers were reminded, included such figures as the saintly Jack Hobbs.[10]

Though Harris and Warner were supportive in public it seems likely that they regretted the bluntness of Hawke's language: to talk openly of social exclusion exposed 'the republic of the playground' as a convenient fiction. Warner, in particular, while as concerned as Hawke to safeguard the hegemony of the gentleman amateur, preferred the more subtle strategy of mitigating social distinctions in order to preserve them.[11] By the late 1930s, with no obvious amateur candidate for the England captaincy having emerged, Warner's pragmatism helped to underpin existing authority relations by making it possible for Wally Hammond of Gloucestershire, a professional and one of England's finest batsmen, to become an amateur. Hammond had been on the controversial 'bodyline' tour of Australia in 1932–33 and had become close to Warner, the manager of the England party. Having captained the Players against the Gentlemen in 1936 and 1937, Hammond, after 17 years as a professional, declared himself an amateur in November 1937, captaining the Gentlemen against the Players in 1938. This was made possible for him by a highly paid sinecure with Marsham Tyres, part of the Dunlop empire, arranged by

Warner's contacts at the MCC. Marsham were happy to pay £2,000 a year to have on their books a man likely to become England's captain. In 1938, Warner having failed in his efforts to persuade G.O. ('Gubby') Allen, stockbroker and Middlesex amateur, to continue, Hammond was duly awarded the captaincy.[12]

Writing a few years after his social elevation Hammond embraced 'the republic of the playground' and its mores. 'In England', he wrote, 'we have a way of forgetting differences in technical status in all our games, and cricketers, whether amateurs or professionals, have always been the same jolly crowd of pals to me both before and after I joined the amateur ranks.'[13] Significantly, by the early 1950s, he had come to reflect on these events in a different way:

> It is only the nominal status, not the man or his characteristics, to which objection is taken. I can say this because I captained England, after most of a cricketing lifetime as a professional. I was the same man as before, or perhaps I even had a slightly declining skill by that time. But because I had changed my label all was well. I submit that this is illogical.[14]

It seems clear that Hammond realised that he had become party to the façade that amateurism had been throughout the history of first class cricket. This history is now replete with stories of the (usually large) sums of money paid to amateurs by the county clubs directly and by various intermediaries. Money was paid, in effect, to sustain a certain pattern of class relations. Many cricketers knew this well enough but, unlike Hammond, they chose to retain their social position. Jack Hobbs, Herbert Sutcliffe and Patsy Hendren – stars in the same galaxy as Hammond – were all proud to remain professional cricketers. Indeed, in 1934, when he was the only professional selected to play for the MCC against the Australians at Lords, Hendren refused an invitation to walk out of the pavilion with the other ten, choosing to stride out alone through the professionals' gate, an incident in which the popular press took a significant interest.[15]

Ewart Astill: The First Professional Captain?

Professionals often captained county sides on an occasional basis in the inter-war period when amateurs were playing test cricket or were otherwise unavailable. The first professional cricketer to have been

35

appointed for a season is widely thought to have been Ewart Astill of Leicestershire in 1935 but close examination reveals a more complex story. Leicestershire, like most other counties, were in financial difficulties during the 1930s, relying heavily on fund-raising initiatives and the benefactions of Sir Julian Cahn, a local furniture magnate, also president of Nottinghamshire, who paid off the club's overdraft in 1934. When it came to appointing a first-team captain for 1935 the club first approached Arthur Halezrigg, an Old Etonian and later the second baron, and Wally Beisiegel, an RAF officer serving locally, both of whom turned it down. Charles Packe, from a local landed family, was also approached. Leicestershire, it seems, struggled to find available gentlemen captains at this time – during the 1930s they had seven captains in ten summers – but that did not stop them looking.[16] Early in May the selection committee settled on an Old Reptonian, A.T. Sharp, to lead the first team against Sussex but it 'was decided that Astill should captain the side should Mr Sharp be unable to play'. It subsequently transpired that Sharp, along with another amateur, Bradshaw, who was also offered the captaincy, preferred to play for the Second XI. Ewart Astill, therefore, normally captained Leicestershire in 1935, but only by default. He was never officially appointed and was left in no doubt that his social status, as a professional cricketer, remained unaltered. Indeed, it was re-affirmed, as an entry in the selection committee minutes for 29 May 1935 makes clear.

> Astill. The Secretary reported that Astill's behaviour during the match v. Melton and District had been unsatisfactory. Mr Hilton (the Chairman) undertook to interview Astill.

This sort of incident was unremarkable for a professional cricketer at this time and probably did not reflect personally on Astill, a man known, according to his obituarist, for his 'smiling equanimity'. But no one would have thought to treat an amateur cricketer, let alone an amateur captain, in such a peremptory fashion.[17]

Although Astill's captaincy was conspicuously successful, he was stood down in favour of C.S. Dempster, an amateur and a New Zealand test player, who had been found a job in Leicester by Sir Julian Cahn, managing one of his furniture stores. A public dinner was held in Astill's honour at the Grand Hotel at which he was presented with a gold cigarette case: thanks, as it were, to a humble servant for

Five Counties for Gentlemen Only

At Essex, the captain of the immediate post-war period, T.N. ('Tom') Pearce, was able to play as an amateur because, through Trayton Grinter, an Essex supporter and former player, he was employed by Cockburns, the wine merchants.[27] In 1951 Pearce gave way to ex-Cambridge University captain, Doug Insole, who led the side until his university contemporary, Trevor Bailey, took over in 1961. Insole was employed by George Wimpey, the builders, as an 'assistant public relations officer', a post which he claimed was poorly paid but which, nevertheless, permitted him to play first class cricket. Unusually for this period, Insole offered a robust defence of amateur captaincy: 'Professionals as a whole and there are, I admit, exceptions – do not relish the idea of captaining a side and are generally happy to get on with the game and let some other person be answerable to the authorities for policy decisions.' Moreover, it was wrong, Insole assured his readers, to suggest 'as has been alleged by some extremists, that there is any semblance of a "class" war in cricket'.[28] By 1957 Essex, along with several other county clubs, were in severe financial difficulty, saved only by the revenue generated by a football pools scheme. Insole appears not to have been paid the generous 'expenses' afforded to some other captains and his amateur status may well have assisted the impoverished club. Trevor Bailey, Insole's successor and Essex captain from 1961 to 1966, was employed as club secretary from 1954 to 1967. Here again, since Bailey's post was no sinecure, the county benefited, in this case getting two employees for the price of one.[29]

Derbyshire successfully reformed their captaincy while maintaining its amateur status. Their captains in the immediate post-war period were classically of the old order. Gilbert Hodgkinson (1945–46) was 'never anything more than a good club cricketer' who, because he ran a greengrocery business, was not available for the full season. Eddie Gothard (1947–48) was 'a strict disciplinarian' but he was 42 by the time of his appointment. The record of David Skinner, who led the side for the summer of 1950, averaging a modest 14 with the bat and rarely turning his arm over, suggests that he was a player of below county standard. Some steps towards modernity, however, were evident in the appointment of Guy Willat, ex-Repton and Cambridge University, who captained the side from 1951 to 1954. Willat, who could claim a place in the team on merit, eliminated all amateur–professional segregation at the club.[30] He was succeeded by Donald Carr, ex-Repton and Oxford, another amateur whose abilities could be vouched for by the professionals. For the last two years of his captaincy (1960–62) Carr was also club secretary before moving on to take up the same post with the Test and County Cricket Board.

Post-war politics at Glamorgan County Cricket Club were dominated by Wilfred Wooller, an amateur, who was appointed captain and secretary in 1947, posts he held until 1960 and 1977 respectively. Glamorgan had been a first class county only since 1921 and, perhaps on the principle that traditions are often defended most zealously by those whose hold on them is the most tenuous, the club mounted one of the most determined defences of amateur captaincy in the championship. Moreover, there was much evidence at the club of what Richard Holt has called 'the complex blend of dependency and assertiveness found in the relationship of Wales with England'.[31] For many within the club's establishment in the 1950s, the greatest names in the Glamorgan pantheon were those of ex-captains Maurice Turnbull and J.C. Clay, Welshmen with English amateur credentials. Turnbull, a Cambridge blue and England test player, was killed in action with the Welsh Guards in 1944, while Clay, a Wykehamist and landowner, played through the 1930s with all the amateur insouciance of the Edwardian era.[32] Wooller modelled himself on the autocratic Turnbull and was fiercely competitive, a combination of attributes which seemed destined to attract controversy. For traditionalists Wooller was insufficiently a gentleman, especially after he was accused of unsporting play against Surrey at Cardiff in 1956; for the modernists he was too highhanded. A faction on the Glamorgan committee, which included 'businessmen and industrialists', was keen to replace Wooller with a professional captain and, in 1958, he offered to stand down if a suitable replacement could be found. In defining the latter, however, those sympathetic to the amateur cause prevailed and Wooller remained in post, a trawl of the available Oxbridge blues having come to nothing. This trawl, incidentally, included placing advertisements in the press, a practice adopted by several counties in the 1950s.[33]

The only other amateur on Glamorgan's books at this time was Tony Lewis, then an undergraduate at Cambridge but earmarked at the age of 17 as a future club captain. Lewis later wrote vividly of the social world into which he was propelled at this early age by his skipper. Wooller made it clear to Lewis on only his second appearance that he wanted him to captain the side one day, pointing out that 'it would mean being an amateur'. 'You'll get your expenses but no match fees,' Wooller explained. 'Stay close to me, I'll show you the ropes.'

> At Old Trafford, Mr Wooller and Mr Lewis, the only two amateurs, went through the players' dining room where they were tucking into steak and kidney pie, to join the Lancashire committee who always lunched with some formality. Impeccably uniformed waitresses offered aperitifs and handed out menus indicating choices of meats hot or cold and often salmon. If an amateur had the misfortune to lose his wicket during the morning's play he could settle into Stilton and port with abandon.

On other major grounds, Lewis discovered, the amateurs had their own dressing rooms. At the Oval the accommodation was especially spacious. It came replete with 'wicker armchairs for viewing the game, dressing table with clothes brushes, a basket for used hand towels'. Five minutes before the start of play Lewis and his captain were informed by their personal attendant: 'The umpires are out and your team is ready.' Lewis's induction into the ways of the gentleman amateur was in 1955. In 1960, with the days of port and Stilton drawing gradually to a close, Wooller was replaced by O.S. ('Ossie') Wheatley, a Cambridge blue who had previously played for Warwickshire, and Lewis was installed as his vice-captain and heir apparent. Both were 'modern' amateurs in the sense that they were cricketers of first class standard who, while by no means impoverished, lacked substantial private wealth. Both were found employment – Wheatley in advertising and Lewis within the club as another of the growing cadre of county 'assistant secretaries'. Lewis plunged deeper still into modernity in the early 1960s when he and his wife opened a boutique in Cardiff called 'Popsie'.[34]

Of all the counties, Hampshire were probably the most successful in negotiating the 1950s without undue controversy or radical change. This seems to have been achieved through a steadily paternalistic regime, in which gentlemanly government was neither very officious nor obviously under threat. For much of its history the club had especially strong links with the cricket culture of the public schools. H.S. Altham, historian of the game and Hampshire's president until his death in 1965, had been cricket master at Charterhouse for 20 years. There was also a noticeable Winchester connection; by the late 1980s 34 Wykehamists had played for the county. Desmond Eager (Cheltenham and Oxford), club secretary and captain from 1946 to 1958, 'believed in the standards of the "Golden Age" of cricket and in later life was concerned that cricket was becoming too much part of show business'.[35] When he retired the captaincy passed to Colin Ingleby-Mackenzie, Old Etonian and *bon viveur*, under whose leadership Hampshire developed a style that might have might have been scripted in Hollywood. At a time when English cricket was tentatively embracing a more professional, business-orientated approach Ingleby-Mackenzie ordered his players to go out and have fun, requiring only that they should 'be in bed by breakfast time'. Improbably, Hampshire won the championship in 1962, thereby giving hope to every romantic conservative in the English game. Later that year Ingleby-Mackenzie published his autobiography, a breathless chronicle of cricket in the colonies, race meetings and all-night parties with fun-loving debutantes. Some cricket writers, including Hampshire's favourite son, John Arlott, felt compelled to marry the playboy to the new technocratic age, insisting that Ingleby-Mackenzie was tactically shrewder than he appeared.[36]

At the Oval, generally seen as second only to Lords as a centre of English cricket power and prestige, Surrey's determined pursuit of an amateur captain in the immediate post-war years took on an element of farce. Seeking a replacement for their pre-war captain, the dashing Monty Garland-Wells, who had been wounded in action, the county were told of a good amateur player, named Bennett, currently playing club cricket in London, who might possibly fill the gap. When H.N. Bennett, an ex-public schoolboy and club cricketer with no first class experience, called in at the Oval one day to ask for some second eleven cricket, he was surprised to be offered the captaincy of the first team. He took the job, leading Surrey during 1946, but had almost certainly been mistaken for A.C.L. Bennett, another ex-public schoolboy, who had occasionally captained Northamptonshire.[37] One of the club's historians insists huffily that 'no useful purpose can be served by compiling a thesis on this subject', which strongly implies that the story is true.[38] Bennett lasted only one season, whereupon Surrey brought back a pre-war captain, a throwback to gentler times. The faint praise bestowed by the club on E.R.T. Holmes, an Old

Malvernian, Oxford blue and member of the Stock Exchange, speaks largely for itself. 'Not a master tactician', he was said to possess 'great charm and sweetness'. Holmes captained Surrey for only two years, possibly because he believed that 'county cricket was becoming dull and stagnating'.[39] His successor, Michael Barton, had played no first class cricket after Oxford but did manage a thousand runs in 1951, his last season.

Surrey effectively embraced modernity in appointing Stuart Surridge to follow Barton. Surridge was, by then, 34 and comfortably off through his family's sports goods business. Although he was an amateur, leading professionals, like Dollery, recognised him as a kindred spirit. 'He was a tough competitor but he always gave the impression that he was one of the boys so far as the Surrey team were concerned.'[40] Surrey won the County Championship in every year of Surridge's captaincy from 1952 to 1956. Peter May (Charterhouse and Cambridge), who took over in 1957, was not one of the lads in the way that Surridge had been, but he was an England batsman who, at his own estimation, 'did not always play in the obviously light-hearted way that had been associated with some amateurs in the past'.[41] Significantly, May was assisted by an experienced professional vice-captain in Alec Bedser. Thus arrangements at the Oval came to resemble the cross-class alliance so often portrayed in British war films of the time: the diffident upper-class major and his faithful, straight-talking NCO. May relied heavily on the devoutly conservative Bedser but was unable to stifle insubordination in the ranks, clashing especially with Jim Laker, his colleague in the England test team, who made public his resentment of the expenses paid to amateur cricketers. Laker once outraged England selector 'Gubby' Allen by asking if he could become an amateur so as to make more money. When, in 1960, he published a book criticising May as aloof, Surrey withdrew his honorary membership of the club.[42]

Keeping Up Appearances

The midland counties of Northamptonshire and Worcestershire, like Leicestershire, stood well down cricket's hierarchy of prestige. And, though it staged test matches, so too did Nottinghamshire. The committees of these clubs, heavily reliant on the local gentry, sought for much of the 1950s to maintain a vestige of respectability by appointing amateur captains, settling for professionals only when no suitable candidate could be attracted. With the emphasis now increasingly on cricketing ability as much as on the personal attributes deemed necessary for captaincy, these lesser counties were often pursuing a very small list of candidates. This might include, typically, the current Varsity captains along with any amateurs at other counties with blocked leadership aspirations. Sometimes such men said 'Yes'; more often they said 'No'.

At Northamptonshire, the late 1940s are referred to dryly by the club's historians as 'the double-barrelled years'. At the end of 1946 P.E. Murray-Willis gave way as captain to A.W. Childs-Clarke, whose principal credential appears to have been that he had played a few games for Middlesex, the last one in 1934. Childs-Clarke appeared shaken by the committee's expectation that the team, rooted at the foot of the league table, should do better. 'Where have I let you down?' he asked plaintively in 1948. Childs-Clarke was replaced by Freddie Brown, an ex-England player, who was prepared to make himself available provided that he was 'given a job'; local patron John Pascoe of British Timken obliged and Brown served as captain from 1949 to 1953. During the autocratic Brown's captaincy, showering at Northampton still took place in order of seniority and a bath was reserved for the captain's use. After Brown's retirement the club advertised for a replacement but settled in the end for Dennis Brookes, one of their own professionals. The committee, however, insisted on an amateur vice-captain, one member being of the opinion that to have two professionals on the bridge would be 'an enormous mistake'. Though Brookes served for three years, from 1954 to 1957, the club continued to seek an amateur captain, finally settling on Ramon Subba Row, a Cambridge blue of Bengali and English parentage then playing for Surrey. He arrived in 1956, having been offered flexible employment with a local accountancy firm and the county captaincy from 1958.[43]

At Worcester amateur captaincy was also maintained until the mid-1950s, being entrusted to, amongst others, Alexander Parkinson ('Sandy') Singleton – 'a lively joyful cricketer and an adventurous leader' – and R.E.S. Wyatt, the ex-Warwickshire and England player, 48 years old at the time of his appointment.[44] As Worcestershire professional Don Kenyon recalled later, the county at that time often 'included amateurs who weren't quite up to it and that did cause resentment... When it came to the captaincy', he added, 'the same situation applied.'[45] Reg Perks became Worcestershire's first professional captain in 1955 but was replaced a year later by Peter Richardson, an amateur, who was given an administrative position at the club. In 1958 Richardson gave way to Kenyon, by then 35, and a professional at Worcestershire since 1946.

During this period no county appears to have had as much difficulty in attracting gentlemen of the 'right stuff' as Nottinghamshire. It was not until 1961, however, that they appointed their first professional captain and, even then, John Clay was only a caretaker because Andrew Corran, an Oxford blue, was unavailable until July. Immediately after the Second World War Nottinghamshire had been captained by G.F.H. Hearne, who had played under the patronage of Sir Julian Cahn since the late 1920s, leading the side from 1936. It is said that he was withdrawn in 1946 because one of the senior professionals 'objected to being shouted at'. Hearne's replacement, William Sime, was an Oxford graduate with little experience of first class cricket, who practised as a barrister in Nottingham. Sime lasted for four summers, giving way in 1951 to Reg Simpson. Simpson, the only amateur to lead Nottinghamshire after 1945 who had credibility as a first class cricketer, was another 'assistant secretary', later admitting that 'they didn't see much of me at the office', and was also employed by Gunn and Moore, the local cricket equipment firm. When Simpson retired in 1960 his replacement, Corran, lasted only one season, possibly because his experience of first class cricket was limited, a handicap which, by then, was unlikely to be tolerated in the average county dressing room.[46]

Ructions in the Rural South

Sussex, too, negotiated the 1940s and 1950s with little recourse to professional captaincy. Despite a better endowment of gifted amateur cricketers than the midland counties – six of the seven men who captained Sussex between 1946 and 1965 were Cambridge blues – it proved impossible to avoid public controversy. The county were captained immediately after the war by S.C. ('Billy') Griffiths, who was also club secretary, succeeded in 1947 by Hugh Bartlett, who had been a friend of Griffiths at Cambridge. By the end of the 1940s, however, the membership became dissatisfied with the team's performance, prompting both Griffiths and Bartlett to resign in 1950. The club now announced a joint captaincy of R.G. Hunt and Hubert Doggart, Hunt to cover for Doggart until the end of the Cambridge term. It was not unusual, of course, for county clubs to organise team selection and captaincy around the restricted availability of Oxbridge players but, significantly, the plan was angrily attacked at the annual general meeting in 1950, members expressing concern at what was seen as a haphazard approach unlikely to promote continuity in team affairs. In these unhappy circumstances Jim Langridge was appointed captain, the first professional to lead the club. This was, however, but a temporary expedient; amateur captaincy was restored in 1953 when David Sheppard, former Cambridge captain and only 24 years old, took up the reins. The following summer saw Hubert Doggart in post before returning to teach at Winchester. Leadership responsibilities then passed on to a third ex-Cambridge University captain, Robin Marlar, who captained the side until 1959.[47]

Sussex, in the mid 1950s, had 31 registered amateurs and, though the strength of the side derived largely from the 25 contracted professionals, it was remarkable that professional captaincy should have occurred at all in these circumstances. The committee generally held out for amateur captains, but the issue was at times vigorously contested. Ted Dexter, the county's last amateur captain, appointed in 1960, represented little in the way of compromise with the professionals. As his predecessor noted, Dexter was 'never one of the boys' but, in other ways, he was a bridge between tradition and modernity. There was something of the old-style Corinthian about Dexter. At Cambridge he had played much sport but was said to have attended no lectures. In 1956, having promised to play a few games for the county, he sent a postcard cancelling the arrangement, having met an attractive woman in Copenhagen. But, significantly, Dexter developed his own business interests, not in the City, but in the emergent field of sports media and public relations.[48]

Elsewhere among the southern counties questions of captaincy, contoured by emergent notions of meritocracy and professionalism, were a visible source of conflict. At Kent, the first two captains of the post-war period were the amateurs Bryan Valentine and D.G. Clark. The idea of professional captaincy was first mooted in 1951 when Les Ames, then the senior professional, was approached with a view to succeeding Clark, initially on the condition that he turned amateur.

Ames had declined and the Oxford-educated William Murray-Wood, who had first played for Kent in 1936, took over, though it soon became clear that he did not enjoy the confidence of his team. Dressing-room dissent culminated in an incident at Canterbury in 1953 when the entire Kent side made it clear that they would not play for the county again unless the captaincy was removed from Murray-Wood forthwith. This led to the appointment of Kent's first professional captain, Doug Wright, in 1954, though three years later the leadership reverted to an amateur, Colin Cowdrey, who had served as a stop-gap replacement for Murray-Wood following his hasty departure the previous season.[49] Cowdrey, however, considered himself one of the 'new-style amateurs', primarily a cricketer worth his place, anxious to win matches and to govern, where possible, by consent. He consulted closely with his senior professional, Les Ames, and tactfully restricted amateur access to the side. Some had come to expect a place to be made available for them each year during 'Canterbury week'.[50]

The difficulty in finding gentlemen of sufficient cricketing calibre to lead the team seems to have been especially acute at Somerset; the county had seven captains during 1948 alone. These included Norman Mitchell-Innes, an army officer recently returned from the Sudan who regarded the burden of captaincy as 'great fun'. Somerset settled on George Woodhouse (Marlborough and Cambridge) for 1949 and then on Stuart Rogers, another army officer, from 1950 to 1953. The club's official history describes Rogers as 'a modest player' and, equally significantly, his successor, Ben Brocklehurst, as 'a disciplinarian'. Cricket culture in the 1950s was increasingly intolerant of both inferior players and autocrats and, in the summer of 1953, three local journalists, possibly speaking for disgruntled players as well as members, began a campaign against the county committee. Though rebuffed at first the modernisers eventually triumphed in 1956 when Somerset, having finished last in the championship for the previous four seasons, turned for the first time to a professional captain, appointing Maurice Tremlett to lead the side.[51]

There was an equally turbulent turn of events at Gloucestershire resulting in one of the *causes célèbres* of English cricket during the last days of amateurism. Once again the issues of cricketing ability and of where, in the new age of efficiency, the true qualities of modern leadership might reside, were at the heart of the dispute. At Gloucester the pendulum seemed to swing more violently between amateurs and professionals than at any other club. There was also a background of severe financial difficulty, increasingly likely in the post-war era to be linked to playing performance and thence to captaincy. Walter Hammond had been followed by two amateurs, B.O. Allen in 1947 and then Sir Derrick Bailey in 1952. For 1953, however, the job was entrusted to a professional, Jack Crapp, who captained the side for two summers before retreating to the ranks on the grounds that the responsibility was affecting his form. Perhaps seeing this as proof that professionals were not cut out to lead, Gloucestershire now went for George Emmett, an autocrat with a 'curmudgeonly exterior', known among the team as 'Captain Bligh'.[52] For Emmett's replacement in 1959 the club chose a professional, Tom Graveney, by then an experienced test cricketer, but later engaged C.T.M. Pugh, a London-based Old Etonian, with the promise that he would shortly be elevated to the captaincy. Having failed to persuade Graveney, who had not been told of the promise to Pugh, to remain as senior professional, the club agreed to release him to join another county but then reneged on this arrangement, leaving the player stranded and temporarily out of county cricket in 1961. The popular press was predictably keen to probe this strife between master and high-profile servant and Graveney was offered £2,000 for his story by *The People*. But the most important aspect of the saga, from the standpoint of contemporary dressing-room politics, was rarely mentioned: Pugh was probably not a cricketer of county standard. When captaining the side Graveney had been reluctant to play him 'because I did not think he was up to scratch'. But, in a sense, the reason given by the county for dismissing Graveney also reflected more modern thinking, the covert promise to Pugh notwithstanding. It was, the county explained, not a question of Graveney's social status; Gloucestershire had made a loss of £15,000 over the summer of 1960 and it was this that had compelled the club to review its captaincy arrangements.[53]

Trouble up North: Yorks and Lancs

Yorkshire ended the 1950s as county champions, bringing Surrey's run of seven titles to a close. Surrey's success had been attributed in large part to captaincy, to Surridge as *primus inter pares* and to May ably supported by Bedser. Yorkshire, the county of Lord Hawke, persisted with amateur captains throughout the 1940s and 1950s, despite having

England's first professional captain, Len Hutton, on their books. When they won the title in 1959 some observers were inclined to attribute this success to the captain, Ronnie Burnett. This no doubt encouraged the club's historian to describe Burnett's contribution as 'immeasurable' despite decidedly modest totals of runs and wickets. Averaging only 11.47 with the bat, Burnett took only six catches and captured only one wicket in two overs. 'But few who watched that side would deny that he had a tremendous hand in leading the team to success.'[54]

Opinion among the players, however, seems to have been divided. Brian Close, in his memoirs, described both Burnett and Billy Sutcliffe, his predecessor, as nice men who, nevertheless, should have had neither the captaincy nor a place in the side.[55] Sutcliffe, who had succeeded Norman Yardley in 1955, stood down after much abuse from Yorkshire crowds and a dressing-room petition demanding his resignation. Burnett had strong support from some players but rowed persistently with Johnny Wardle, his senior professional, whom others believed should have had the captaincy.[56] Wardle was sacked at the end of 1958 having criticised Burnett's leadership in *The Daily Mail*. Yorkshire's captaincy controversies in this period seem more overlaid with personal feuding than at other counties but the lines of contestation were clear and, for the time, not unusual: amateur versus professional and team selection on merit versus the tradition of the captain born to lead. Despite the championship of 1959, Yorkshire did not risk another amateur as Burnett's successor and, in 1960, Vic Wilson became the county's first professional captain since the 1880s.

Across the Pennines virtually all the ingredients of contemporary cricket strife were present during this period – status divisions, disgruntled spectators, militant members, a discontented dressing room, an intransigent committee wedded to tradition. 'At Lancashire', according to Frank Parr, who signed as a professional in 1946, 'you were kept in your place.' 'The committee', he recalled, 'were firmly rooted in the 1920s – or even before that.' Any member was entitled to come at any time after work and have the services of two professionals to bowl at him.[57] In 1946 the captaincy had been offered to Tommy Higson, a solicitor and son of a former captain, who had led the side for a few games before the war but he had turned it down, feeling that his cricket was not of the required standard. The job went instead to an Old Worksopian, Jack Fallows who, according to club historian Keith

Hayhurst, 'was even worse than Tommy'.[58] Fallows was succeeded by two cricketers of acknowledged ability: Ken Cranston (1947–48), a dentist waiting to take over his father's practice, and Nigel Howard, son of Major Rupert Howard, the club secretary. Under the latter's leadership Lancashire were joint champions in 1950 but, when Essex visited Old Trafford a year or two later, Trevor Bailey 'was sorry to note that the attitude of their supporters had changed'. Howard, who was still captain, 'was jeered all the way to the wicket, not just by the paying spectators but also by members whose committee had appointed him'.[59]

Howard's successor, the England player, Cyril Washbrook, thought by many to have run the side under Howard, was Lancashire's first professional captain and his appointment was hailed as a blow for modernity. 'Tradition has been thrown overboard,' declared the *Manchester Evening News*, 'and for once public opinion has triumphed.' The professional cricket captain, it explained, 'is just as much a sign of progress as is the jet plane or a television set.'[60] But neither Washbrook nor the committee that appointed him was as modern as they seemed. Washbrook, one of the first grammar school boys to become a professional cricketer, was widely perceived at Old Trafford and beyond as an autocrat in the mould of Wooller and other 'Captain Blighs' of the county circuit. Many regarded him as an amateur in all but name and he himself had stated that he might prefer to play as one if he could afford it.[61]

Washbrook's stern regime lasted for six years and, on his retirement, his young amateur vice-captain, the Cambridge blue, Bob Barber, took over. Moreover, on the committee's instructions, apparently conveyed by Colonel Leonard Green, who had captained the side in the 1920s, Barber revived the pre-war practice of staying in a separate hotel from the other players. In 1961, amid continuing grapevine and press stories of player unrest, a Lancashire player, Peter Marner, was sent home from the county's match against Kent at Folkestone 'after ignoring a committee edict on wearing blazers at lunch'.[62] Barber resigned that year but the Lancashire committee determined to persist with amateur captaincy. They appointed Joe Blackledge, an Old Reptonian waiting to assume management of the family mill, who had played for Lancashire's Second XI in the 1950s. Both Blackledge and the team had a poor season, the former with a highest score of 68 and the latter finishing next to bottom of the table. Blackledge's appointment, he thinks now, was partly inspired by the notion, generated by Burnett's achievements at Yorkshire, that a modest cricketer could nevertheless bring success through applying skills of leadership. 'The thinking must have been that Ronnie Burnett had done a great job for Yorkshire – and he didn't get many runs, did he?'[63] Lancashire reverted to professional captaincy in 1963 with Ken Grieves; when he was sacked in 1964 the committee lost a vote of no confidence. One of its final acts, prior to new elections, was to advertise in *The Times* for a new captain.

Lords, and the Quiet Death of Amateur Status

It has become evident in the course of this survey that the English county clubs adhered to the principle of amateur captaincy with great tenacity in the post-war period. Circumstances might persuade them to depart from the principle on occasion but it was rarely abandoned comprehensively; indeed, some counties appear to have gone to extraordinary lengths in pursuit of leaders in the traditional mould. At Middlesex, as at Lancashire, the club persisted in this course right through to the early 1960s. Middlesex had long suffered from a shortage of good amateur cricketers; as early as 1935 Walter Robins had been appointed to captain a side that was already 'essentially professional'. Robins, who retired in 1947, was succeeded by another amateur, George Mann, but on his retirement in 1949 there was no obvious successor and the committee was obliged 'to investigate the future availability of amateurs to see who could be asked to lead the side'. Finding a new captain with the appropriate gentlemanly and cricketing qualifications proved difficult; Middlesex had seven different captains during the summer of 1950.[64] In these circumstances the county had little alternative but to appoint its first professional captain, Denis Compton, in 1951, albeit jointly with Bill Edrich, newly-turned amateur. Edrich, however, had sole captaincy from 1952 to 1957 and was succeeded by J.J. Warr, another amateur, from 1958 to 1960. Both Edrich and Warr were accomplished cricketers but, in 1960, with no amateurs available within the club to fill the vacant captaincy, Middlesex turned to Ian Bedford, a relatively unknown London club cricketer. Bedford served for two years before giving way to Oxford blue Colin Dryborough.

Bedford's appointment, like that of Blackledge at Lancashire, seems extraordinary. It defied the new meritocratic thinking among county professionals and it was made barely two years before the distinction between amateurs and professionals was abandoned. But the Middlesex officials, as we have seen, were not out of line in their reluctance to appoint a professional captain. The sustained resistance to professional captaincy can be explained. Many cricket administrators in the 1940s and 1950s – retired officers from the armed forces, members of the gentry and men of private means – were drawn from social worlds in which status was still ascribed rather than earned. They preferred their captains to be of a similar stamp. This is illustrated by an incident from the early 1950s recalled by David Sheppard.

> When I was at Cambridge we played against Gloucestershire at Bristol. I made some runs, and, as we came off the field, Tom Graveney, with whom I had made friends in 2nd XI matches said, 'Well played, David.' A few minutes later the Gloucestershire captain for that match walked into our dressing-room and came over to me. 'I'm terribly sorry about Graveney's impertinence,' he said. 'I think you'll find it won't happen again.'[65]

Relations, of course, were not always as bleak as this, but county captains administered an often severe discipline and, as we have seen, county committees strove to maintain the decorum of a bygone age. The greater the threat to this decorum – be it from dressing-room unrest or from the thriving commercial culture of the wider world – generally, the greater their determination. Moreover, adherence to tradition and what were increasingly perceived as oppressive workplace relations helped to ensure that wage costs remained relatively low. The amateur captain, always canvassed as the man who would stand up to the committee, was more likely to be the instrument of the committee's will in this regard, standing 'no nonsense'. This policy was given an extra edge when clubs spurned other possible sources of income as at Essex, in the early 1950s, where Sir Hubert Ashton, the club's president, refused to allow the club to run a football pool, believing that cricket should not profit from gambling.[66]

But, despite the tenacity with which the counties adhered to amateur captaincy, the writing was on the wall. In a post-war world where the phrase 'got to earn a living' was gaining greater currency, there were fewer men either willing or able to suspend a business career to play a summer's cricket, however generous the 'expenses'. By the late 1950s English county cricket was haemorrhaging spectators, gentlemen and benefactors, each loss exacerbating the others. An attempt to re-present the amateur captain as a born manager and as someone who could 'get results' in the new technocratic universe was generally unsuccessful, especially when they were transplanted from outside county cricket. The increasingly common practice of employing amateur captains as secretaries or assistant secretaries appeared to offer a way forward for some counties but, as a strategy, its value was limited. Though it represented a compromise between tradition and modernity it displeased the socially conservative elements on county committees who, because the men concerned were paid servants of the club, regarded it as a perversion of the true amateur spirit.

With attendances at county matches falling and most clubs in a state of seemingly permanent financial difficulty, those administering the English first class game came, belatedly, to a realisation that it was necessary to court the new, populist mass media. This meant developing a sense of cricket as a 'product' and learning what constituted 'good' and 'bad' publicity in the marketing of this product. The MCC needed the popular press and, in time, television and advertisers on their side. To the population at large and also to a growing proportion of its own public, a sport in which team leaders were selected primarily on the basis of birth and private education was plainly off-putting. The modern marketplace demanded images of achievement through openness and merit rather than sensational stories about talented cricketers, like Wardle, Laker and Graveney, who had been slighted by 'the toffs'. Newspapers were prepared to pay handsomely for such stories but they represented negative publicity for the game as a whole.

It also became increasingly clear to the MCC that the persistent controversy regarding payments to amateurs, captains and otherwise, was disabling the England team, the commercial and political significance of which had never been higher. Test matches, which usually sold out, now generated additional revenue through television and, with the British Empire in the process of being dismantled, matches against newly independent states placed the reputation of the old colonial power permanently at stake. After an acrimonious tour of Australia in 1958–59, professionals in the England side began to raise the question of differential expenses. Two years later the MCC Cricket Enquiry Committee, which had been prevaricating on the issue of the amateur–professional distinction since 1957, recommended that it should go, and the debate on the merits or otherwise of amateur captaincy began to fade from view. This did not mean, of course, that captains of first class teams no longer came from the public schools; far from it. It simply meant that such players were reconstituted as part of the reservoir – the market – from which counties could draw. This was a significant step in the direction of modernity, not least on account of the comparatively early stage at which an apparently reactionary body was prepared to make it. As leading cricket commentator Christopher Martin-Jenkins has pointed out, the abolition of the amateur status was 'more a reflection of changing attitudes in society than a radical shift in the character of cricket'. The new dispensation arrived at the same time as England's first commercially sponsored competition, a limited overs, knock-out tournament backed by the Gillette razor company.[67] This was clearly no coincidence.

ACKNOWLEDGEMENTS

My thanks to David Collier, chief executive of Leicestershire CCC and to Roger Knight, secretary of the MCC, for allowing me access to the records of their respective clubs. Many thanks also to Stephen Green and Glenys Williams at the Lords library; Sue Wilson and Harjeet Singh at Lancashire CCC; Campbell Burnap, Frank Parr, Paul and Les Corrall, Keith Hayhurst, Chris and Pam Lee, Joe Blackledge, Dil Porter, Adrian Smith and Jon Gemmell.

NOTES

1. The keynote quotation is taken from pp.12–13 of the 1974 edition of *The Bridge on the River Kwai*, published in London by Secker & Warburg; Pierre Boule's book was originally published in 1956.
2. Michael Marshall, *Gentlemen and Players: Conversations with Cricketers* (London: Grafton Books, 1987), p.222.
3. Christopher Brookes, *English Cricket: the Game and its Players throughout the Ages* (London: Weidenfeld & Nicolson, 1978), pp.96–7, 101–19; Ric Sissons, *The Players: A Social History of the Professional Cricketer* (London: Kingswood Press, 1988), pp.71–82; Mike Marquese, *Anyone but England: Cricket and the National Malaise* (London: Verso, 1995), pp.59–64; see also G. Derek West, *The Elevens of England* (London: Darf Publishers, 1988).
4. David Lemmon, *The Crisis of Captaincy: Servant and Master in English Cricket* (London: Christopher Helm, 1988), p.14. Both Yorkshire and Nottinghamshire had

appointed professional captains in the nineteenth century, William Clark leading Notts for 20 years from 1835.

5. Marquese, *Anyone but England*, p.75; Eric Midwinter, *The Illustrated History of County Cricket* (London: The Kingswood Press/Bass, 1992), pp.21, 26.
6. Steel, quoted in Lemmon, *Crisis of Captaincy*, p.28.
7. John Arlott, *Jack Hobbs: Profile of 'The Master'* (Harmondsworth: Penguin Books, 1982), p.64; Warner cited in Rowland Bowen, *Cricket: A History of its Growth and Development throughout the World* (London: Eyre & Spottiswoode, 1970), pp.141–2.
8. James Bradley, 'The MCC, Society and Empire: A Portrait of Cricket's Ruling Body 1860–1914', in J.A. Mangan (ed.), *The Cultural Bond: Sport, Empire, Society* (London: Frank Cass, 1992), pp.27–8.
9. James Coldham, *Lord Hawke: A Cricketing Biography* (Ramsbury: Crowood Press, 1990), pp.9, 183–4.
10. Sissons, *The Players*, p.245
11. It was under Warner's captaincy in Australia during the 1903–4 MCC tour that amateurs and professionals stayed at the same hotels for the first time. See Gerald Howat, *Plum Warner* (London: Unwin Hyman, 1987), p.42.
12. David Foot, *Wally Hammond: The Reasons Why* (London: Robson, 1998), pp.234–5; Howat, *Warner*, pp.162–3; Sissons, *The Players*, p.248.
13. Walter Hammond, *Cricket My Destiny* (London: Stanley Paul, 1946), p.136.
14. Walter Hammond, *Cricket's Secret History* (London: Stanley Paul, 1952), p.55.
15. Sissons, *The Players*, p.257; Brookes, *English Cricket*, p.254; Marshall, *Gentlemen and Players*, pp.120–21.
16. Leicestershire were not unusual in this respect. Hampshire had six captains in the summer of 1933 alone when the regular incumbent, the Hon. Lionel Tennyson, was ill. See Peter Wynne-Thomas, *The History of Hampshire County Cricket Club* (London: Christopher Helm, 1988), p.105.
17. Denis Lambert, *The History of Leicestershire County Cricket Club* (London: Christopher Helm, 1992), pp.108–34.
18. Marshall, *Gentlemen and Players*, p.137.
19. Lambert, *History of Leicestershire*, p.189
20. Marshall, *Gentlemen and Players*, p.137.
21. Ken Barrington, *Running into Hundreds* (London: Stanley Paul, 1963), p.173.
22. Jack Bannister, *The History of Warwickshire County Cricket Club* (London: Christopher Helm, 1990), pp.99–101; 109–10, 114.
23. H.E. 'Tom' Dollery, *Professional Captain* (London: Stanley Paul, 1952), p.161.
24. Bannister, *History of Warwickshire*, p.124.
25. Dollery, *Professional Captain*, p.170.
26. Gerald Howat, *Len Hutton: the Biography* (London: Mandarin, 1990), p.105; Sir Leonard Hutton, *Fifty Years in Cricket*, (London: Stanley Paul, 1954), p.64.
27. David Lemmon and Mike Marshall, *Essex County Cricket Club: the Official History* (London: Kingswood Press), pp.158–9.
28. Douglas Insole, *Cricket from the Middle* (London: William Heinemann/The Naldrett Press, 1960), pp.36, 47.
29. Trevor Bailey, *Wickets, Catches and the Odd Run* (London: Willow Books, 1986), pp.62–3.
30. John Shawcroft, *The History of Derbyshire County Cricket Club* (London: Christopher Helm, 1989), pp.139, 142, 151–2, 161.

31. Richard Holt, *Sport and the British* (Oxford: Oxford University Press, 1992), pp.203–4.
32. Tony Lewis, *Playing Days* (London: Stanley Paul, 1985), pp.72–5.
33. Andrew Hignell, *The History of Glamorgan County Cricket Club* (London: Christopher Helm, 1988), pp.172–6; see also Wilfred Wooller, *A History of County Cricket: Glamorgan* (London: Arthur Barker, 1971), pp.90–97.
34. Lewis, *Playing Days*, pp.70–71, 92–3.
35. Wynne-Thomas, *History of Hampshire*, p.128.
36. Colin Ingleby-Mackenzie, *Many a Slip* (London: Oldbourne, 1962).
37. David Lemmon, *The History of Surrey County Cricket Club* (London: Christopher Helm, 1989), p.200.
38. Gordon Ross, *A History of County Cricket: Surrey* (London: Arthur Barker, 1971), p.98.
39. Lemmon, *History of Surrey*, p.177.
40. Marshall, *Gentlemen and Players*, p.181.
41. Peter May, *A Game Enjoyed* (London: Stanley Paul, 1985), p.xiii.
42. Marshall, *Gentlemen and Players*, pp.253–4; see also Jim Laker, *Over to Me* (London: Frederick Muller, 1960), pp.177–8.
43. M. Engel and A. Radd, *The History of Northamptonshire County Cricket Club* (London: Christopher Helm, 1993), pp.142–78.
44. David Lemmon, *The History of Worcestershire County Cricket Club* (London: Christopher Helm, 1989), p.110.
45. Marshall, *Gentlemen and Players*, p.149.
46. Marshall, *Gentlemen and Players*, pp.146–7.
47. Christopher Lee, *From the Sea End: the Official History of Sussex County Cricket Club* (London: Partridge Press, 1989), pp.188–96.
48. Alan Lee, *Lord Ted: the Dexter Enigma* (London: Cassell, 1996), p.74.
49. Dudley Moore, *The History of Kent County Cricket Club* (London: Christopher Helm, 1988), pp.120–28.
50. Colin Cowdrey, *M.C.C.: The Autobiography of a Cricketer* (London: Coronet, 1977), p.81; Marshall, *Gentlemen and Players*, p.198.
51. David Foot, *Sunshine, Sixes and Cider: A History of Somerset Cricket* (Newton Abbot: David & Charles, 1986), pp.142–78.
52. David Green, *The History of Gloucestershire County Cricket Club* (London: Christopher Helm, 1990), pp.108–9, 119.
53. Tom Graveney, *The Heart of Cricket* (London: Arthur Barker, 1983), pp.18–19.
54. Anthony Woodhouse, *The History of Yorkshire County Cricket Club* (London: Christopher Helm, 1989), p.418.
55. Brian Close, *I Don't Bruise Easily* (London: Futura, 1979), pp.41–3.
56. Freddie Trueman, *The Freddie Trueman Story* (London: Stanley Paul, 1965), pp.28–9; Fred Trueman, *Ball of Fire: An Autobiography* (London: J.M. Dent, 1976), pp.67–71.
57. Frank Parr interviewed by the author, 11 June 1999.
58. Keith Hayhurst interviewed by the author, 29 September 1999.
59. Bailey, *Wickets*, p.93.
60. *Manchester Evening News*, 17 February 1954.
61. Cyril Washbrook, *Cricket – The Silver Lining* (London: Sportsguide Publications, 1950), p.200.
62. Brian Bearshaw, *From the Stretford End: the Official History of Lancashire County Cricket Club* (London: Partridge Press, 1990), pp.301–3.

63. Joe Blackledge interviewed by the author, 30 September 1999.
64. David Lemmon, *The History of the Middlesex County Cricket Club* (London: Christopher Helm, 1988), pp.212–13.
65. David Sheppard, *Parson's Pitch* (London: Hodder & Stoughton, 1964), pp.165–6.
66. Bailey, *Wickets*, p.63.
67. Christopher Martin-Jenkins, *Twenty Years On: Cricket's Years of Change 1963 to 1983* (London: Willow Books, 1984), p.11.

'Big Money': The Tournament Player and the PGA, 1945–75

RAY PHYSICK and RICHARD HOLT

Professionalism and commercialisation can easily be confused, especially in Britain where amateurs frequently retained overall control of sports in which players were paid for their services. Historically, both cricket and association football, for example, saw an accommodation between the employment of professional players and a broadly non-profit-making philosophy of sport. So, too, did golf. The Professional Golfers' Association (PGA) was begun in 1901 primarily to promote the interests of those who were employed by golf clubs to teach the game, mend clubs and help maintain the course. The PGA encouraged the holding of tournaments with cash prizes for their members as an occasional supplement to regular earnings rather than as end in itself. Although the idea of a tournament circuit supporting a specialised group of top players was born before the First World War, the full implications of golf as a commercial sporting entertainment were not apparent until very much later. Failure to grasp the new commercial possibilities of the sport became a major grievance among the post-war generation of top tournament professionals, who increasingly challenged the decisions, structures and ethos of what they saw as an ageing and inflexible association. For their part, the PGA was understandably disinclined to risk the interests of its wider membership for the sake of the few. There were around 1,400 professinal golfers in post-war Britain including assistants. Around 250 played in tournaments but no more than 20 were in serious contention.

Post-war affluence, however, made it increasingly difficult to maintain the cosy pre-war consensus. The PGA was both an organiser of tournaments and provider of benefits. As the sport grew as a competitive spectacle, the top players became increasingly wealthy and beyond PGA control. A more democratic post-war generation were less inclined to accept direction from the PGA secretary simply because he was a 'gentleman'. Economic and technological change created exceptional and unforeseen possibilities for expansion, which called into question the PGA's traditional values and complex regional structure. The number of amateur golfers rose from around half a million in the 1950s to a million by the early 1970s, largely concentrated in the expanding middle-class commuter suburbs. Wider car ownership made access to golf easier, as did the provision of municipal courses.[1] Although still strongly male, middle aged and middle class, the audience for professional golf was changing and expanding quickly. Just as the crowds for established team sports like football and cricket were starting to fall in large numbers, so a new breed of more affluent spectators flocked to watch golf tournaments. These events were increasingly sponsored not by golf manufacturers, but by tobacco and drinks firms attracted by television coverage.

By the 1960s almost 90 per cent of British households had a television. With its sea vistas and gorgeous parkland, golf made good scenic television, especially with the spread of colour reception in the early 1970s.[2] From the first televised Open Championship in 1955, golf was established in the BBC's sporting canon. The mechanics and tempo of the swing, the choice of club, the depth of the rough and the roll of the greens and the other mysteries of the game were explained to the masses by Henry Longhurst, whose Oxbridge drawl gave way to the relaxed, chatty style of his successor, Peter Allis, a successful player and influential member of the PGA as well as a key figure in the popularising of the sport on television.

American golf was a significant influence on its older and more staid British relative, especially at the top level of tournament play where Samuel Ryder inaugurated a biannual competition between the best British and American players in 1927. There were 6,000 golf clubs in America by the 1930s and the top Americans eclipsed their British counterparts, starting with Walter Hagen in the 1920s who won four Open Championships and challenged the ban on professionals entering private clubs. The vast commercial value of sustained media exposure for golfers was first apparent in the United States, where a Florida and West Coast tournament circuit blossomed into a vast national tour by 1970. Eisenhower famously played golf throughout his presidency while middle America's appetite for the game fed a multi-million dollar equipment industry selling clubs endorsed by the great players of the 1940s and early 1950s: Byron Nelson, Sam Snead and Ben Hogan.

The scene was set for the 'Big Three' in the early 1960s: the Americans Arnold Palmer and Jack Nicklaus, and the South African Gary Player. The new stars had a big following in Britain as well as the United States, where they became extraordinarily rich and successful. They were managed by a new sports entrepreneur and agent, Mark McCormack, who operated on a global basis. As McCormack observed in 1967, 'there is no precedent for a sports figure becoming the centre of the kind of merchandising empire that now surrounds Arnold Palmer.'[3] Palmer endorsed everything from golf clubs to lawn mowers and hotel chains. McCormack soon began to spread his interests to Great Britain, snapping up Tony Jacklin after his British and American Open victories of 1969–70, and subsequently managing almost all the top British players.

How could an organisation set up to look after men who spent their time repairing clubs and giving lessons develop the commercial and entrepreneurial skills to exploit the opportunities open to the best British players? The PGA wanted to profit from the boom in tournament golf without changing its structure or relinquishing power to the playing elite. This was a recipe for conflict with a group of increasingly wealthy and assertive championship players. The first battles were fought in the late 1950s over representation; the second in the early 1970s over power and finance.

Early Developments, 1901–c.1950

Like cricket, golf originated as an eighteenth-century gentleman's game in which professionals emerged from the ranks of caddies as club makers, teachers and green-keepers. The greatest player of the Victorian age, 'Old' Tom Morris, was 'Keeper of the Green' at St. Andrews from 1864 until his retirement in 1903. Large scale urbanisation in the later nineteenth century led a boom in golf, which in turn created a critical mass of club professionals.[4] Around 1,800 courses and 2,800 clubs were founded before 1914. It was the interests of those who worked in the new suburban courses which were represented by the new body, the Professional Golfers' Association. The PGA was founded with 'the primary object of promoting the welfare of professional golfers…by the establishment of an agency for those in want of employment, either as professionals or club makers; and by instituting a fund for the benefit of deserving members'. Holding 'occasional tournaments for the purpose of bringing forward young talent' was a secondary objective.[5]

The PGA secured its first commercial tournament sponsor, *The News of the World*, in 1903. Tournament golf developed steadily in the Edwardian years, and was boosted in the 1920s by the emergence of great American players like Walter Hagen and Bobby Jones, the last amateur to win the Open. However, only a handful of players could ever hope to earn enough to live as tournament players and virtually all of them supplemented their winnings by working as a club professional. In 1934 there were just nine professional tournaments, including the Open, with a total of under £7,000 in prize money. The Ryder Cup had been founded as a team competition between British and American professionals, but players were not paid to take part in it. They were expected to play – like amateurs – for the honour of their country.

J.H. Taylor, who had been the first English professional to win the Open in 1894, and went on to win on four further occasions, was a crucial figure in the PGA between the wars and for some time after – he lived to the age of 91. It was Taylor who recruited a golf partner and recently retired naval commander, Charles Roe, as the new PGA Secretary in 1934. Taylor wanted 'someone with a handle to his name, someone with a title', to replace the outgoing Secretary, Percy Perrins, a stockbroker who had been very much an honorary and part-time official. Roe was a 'tall, imperious, stiff-backed and martial figure whose idea of good fun was to be downright rude to you and whose everyday greeting was "Well, what do you stiffs want?"' Beneath this bluff, autocratic exterior there was a dedicated, well-organised but utterly uncompromising man, who ruled the PGA for nearly 28 years. Roe did not retire until he was nearly 77, and for as long as he was there, 'the Commander's way was unquestionably the only way'.[6]

The PGA's attitude to Roe reflected an ingrained respect for the social order. The Executive, headed by J.H. Taylor, laid down no policy other than to tell Roe: 'Whatever decisions you give, we will uphold.' Roe for his part decided that the 'best way of running a tournament was the same way I would want to run a happy ship. I would decide on all the people who were to be involved in the promotion, people such as the press, and then I would simply find out what they wanted and how that fitted in with what we wanted.' Roe felt that, if the professional golfer was presented in 'his true light', sponsors would approach him, 'rather then me having to go and knock on boardroom doors and putting up the idea of golf sponsorship'.[7]

Tournament golf commenced quickly after the war with 12 tournaments in 1946 (in addition to the Open and the Irish Open) as golf benefited like other sports from the pent-up wartime demand for entertainment, with record prize money of £23,463.[8] However, this boom was short-lived. Total prize money of £30,000 in 1953 fell back to £25,000 in 1954. The number of qualifying tournaments for the Harry Vardon Trophy, which was awarded to the best player over the entire year, was reduced from seven to five. This reflected a wider crisis for the PGA, which saw its income from tournament proceeds decrease and therefore its ability to distribute funds to needy members. The situation was discussed by the PGA's Executive Committee in August 1954, which agreed to refer it for debate at that year's AGM. At this meeting it became clear that there was a sharp difference of opinion between the top players and the rest of the Association over prize money and the large number of competitors entering tournaments.[9] The scene was set for the first of several confrontations between the players and the PGA – or, more precisely, between those early post-war professionals with a more commercial and democratic agenda and the Commander with his benevolent dictatorship.

The Principle of Player Representation, 1954–55

Roe's management style reflected the power of gentlemanly values at the heart of the professional game. Here was an ex-naval officer, running a group of professional sportsmen rather like a collection of naval ratings, using his 'old boy' contacts with 'men of tea and timber, money and shipping' to develop commercial support for a tournament circuit. Roe's overall achievements were impressive and his commitment to the cause of the professional unquestioned. When he retired in 1961 there were 19 professional tournaments to play for, including the Open, worth over £74,000. However, his traditional methods and the slow pace of change were increasingly unacceptable to a new generation of tournament players who wanted more control over their own affairs.[10]

The tournament players demanded greater representation on the tournament sub-committee of the PGA and the appointment of a tournament manager. Henry Cotton thought Roe was responsible for the loss of the *Daily Telegraph*, the *Daily Mail* and the Goodwin tournaments. Appointing a tournament manager implied greater control by the top players, and this was something Roe and the PGA Executive were loath to concede at this stage. Indeed, such an appointment was perceived as a way of bypassing Roe, whom the players now regarded as a barrier to tournament promotion.[11]

The issue was now in the public domain. At the PGA Annual Dinner in November 1954, Henry Cotton, three times Open Champion, issued a statement on behalf of 24 leading players to the effect that they would not play in any international match sponsored by the Association unless they were satisfied with the selection committee and the captain. Henry Cotton had a special place and influence among professionals as the greatest British player of that era and a man who had shrewdly exploited the commercial possibilities of the game. He was also a public schoolboy who had chosen to be a professional player and pressed for the middle-class club house to be opened up to professionals. Within three days nearly 100 professionals had expressed their support for Cotton's stand. This was largely a tactic by the players to force the hand of the Executive Committee. Earlier, in the summer of 1954, 30 professionals had sent a letter to the Executive Committee asking for a meeting to discuss the declining tournament situation, but the PGA had procrastinated. Hence the speech by Cotton at the Annual Dinner was a calculated move to bring the issue into the open. Matters were complicated by the fact that powerful figures within the PGA did not wish to appoint Cotton as the Ryder Cup Captain for 1955. The problem, however, went far deeper than a clash of personalities. As *The Times* observed, 'in general terms this amounts to a feeling that the tournament-playing professionals, and therefore the younger men, are not adequately represented on a committee which, it is claimed, is out of touch with the requirements of professional golf since the war'.[12]

There was some strong player criticism of the way the PGA ran tournaments. There was a feeling that prize money should be more concentrated; that too many mediocre players entered; and that the rule fining golfers who entered but did not appear should be modified. More generally, there was alarm at the decreasing number of tournaments being sponsored. In other words, those who made their living by playing were no longer willing to put up with a structure that had been devised to let the club pro play when he felt like it and earn enough to cover his expenses.

Following Cotton's speech the PGA's tournament sub-committee agreed to meet the players, who reiterated their demand for a tournament manager and eight places on the tournament sub-committee itself, which would have given them a majority. They also wanted greater influence in Ryder Cup selection, with the team rather than the PGA Executive choosing the captain.[13] The Executive was forced to make concessions. They agreed to reduce their representatives on the tournament sub-committee from six to four, and invited three tournament players – Rees, Jacobs and Adams – to serve on it. However, this proved unacceptable to the players, who had formed their own negotiating committee in December 1954. Dai Rees on behalf of the tournament players agreed to meet the PGA, if Cotton was included in the party. F.H. Taylor, the PGA Chairman, stated publicly that he was 'willing to meet them with their spokesman, Henry Cotton, for a round table conference'; but he was careful to add that 'of course, the committee must agree to the next step'.[14] Commander Roe was not going to stand for mutiny in the ranks – not even from the urbane figure of Henry Cotton – but he would agree to better representation, providing he kept firm hold of the reins of power.

The next step was decided at the Executive meeting of 25 January 1955. Seemingly important concessions were made to the players, who were given eight representatives on the tournament sub-committee and were to be consulted in the choice of Ryder Cup captain. The players had flexed their economic muscle. One estimate suggested around 80 per cent of PGA funds came from tournaments. F.W.H. Kenyon, one of the players' representatives, argued that this revenue could be used to help finance a tournament manager on a 10 per cent commission basis.[15] The players pressed for more concessions and reaffirmed their demand for a tournament manager. A compromise was reached when it was agreed to appoint an assistant secretary. This would allow Roe more time to devote to the promotion of tournaments. While this might have seemed provocative to the players, who regarded Roe as part of the problem, the concessions already won were sufficient to satisfy them. The first round of the conflict was over. The tournament players had made their presence felt and won significant concessions, although the structure, values and purpose of the PGA remained largely unchanged.

It was no accident that the attack on the old order was led by Henry Cotton. Cotton lived lavishly – once, mistakenly, feeding his best caviar to the cat – and felt golf should offer the highest rewards to the greatest players, rather than spreading the jam too thin to give everyone a few pounds.[16] 'The best is always good enough for me' was one of his favourite expressions as he poured out champagne from the boot of the limousine he took to big events, just as Walter Hagen had done before him. Cotton had been strongly influenced by Hagen's commercial skills and star quality on an early trip to the United States in 1928. He believed tournament golf was the sport's shop window, and that ordinary pros would benefit from the publicity and equipment sales generated by the stars.

Cotton, of course, for all his influence was hardly typical of top professionals. Men such as Fred Daly, the 1947 Open champion and the son of an Ulster artisan golfer, or Dai Rees, whose father was a professional from Barry in South Wales, had more in common with the average professional. They retained a sense of loyalty to the PGA despite their evident frustration with it. Family ties, and close friendships with the club pros who guided their early careers, help explain why top players refused to break away. Dai Rees, in particular, emerged as an important figure, being runner-up in three Opens to Hogan, Thompson and Palmer, in 1953, 1954 and 1961 respectively. He was captain of the victorious Ryder Cup team in 1957. That year's contest drew such large crowds to Lindrick, near Sheffield, that the PGA ran out of tickets and let thousands in free. This was just the sort of thing that exasperated the tournament professionals, who were providing the entertainment without payment in order to represent their country and raise funds for the PGA. However, the Ryder Cup victory, after 20 years of American dominance, did a great deal for the public image of British professional golf. Rees was voted BBC Sports Personality of the Year and made a CBE in the New Year's honours list. This popularity and prestige was to prove important when the little Welshman led a second challenge to the PGA hierarchy in 1960.

A Share of Executive Power, 1960–61

The second half of the 1950s saw a reversal of the problems of the first. Instead of a declining number of tournaments, the economic boom brought extra sponsors into golf. At the 1958 AGM Roe was able to boast a tournament programme, with weekly events from March to October. In 1959 there were even complaints about tournaments clashing. This tremendous growth, however, did not solve the underlying problem between the PGA and the tournament players. The reforms of 1955 were proving less effective than the players had hoped. The functions of the new tournament sub-committee established in 1955 were 'limited to last minute suggestions for tournaments already about to start. It was not even consulted beforehand about proposed changes put forward by the PGA for the next Ryder Cup matches'.[17] Far from appeasing the players, the boom in tournament golf had increased their self-confidence, and highlighted what appeared to be a continued weakness within the PGA when it came to driving a hard bargain. Such was the rising demand for tournament golf that Henry Cotton successfully moved a motion at the Association's 1958 AGM that promoters should be approached and asked for a minimum of £2,000 for any promoted tournament.[18]

By 1960 the players had gathered sufficient strength to make another attempt to extract more control over tournaments, and Commander Roe had finally made clear his intention to retire. A special meeting between the Ryder Cup players and the Executive heard Dai Rees deliver a players' manifesto outlining the policies the PGA should adopt to make it more responsive to the players' needs. Rees noted the increasing economic wealth of the country and, by implication, the increased wealth of the sponsors. The players wanted 'a more dynamic relationship' with a more diverse group of sponsors; they thought the golf equipment manufacturers had too much power and got 'promotions too cheaply'. They were keen to attract sponsorship from big multinational vehicles, petrol, tobacco, beer and whisky companies. They saw this as essential if they were to secure their aim of a minimum of £2,500 for a three-day 72-hole stroke-play tournament. They wanted a more thoroughgoing commercial approach to sponsorship, involving local chambers of commerce. To do this, the players resurrected their earlier demand for a separate tournament bureau run by a tournament manager, who should be 'a distinctive but not overpowering personality' – a clear reference to the notoriously abrupt style of Commander Roe.[19]

The players wanted to give real power to the tournament sub-committee, by making it 'solely responsible for the running of all tournaments'.[20] The committee was to consist of four players and four executive members. They also wanted a tournament manager whose job it would be to raise total prize money to £100,000 p.a. by 1963 at the latest. The players estimated that running costs would total £4,500, which included a salary of £2,500 for the manager. This would be met from a ten per cent levy on all prize money, which was to be paid into a separate 'Promotional Account'. In effect, the players expected tournament promoters to provide more prize money, which would fund further expansion. The new tournament manager would be wholly responsible for the running of tournaments, negotiations with the promoter, and all public and press relations and promotions. Given that the elderly Roe was at long last due to retire, the person appointed to run tournaments would be in a very strong position to assert his authority in the new system.

The players took their argument for reform to the golfing press. John Jacobs emerged as a key figure, arguing strongly that the PGA must adapt to the needs of the modern tournament player. This included allowing amateurs to turn professional without going through the prolonged PGA apprenticeship. This would revitalise the tournament scene, and bring greater competition, which would 'boost the game of golf to the benefit of all professionals'.[21] In the time-honoured fashion of bureaucratic bodies the PGA set up a special sub-committee to consider the players' demands and report back to the Executive in September 1960. Relations were clearly very strained, with one member of the special committee fearing that there 'may come a time, and this may be much nearer than some of us realise, when we shall be faced with the possibility of a split'.[22]

The players maintained their offensive, putting their case to the sponsors. Peter Allis demanded that the tournament sub-committee should have full authority over tournaments. Matters came to a head when he contested the minutes of the previous meeting, which stated that the proposed ten per cent levy would be placed in the PGA general fund, when it had previously been understood that this money would go into a promotional fund for tournaments. The players walked out of the meeting, giving the Executive three days to resolve the matter or face the mass resignation of leading players. Jacobs told *The Times*:

> If they give us the power we ask for we will all be delighted to go on and do our best for the game. But there would be no point in

doing so if they refuse our request for full authority... We are willing to give up ten per-cent of the prize money for the benefit of the game, but we won't give it up so that it can go into the general funds of the P.G.A. The money must be spent on and for tournaments.[23]

This was the crux of the matter. The traditional role of the PGA, as a body which distributed funds across the whole range of professional golf, was called into question once the more successful players refused to subsidise the rest. The old idea of the trade association based on mutual solidarity and fraternity had gone. The players wanted a 'modern thinking businessman as manager', and Peter Allis 'envisaged the prize money reaching the £100,000 mark in a few years. This is big money and this surely warrants special business-like arrangements. We should have both a secretary to look after the ordinary affairs of the association and a tournament manager whose sole job would be the betterment of the tournaments with a view to attracting a wider public.'[24]

Facing the stark choice of compromise or a revolt, Ernest Bradbeer, the Chairman, moved a resolution agreeing to co-opt the leading players' spokesmen – Allis, Hunt, Jacobs and Weetman – directly on to the Executive, and to elect future tournament representatives to the Executive by postal ballot. This was a major change. Usually in the past no more than one tournament player had managed to get on the committee of 18. By giving the top players a share of power without a majority, the Executive might reasonably hope to keep them on board without giving too much away. In addition the 1960 AGM eased restrictions on amateur golfers becoming tournament players, requiring them to play as assistant professionals for only six months before being allowed to retain prize money. This was a key demand of the tournament players, who wanted to scrap the old apprenticeship structure, which harked back to the artisan origins of the profession. This marked the beginning of the modern tournament player whose dependence upon passing through the full PGA apprenticeship was ended. The result, according to *The Times*, was a 'triumph for the tournament players, led by Jacobs... They have not got everything they are working for but they cannot have expected at this stage to achieve more than they did. What they have done is rouse the P.G.A. into adopting a more up-to-date outlook.'[25]

The Formation of a Tournament Players' Division, 1974–75

The 1960 agreement was certainly a major advance for the tournament players, as the disgruntled attitude of some of the club professionals revealed. F.H. Taylor wrote to the *PGA Journal* in 1962 complaining of the special rights of representation which enabled top players 'primarily to look after their own interests' at the expense of the 'legitimate rights and benefits of others'.[26] On the other hand, the professional elite had not succeeded in getting a separate tournament director. Roe's successor was another retired officer, Lieutenant-Colonel J.H. Reid, who was groomed for the job by Roe and initially made it clear he expected to speak on behalf of all members of the PGA. However, there were now club pros and tournament players within the same governing body and Reid found it difficult to work for both groups, resigning in 1965 and insisting that 'golf has changed radically in the last five years; a half a million pound business needed businessmen to run it.'[27] The Executive Committee agreed that someone with 'great business experience who would act as a consultant in the matter of tournament promotion and encourage new sponsorships' was needed.[28] The natural candidate was Brian Park, a rich businessman who had sponsored the 1965 Ryder Cup. Park became an unpaid Executive Director, appointed for two years on his own terms but responsible to the Executive Committee. This was the first tentative step on the road to creating a dedicated tournament directorate. The day-to-day administration was handled by a new tournament administrator, Commander Fell, leaving the new PGA secretary, Major Bywaters, free to run the rest of the Association. The PGA kept a foot in both camps. Dai Rees, an influential critic of the old order, was made PGA Captain in 1967, but the tradition of appointing retired military men of senior rank was maintained.[29]

Two new factors had an important influence on relationships within the PGA in the late 1960s. First, in August 1968 top American golfers announced a complete break with the US PGA. *The Times* made a direct comparison with the British situation, noting that the players have 'the whip hand because it is the big names who attract the sponsors and the crowds'.[30] The rival American bodies eventually patched up a compromise deal, which involved the formation of a ten-man board with absolute control over the tournament programme.

This comprised four players, three PGA officials and three businessmen. The implications of this were only too obvious to top British players, who had long hankered after just such an arrangement. They now had a working model of what they wanted.

Second, there was the formation of a European Circuit. Towards the end of the 1960s European golf tournaments were beginning to attract top fields, especially in the various national championships. Indeed, the PGA facilitated this by including the 1970 French Open in the Order of Merit for Ryder Cup points, and merging the British Circuit with the European Circuit from 1971. It was essential for the PGA to adopt the same procedure as the United States and Australia, whereby their members had to support a certain number of tournaments on their own circuit each year. This was to ensure attractive fields for sponsors, who were continually urged to provide greater sums in prize money. A report by Peter Thompson, the Australian five times Open winner and a great favourite in British golfing circles, indicated how a continuous circuit of tournaments could be established by bringing Europe into the fold.

The growth in domestic golf, combined with this new European dimension, was proving too much for the PGA's administration. The sheer volume of work began to push the PGA itself towards reforming tournament golf. As *Golf Illustrated* observed, 'for long enough an overworked office staff has been looking after administration, trying to get sponsors for new events and a hundred and one other tasks.'[31] Fearing a repeat of the American debacle of the previous year, the PGA established an Advisory Council in 1969, comprising three members of the Executive and three businessmen, the latter reflecting the growing influence of big business in golf. Park had departed in 1968, leaving a commercial vacuum. There was a need for men who were 'accustomed to profit-making enterprises and were well known for their interest in the professional game'; who could take quick decisions without always referring to the cumbersome 24-man Executive.[32] Club professionals had other problems. The transformation of sports retailing meant club pros were less concerned with restricting the power of tournament players than preventing the spread of golf shops in big stores and driving ranges.

Faced with a short-term drop in prize money from £290,000 in 1970 to £176,000 in 1971, and given the increasing complexity of merging the British and European circuit, the Advisory Council authorised the appointment of a 'supremo' to be given 'overall direction of the Tournament scene'.[33] The players' candidate for the new post of Tournament Director General was John Jacobs, one of the original 'rebels' of 1954–55, who had been involved in the Executive during the 1960s. A public relations consultant, George Simms, was also appointed. Jacobs and Simms demanded three years 'elbow room' to transform the tournament scene, and also a wide degree of freedom from the PGA. Jacobs was answerable to the Advisory Council, while for the day-to-day running of tournaments he was advised by a three-man committee of tournament players; he was also given an assistant. All the additional costs, of around £19,000, were to be met by a levy on the 300-strong tournament players group.

This was a revolution in all but name. While there was still no formal division of powers, the appointment of Jacobs as Tournament Director General, with a salary paid by the players, was a major step towards self-determination. Jacobs warned that it might be necessary to set up a tournament group similar to the one operating in the United States: 'We must be able to offer a proper deal to the promoters... There will be difficult decisions to make and I shall have to be ruthless at times. I would not be surprised if we lost one or two tournaments in the present set-up.' By the end of three years he hoped to have a British and Irish circuit worth £200,000. Moreover, changes in the rules, if passed, would mean that players would not be permitted to take part in any other tournament run at the same time as big PGA events: 'We must be able to offer a sponsor the top 20 players.'[34]

The results of the reforms far exceeded expectations. Prize money for 1972, including the continental circuit, approached £500,000. Critical to this transformation was the growth of the European tournament circuit. This Jacobs strongly supported, arguing that prize money 'cannot expand much more in the UK and it is for us to set up the proposed [European] administration to our own advantage'. This was done in May 1973, tying together the British and emerging European circuits to their mutual advantage. Meanwhile in Britain a new agreement for a minimum of £8,000 in prize money per tournament, with at least £15,000 for events held in specialised periods, was put in place. By 1974 this was increased to £12,000, with some sponsors actually paying £25,000 at peak periods. Significantly, Jacobs also secured television deals with the BBC and ITV, which ensured the broadcasting of eight tournaments in 1972. Dai Rees's predications in 1960 had come true: the cigarette manufacturers flocked to a sport which offered prolonged media exposure at relatively low cost. The 'Dunlop Masters', which had been run from 1946 to promote Dunlop golf balls, was taken over by Silk Cut, and later by Dunhill. Benson and Hedges founded a new tournament in 1971, and a Japanese whisky manufacturer was one of many new companies to jump on the golf bandwagon in the course of the decade.

The success of Jacobs and the new structure meant in effect that the players had the substance of what they wanted, without formal control over their own assets. Frequent transatlantic trips familiarised top British players with new American arrangements. It was only a matter of time before the best British players demanded equal treatment with their American counterparts, in accordance with the evolving commercial logic of the sport. Bernard Hunt made the case for an autonomous Tournament Playing Division in a letter to the PGA in May 1974. The players wanted their own full-time executive and staff, which would operate from the PGA offices. In particular, they wanted a 'hundred per cent full time Tournament Director General'.[35] Jacobs' contract was up for renewal and there had been rumours he would be offered a part-time position. Hunt warned that the players would go their own way if they were blocked yet again. Clearly the new world of global golf was having an effect upon the players. Tony Jacklin, drawing upon his extensive overseas playing experience since winning the US Open in 1970, told the 1974 AGM that: 'he had been recently in South Africa, and had seen what had happened on the tournament side there…and he was ashamed almost to say that they have overtaken us there in tournament organisation… Golf is big business around the world and we want to take every advantage of this. This is why the Tournament players want to run their own affairs.'[36]

Lord Derby, the PGA President, attempted to use the power of aristocratic prestige to bring both sides together. In the event, he recommended significant concessions to the players. They should be fully responsible for all matters relating to tournaments while remaining within the Association. He proposed that a management committee be formed consisting of three tournament players and three club professionals, with a chairman appointed from outside the Association. The Tournament Director General would be in charge of all tournament matters and the PGA Secretary for all other aspects of the affairs of the Association. Both would be responsible to the management committee. The Executive agreed that Lord Derby would address meetings of the tournament players at the Open Championship.

At the 1974 AGM agreement seemed to have been reached. The Chairman stressed the organisational logic of a change in structure rather than admit the PGA's hand had been forced: 'The Association has expanded over the years. We have got bigger and more complex and the Tournament side and Club Professionals side should be separate entities.'[37] The Board of Management would offer advice and 'judge on what area the Tournament Committee should cover, and what area the General Purposes Committee should cover'. Hunt endorsed the Chairman's remarks. Even *The Times* reported that 'an open rift between the two elements of professional golf, the club professional and the tournament player, has been avoided... [T]he age-old division of interest within the PGA has now been given formal recognition'.[38]

This was not quite the end of the story. To agree to the setting up of a Tournament Players' Section (the Executive preferred the term 'section' to 'division' in order to minimise the idea of a separation of powers) was one thing; to agree what powers it would have, and how money and assets would be distributed, was another. It was over such constitutional and practical matters that the final rift took place in 1975. The Tournament Players' Section was duly formed, with full control of tournaments and its own secretary from 1 January 1975. Conflicts over power and money soon re-emerged. Jacobs protested on behalf of the Tournament Players' Section over the apparent right of the Management Committee to confer about issues that were held to affect both sections. There were continuing disagreements about the proposed move of the PGA to a new purpose-built golfing complex linked in with a leisure development at The Belfry, near Birmingham. This move was linked to a commitment to the developers to hold the Ryder Cup at The Belfry site, which brought the control of the event into sharp focus. The PGA Executive had also agreed a one-year television deal, worth £2,500, with ITV for the Ryder Cup, despite a £14,500 three-year offer from the BBC – a decision which was criticised by the tournament players, and which could have been construed as infringing their rights.[39]

These tensions came fully to the surface when the two sections met to discuss the new constitution. Where did sovereignty lie? How much real power would the new body have? Inevitably there were personality conflicts, but it was around the issue of financial assets that matters boiled over. The tournament fund had a surplus of £18,432, and total assets amounting to £46,031. As the PGA accountant made clear, legally these assets 'belong to *all* members of the Association'. Jacobs warned that, if the whole of the Tournament Fund was not given to the players, 'there was a distinct possibility that the tournament side would wish to break away from the PGA'.[40] The threat worked once again and the Tournament Fund was handed over to the Tournament Players' Section, subject to an audited set of accounts being presented to the Board of Management.

The players were not going to be denied their independence any longer. At a private meeting at the 1975 Open Championship they backed a formal statement by Jacobs. This was released to the press on 15 July, as soon as the Open was over. He stated unequivocally that he would not accept any discipline of the PGA Executive, or pay any fine or accept admonition, and that as Tournament Director General he was responsible only to the players. In effect, the players, led by Jacobs, were forcing the issue of autonomy, while refusing to take the risk of breaking away to form a new body.[41] Fearful of provoking the long awaited schism, the Executive backed down from outright dismissal of Jacobs. A full Executive meeting was called for 12 August at Fulford, to which all tournament players were invited.

This turned out to be the last piece in the jigsaw. Around 100 members attended, including some club pros. A draft constitution was agreed, and ratified at a subsequent special meeting. In a press statement the PGA Chairman, Douglas Smith, announced the 'intention to have two divisions, a Tournament Players Division completely responsible for all tournament matters and a General Purposes Division looking after the remainder of the Association. The Management Committee will be responsible for such matters as the AGM, Annual Dinner, Ryder Cup, etc.' Neil Coles, for the players, endorsed the proposed arrangement whereby both sides would 'largely be running their own affairs'.[42] This time there would be no semantic confusion. From 1 January 1976 a Tournament Players' Division was firmly established, with full control for the promotion of all professional golf tournaments in Britain and Ireland. This played a key role in the development of competitive golf in Europe, just as Jacobs had envisaged. The General Purposes Division developed its role on the club side of the Association, serving its members from youth through to retirement. The move to The Belfry went ahead as planned, creating both a training centre for European club professionals and a site for major tournaments, including the Ryder Cup.

Conclusion

A variety of sports were affected in a variety of ways by the market forces unleashed during the long post-war boom. Professional footballers demanded and won the abolition of wage controls in 1961; cricket abolished the social distinction between gentlemen and players in 1963; and even Wimbledon embraced the logic of professionalism in 1968. Each sport adjusted to a changing post-war commercial context, and the resulting pressures, in its own way, depending upon its particular traditions and circumstances. The PGA originated as a trade association set up to defend the interests of working men who made a living by serving the needs of middle-class club members. Unlike the Professional Footballers' Association, which was created around the same time and with a similar welfare role, the PGA was more concerned with the professional as a craftsman and a shopkeeper rather than as a public performer. This inevitably led to problems as soon as the best players were able to live without running a shop.

The struggle within the organisation had three phases. First came the battle for representation within the old structure, dominated by an autocratic ex-naval officer. It was not until the 1950s and the advent of television that the vast economic potential of professional golf began to become apparent. The PGA was caught between its traditional role and rapidly changing commercial realities. It wanted to profit from the growth of tournament golf, but did not want to change its structure or acknowledge the new bargaining power of the top players. The threatened revolt of 1955 was averted by giving the top players control of the tournament sub-committee, but this turned out to be a hollow victory until a second confrontation five years later won direct access to the Executive itself. The second stage involved using the influence the players had gained to push the organisation in a more commercial direction. Roe's successor, Lt. Col. Reid, was clearly tired of divisions between club and tournament players, and the modernisers increasingly got their way within the existing structure.

Further change came about initially as a result of pressure of business, and the developing commercial logic of events. The PGA needed the tournament side to be profitable but it had become too big to manage through the old structure. This factor, combined with the example of the temporary schism that had taken place in the United States, and the coming of really big sponsorship money in the early 1970s, strengthened the bargaining position of those tournament players who demanded effective autonomy.

Tournament players themselves were an increasingly articulate, affluent and confident group, travelling widely and increasingly independent of club attachments. The 20 years spanning the first skirmishes to the final separation saw a ten-fold increase in prize money, with greatly enhanced opportunities for endorsing products and making personal appearances. Although it was still a hard struggle for the aspiring tournament player, there were big rewards for the best – and it was the best which the public demanded to see, both in person and on television. Golf was a global media commodity, which could no longer be run by a part-time committee of club pros, or a man like Commander Roe who had joined the Royal Navy in 1901. The gulf between the best and the rest had become too big. In the 1950s even a good tournament player would have expected to spend some of the winter months at his club, to which he might retire when his competitive days were over. By the 1970s there was a world market for good players who could play all year round. The logic that had held the two sides together for so long had gone.

ACKNOWLEDGEMENTS

This article is based upon ongoing doctoral research into the history of the PGA by Ray Physick, supervised by Professor Richard Holt, and forms part of a wider study commissioned by the PGA from the International Centre for Sports History and Culture at De Montfort University. The authors wish to express their gratitude to the PGA for access to their records, to Adrian Smith for his editorial advice, and to Peter Lewis, Director of the British Golf Museum at St. Andrews, for his careful reading and expert criticism of the article.

NOTES

1. For a good essay on twentieth century golf see J. Lowerson, in Tony Mason (ed.), *Sport in Britain: A Social History* (Cambridge: Cambridge University Press, 1989), especially pp.187–214. J. Lowerson, *Sport and the English Middle Classes, 1870–1914* (Manchester: Manchester University Press, 1993) sets the context expertly. See also Geoffrey Cousins, *Golf in Britain: A Social History* (London: Routledge, 1975).
2. Garry Whannel, *Fields of Vision: Television Sport and Cultural Transformation* (London: Routledge, 1992), pp.88–9.
3. Stephen Aris, *Sportsbiz: Inside the Sports Business* (London: Hutchinson, 1990), p.16.
4. Peter Lewis, *The Dawn of Professional Golf, 1894–1914* (London: New Ridley and Ballater, Hobbs and McEwan, 1995) provides the best account of the early years.
5. *Professional Golfer*, Sept. 1923.
6. 'Ask the Commander', a portrait by Ronald Heager, *Golf Monthly*, Dec. 1961, pp.24–8.
7. *Golf Trade Journal*, Sept. 1974, 'The Story of the PGA', part 8.
8. *Golf Trade Journal*, Sept. 1974, 'The Story of the PGA', part 8. The prize money total excludes the Open and Irish Open.
9. PGA records (hereafter PGA), held at PGA headquarters, The Belfry, Sutton Coldfield: PGA Executive Committee Minutes, Aug. 1954.
10. *Golf Trade Journal*, May 1976.
11. For Roe's reply see *Professional Golfer*, Feb. 1955.
12. *The Times*, 27 Nov. 1954.
13. PGA Executive Committee Minutes, 24 Jan. 1955.
14. *The Times*, 15 Dec. 1954.
15. PGA Executive Committee Minutes, 24 Jan. 1955.
16. Renton Laidlaw, *Golfing Heroes* (London: Stanley Paul, 1991), pp.32–4.
17. *Golfing*, Jun. 1960.
18. PGA Annual General Meeting Minutes, 1958.
19. PGA, Minutes of a special meeting between the Ryder Cup players and the PGA Executive, 25 Jan. 1960.
20. PGA, Minutes of a special meeting between the tournament players and the PGA Executive, 6 May 1960.
21. *Golfing*, Sept. 1960.
22. PGA Executive Committee Minutes, 8 Feb. 1960.
23. *The Times*, 15 Nov. 1960.
24. *The Times*, 15 Nov. 1960.
25. *The Times*, 24 Nov. 1960.
26. *PGA Journal*, Nov. 1962.
27. *Golf Illustrated*, 31 Jan. 1966.
28. PGA Executive Committee Minutes, 16 Dec. 1965.
29. *PGA Journal*, Nov. 1966.
30. *The Times*, 14 Aug. 1968.
31. *Golf Illustrated*, 26 Aug. 1971.
32. *Golf Trade Journal*, 'The PGA Story', January/February 1975.
33. *Golf Trade Journal*, 'The PGA Story', January/February 1975.
34. John Jacobs, quoted in *The Times*, 9 Sept. 1971.
35. PGA Executive Committee Minutes, 11 June 1974.

36. PGA Annual General Meeting Minutes, 1974.
37. PGA Annual General Meeting Minutes, 1974.
38. *The Times*, 29 Nov. 1974. At the AGM all proposals on the restructuring of the PGA had been passed without dissent but required there to be a special meeting for final approval.
39. PGA, Executive Committee Minutes, 24 Mar. 1975.
40. Meeting between the PGA Executive and the Tournament Players' Section, 6 May 1975.
41. *The Times,* 15 July 1975.
42. PGA Special Meeting Minutes, 27 Oct. 1975.

'The Amateur Rules': Amateurism and Professionalism in Post-War British Athletics

MARTIN POLLEY

> The hard-working, driven amateur made for great Olympic stories. All you would hear about was dedication and sacrifice. The stories of the greatest Olympic champions would make you feel like crying... Now, if you hear the real stories of Olympic champions, the reason you're crying is because you don't make the money we do.
>
> Carl Lewis[1]

After Harold Abrahams won the 100 metre gold medal at the 1924 Paris Olympics, he received his medal by post. He returned to his career in the law in London, and continued to compete as an amateur athlete until he broke his leg competing in the long jump in 1925. He continued to practise as a lawyer, while diversifying into athletics administration, broadcasting and writing on the sport. He remained an influential figure in the sport until his death in 1978, and soon became mythologised for a new generation through Hugh Hudson's celebrated film *Chariots of Fire*, which portrayed his 1924 triumphs as those of a dedicated and talented athlete of a golden age. After Denise Lewis won the bronze medal in the heptathlon at the 1996 Atlanta Olympics, she became a media star in heavy demand. Appearances on television chat shows, colour features in magazines as diverse as *Total Sport* and *Pride*, and a fashion photograph in Powergen's celebrity 1999 calendar alongside such entertainers as Christopher Lee, Louise, Michael Flatley, and Honor Fraser, ensured her high profile.[2] She was promoted as 'one of the best athletes in the world' who, in her own words, 'wouldn't say no to a catwalk for Chanel for an afternoon'.[3]

While it may seem invidious to begin a survey of professionalism and amateurism in athletics with cameos of such vastly different individuals, the comparisons and contrasts are telling. For Abrahams, amateurism in the sport itself was a fundamental ideology: and while he made money from his sport-related activities, such as broadcasting and writing, he was very much part of a voluntary tradition in British sport which prioritised the performance of the activity and its administration as worthwhile ends in themselves. As he put it in a 1977 lecture on 'Sport, Professionalism and the Olympics',

> we must strive to maintain a proper balance in favour of the principle that the primary purpose of sport is the enjoyment of participation, and that if competitors are *paid to compete* there is a very real danger – I think a certainty – that the main motive will be to see what can be gained financially not to enjoy participation [emphasis in original].[4]

For Lewis, operating in a very different context, athletic talent and its careful nurturing over many years came first, but alongside her sporting successes came commercial and professional opportunities: as she put it herself, 'I'm more than just a sports woman. I'm an astute woman trying to take advantage of the privileged position I'm in.'[5] Such contrasts are a useful introduction into the ways in which athletics changed in the UK after 1945, in which a black girl from a single-parent family in West Bromwich, with a BTEC in computing, has become an icon in a sport dominated in earlier generations by a white, male, public school and Oxbridge elite.

The Historical and Historiographical Background

Athletics, as it emerged as a modern sport during the nineteenth century, was strongly associated with predominantly university-based clubs, whose members were keen to distinguish it from the professional sport of pedestrianism; and professionalism was explicitly excluded from the clubs that took over the control of athletics, particularly the Amateur Athletic Association (AAA), formed in 1880.[6] While professional pedestrianism survived, particularly in Cumberland, Northumberland and parts of Scotland, it was a specifically amateur version of athletics, with all the social, economic, and cultural implications that went with the concept of amateurism, that took off in the rest of the UK.[7] This became consolidated as the predominant form of the sport through its close association with the Olympic movement from 1896, and more particularly through the formation of the British Olympic Association (BOA) in 1905. Amateur traditions remained strong in the sport throughout the inter-war period: and while the AAA had to cede some control to the British Amateur Athletic Board (BAAB) from its foundation in 1932, the sport remained strongly tied to a culture of voluntarism in management and administration, and to one of amateurism in performance and participation.[8]

However, the wider societal changes that took place after the Second World War redefined the context in which athletics took place. After 1945, the apparent certainties over the traditions of amateurism were increasingly under attack in British athletics. In part, athletics was just one sport among many which had to re-examine its terms and definitions in a time of dramatic social change. Sports with relatively long histories of accepted professionalism experienced changes in the occupational cultures and industrial rights of their professionals, such as the abolition of the maximum wage and the retain and transfer system in football in 1961 and 1963 respectively, and the discarding of the distinction between players and gentlemen in cricket in 1963. Other sports with historical and cultural traditions of amateurism, such as lawn tennis and rugby union, were also sites of struggle between players, administrators, promoters, and publicists over the issues of payment, sponsorship, and advertising.[9] Debates here were similar to some of those that took place in athletics. However, while modern athletics must be seen in this broader context of sports which held out against professionalism well into the post-war period – it was not until 1981 that payment for performances was legally accommodated - it is also instructive to explore the specifics of the sport's own professional–amateur debate. This discussion sheds light on many aspects of the sport, including its social relations, its internal politics, its position in international structures, its financial condition and its popularity. Together, they help to show how amateurism went from being seen as 'something which is infinitely worth while'[10] to being criticised as 'antiquated'[11] and duly redefined. This redefinition allowed talented individuals to legally make money from their sport, and allowed the sport's administrations to make money out of the sport's appeal.

Athletics is a complicated sport to deal with historically for the basic reason that it is an umbrella term for a range of activities. Even the more specific American usage 'track and field' does not fully do justice to the various activities – running, jumping, walking and throwing – and events, which range from 60 metre sprints to 24-hour endurance races, from throwing various objects to jumping in various ways, to such multi-discipline events as the heptathlon and the decathlon, designed to test an individual's all-round ability. At the 1992 Barcelona Olympics, for example, a tournament which excluded some athletics disciplines (including cross-country and fell running, and tug of war), there were 24 men's athletics events and 19 women's: only the swimming pool-based sports (swimming, diving, water polo and synchronised swimming) rivalled this diversity, with 25 men's water sports, and 19 women's.[12] This multiple nature of the sport has meant that historically, there have been many separate strands of administrative and juridical development. Restricting ourselves to the UK, each of the separate sports has developed its own governing body, with further subdivisions on gender and national lines in some cases, while organisations designed to act as a common forum for all the athletic sports, such as the AAA, the BAAB, and the Women's Amateur Athletic Association (WAAA), have had a troubled history of overlapping territories and agendas. As Neil Macfarlane, Minister for Sport from 1981 until 1985, noted in his memoirs, he was surprised when dealing with athletics to come across 'nineteen organizations which had what must be regarded as a controlling interest in the sport'.[13] While there have been some recent attempts to rationalise this situation – as seen in the unsuccessful institution of the British Athletic Federation (BAF) in 1989 and, in 1999, the establishment of UK Athletics – the 'multiplicity of governing bodies', disciplines, and events has given the sport a unique character among modern majority sports.[14] Add to this the fact that the governing bodies within the UK have also been related to international organisations and agencies, such as the International Amateur Athletic Federation (IAAF) and the International Olympic Committee (IOC), as well as to the BOA, then the logistical and juridical issues surrounding amateurism and professionalism can truly be seen to be enormous. It is, in short, a sport with more interest groups than any other, and thus one in which any necessary critical examination of definitions, traditions, and practices has been over-complicated.

With this administrative context in place, it is regrettable but perhaps not surprising that athletics has so far been relatively under-explored by sports historians. In 1995, Tony Mason named it as one of the sports that still 'largely await the scholar's scrutiny',[15] and despite the increasing availability of source material – not least in the University of Birmingham's Special Collections[16] – we still await a synthesis or a monograph that does for athletics what, for example, Mason has done for football, Wray Vamplew for horse racing, and Eric Halladay for rowing.[17] Despite the challenges that the sport offers due to its multiple nature, Jeremy Crump's 1989 essay still remains the main academic secondary survey on the sport.[18] The historiography of the sport is characterised – again, perhaps unsurprisingly given its nature – by Richard Holt's 'book of Chronicles and the book of Numbers' approach:[19] hero-worship and statistical compendia have figured high in the literature.[20] While the AAA's official centenary history provides a useful survey of that body's past,[21] it was not characterised by the qualities assumed in modern academic sports historiography, summarised by J.A. Mangan as an interest in 'sequence, tendencies, outcomes and change' in sport.[22] Even the athletics writing that has concentrated both on development over time and on controversy rather than celebration, most notably Steven Downes and Duncan Mackay's *Running Scared* of 1996, has tended to approach the subject from an idealised and even nostalgic position: athletics is seen to have 'lost its innocence' since the 1970s, with drugs, commercialism, professionalism and political intrigues serving to corrupt the once pure sport of Paavo Nurmi, Emil Zatopek, Harold Abrahams and Roger Bannister.[23] Much of the literature describes the professional–amateur debate in terms of morality, particularly through the evident association of performance-enhancing drugs and professional athletics, a view evident in David Miller's claim that professionalism's 'threat to sportsmanship, to morality and to the health of the athlete' is its deepest 'iniquity'.[24] In this historiographical context, which has also been influenced by the populist athletics history of *Chariots of Fire*, we can see the need for detailed, analytical, contextualised historical research.

Overall, then, it is clear that the sport has been relatively marginalised in the burgeoning academic study of sports history. It is to be hoped that this situation will soon be redressed. The issues explored in this essay can serve as a way into the whole issue of amateurism and professionalism which will figure prominently in that historiography: by using the AAA and selected athletes as samples of the whole history, this piece aims to highlight themes and suggest areas for expansion, comparison and contrast. It concentrates on the period from 1945 until the late 1970s, thus stopping short of what Miller characterised as the 'bonanza' period, in which 'money was pouring into athletics' with 'much of it...finding its way into the pockets of performers'.[25] The bonanza years have been covered well by Downes/Mackay and Ward, and narratives of the exact changes in the sport's laws and culture, and the impact that they had on administration and performance, can be found there.[26] Instead, in order to provide a perspective for the bonanza, which rested on open sponsorship, television income, legalised appearance fees and prize moneys, subventions, trust funds, and increased commercialisation, this piece will explore the struggles and debates that took place over amateurism and professionalism before the latter became accommodated. While we await a greater historiography – which hopefully will show how, like any other sport, athletics has always been characterised by social, national and gender-based power relations, the exact dynamics of which have changed over time – this survey will attempt to provide some longer term contexts for the professional period.

In order to survey this period of struggle analytically, this essay will start with a view of the AAA's amateur rules as they stood at the start of the period, before moving on to look at the timing of subsequent changes, and the reasons for those changes. This will be explored first by looking at the AAA's move towards a more professional and commercial approach to its work by the early 1970s. Within this institutional and administrative framework, we will then study the AAA's attempts to maintain and defend as strict a sense of amateurism as possible, before juxtaposing these against the growth of a more assertive and critical culture among leading athletes, many of whom resented the restrictions that the laws imposed on their freedom and performance. Brought together, these factors will show how amateurism was, by the mid-1970s, looking increasingly untenable. Through these explorations, we can see some of the ways in which two key ideologies were played out and negotiated, including the administrators' idealistic and socially-constrained view of amateurism, and elite athletes' movement towards a professional culture concomitant with their perceived market and prestige value.

The Definition of Amateurism

The cameo approach used above in contrasting the backgrounds and occupational cultures of Harold Abrahams and Denise Lewis is one way into the changing nature of British athletics: but a more empirical view of the change can be seen by looking at how the rules relating to amateurism were enforced at different points throughout the period. While the rules applied in the UK have to be seen as being constrained by the international rules of the IAAF, it is clear that governing bodies in the UK, particularly the AAA, fought something of a rearguard action against major changes.

In 1946, any athlete wishing to compete under the AAA's laws had to match the organisation's definition of amateurism. The definition was influenced by the organisation's history. As Jeremy Crump shows, the original rules of 1889 were 'relatively liberal' in their statements on amateurism:[27] for example, they did not contain the explicit bars on mechanics and artisans that the Amateur Rowing Association imposed.[28] However, there were some elements of the late-Victorian legacy which were out of keeping with the post-Second World War period. The definition barred amateur athletes from a number of activities, and, when enforced, made anyone who did engage in these activities ineligible to compete in AAA events. The proscribed activities included competing for 'a money prize', betting on one's own event, teaching athletics for 'pecuniary consideration', exploiting one's 'athletic ability for profit', and competing against 'anyone who is not an amateur'. In addition, 11 extra clauses set up activities which, if engaged in, would render an athlete ineligible. These included 'becoming a professional' in any other sport; being paid 'for the exhibition of any prize'; being paid for 'allowing [one's] name as an athlete to be used for advertisement purposes'; receiving broken time payments to cover training, travel, or competition; and 'writing, lecturing, or broadcasting upon athletics...for payment'. There were also strict guidelines on travel expenses.[29] These were added to in 1948, when the acceptance of a fee for officiating at a professional athletics event became a proscribed activity under what the rule book now called its 'Amateur Definition'.[30]

These rules, and the assumptions behind them, were clear evidence that Jeremy Crump's 'cult of the gentleman amateur', underpinned by a predominantly Oxbridge environment, was still influential after the war, particularly through such men as Abrahams and the Marquess of Exeter, both of whom had achieved their own athletic triumphs in the 1920s.[31] However, since the 1940s, a number of changes have been introduced, the accumulated impact of which has been revolutionary. These have all made the sport different in many significant areas in 2000 to how it was in 1945: the sponsorship of events and the use of advertisements on vests and on track perimeters; the effective professionalisation of elite athletes through subventions, trust funds, and commercial freedoms; the growth of a promotions, marketing, and agency culture around the sport and its stars; and the emergence of a mixed sex and non-Oxbridge educated generation of administrators. The reasons for these changes, and the ways in which they made themselves felt, can now be explored.

The AAA: Professional and Commercial Developments

One of the main contexts for change was based in the sport's overall fortunes. Before the late-Victorian reconstruction of professional pedestrianism into modern amateur athletics, sporting events based on individuals' abilities to achieve feats over space and time were frequently big crowd pullers, such as the 'crowds [turning] out in their thousands' to see George Wilson's 1815 attempt to walk 50 miles a day over a 20-day period at Blackheath,[32] and the mid-nineteenth century crowds of 25,000 for big events cited by Peter Lovesey.[33] The infrastructure investments in the development of Lillie Bridge, Stamford Bridge, Belle Vue, Powderhall, and, in 1908, the White City stand as evidence of the sport's popularity and appeal in the late-Victorian and Edwardian periods. While attendances declined relatively in the inter-war period, major events such as the AAA championships could still draw crowds of 22,000 by 1939.[34] In common with other sports, athletics experienced an attendance boom in the immediate post-war period: it was given a particular boost by the first post-war Olympic Games being held in London in 1948.[35] The AAA championships gained their record attendance of approximately 46,000 in 1952.[36] The paying spectators at this event, and at other competitions throughout the year, were central to the sport's survival, as were subscriptions from individual athletes and clubs. However, by the late 1950s, this traditional source of income was in decline again: the AAA championship attendance for 1959, for example, was only 17,000, a fall of 63 per cent in seven years. By 1970, it was down to 4,271.[37]

In part, this decline was linked to the earlier, pre-1939 decline, which had been artificially disguised by the immediate post-1945 boom experienced by all sports after the lifting of wartime restrictions on public recreation. Here, athletics had much in common with football, rugby league, and cricket: peak attendances by the late 1940s and early-1950s, followed by fairly sharp decline. The development of leisure time alternatives, including the cinema and private motoring, were clearly factors in this long-term trend in sport. However, the relative decline in British athletes' international successes was also a factor. The 1948 Olympics helped to develop many people's interest in athletics: and while no British athletes won gold, the six silver medals – including those won by the men's 4 × 100 metres relay team, and by Maureen Gardner, Dorothy Manley and Audrey Williamson in track events – helped to revive and maintain popular interest. The 1952 peak was clearly related to the forthcoming Helsinki Olympics, with great popular following for a team of 'as strong a squad of gold-diggers as ever left these shores', including McDonald Bailey, Roger Bannister and Gordon Pirie.[38] The relative failure of this team, compounded by Great Britain's poor athletics showing at the Melbourne Olympics four years later, dented the sport's popularity: and while this was partially offset in 1954 by Bannister running the world's first sub-four-minute mile, and by the domestic popularity of Pirie's distance achievements, there was no major recovery in the traditional forms of income on which athletics relied for investment, development and administration. In this environment, and with the costs of running athletics and staging events rising, the AAA and other organisations began slowly to diversify: and the form that this diversification took was a factor in the revolutionary changes outlined above. Although some new funding came from central government, the main initiatives were directed towards gaining commercial support. Commercial sponsorship had been used before: Oxo had been commercially involved with the marathon at the London Olympics of 1908,[39] for example, while more significant support for the AAA came from *The News of the World*, which sponsored, among other athletics events, the new coaching scheme launched in 1947.[40] In 1952, the *News of the World*-sponsored British Games raised £2,663 for the AAA's coaching and equipment funds,[41] with £5,000 provided by the same backer in 1954,[42] signs of the growing relationship between the sport and commercial sponsors. In

1955 the AAA also signed a three-year television agreement with the BBC for the annual championships, non-exclusive in case a higher offer was made by another company.[43] The 1960s saw an increased interest in sponsorship from the AAA and other bodies as a means of replacing the lost live-spectator income. This took various forms. The 1961 AAA championships were the first to be sponsored, by Carborundum, while *The Daily Herald* supported the 1962 indoor championships at Wembley,[44] and *Tit-Bits* backed the AAA's relay championship from 1965.[45] Experiments with corporate hospitality started in 1961, when the AAA's Finance and General Purposes Committee initiated the leasing of restaurant tables at White City to businesses for the whole of the athletics season, the fee covering the price of admission and the chosen meal, plus 'a donation to the A.A.A. funds'.[46]

In addition to these sponsorships, the AAA began to carry more advertising in its annual handbooks and rule books: the 1964 edition of the rules, for example, carried a full page athletics-themed advertisement for Ovaltine,

The champion of drinks – THE DRINK OF CHAMPIONS: Over 42,000 cups of 'Ovaltine' were served to athletes at the 1962 Empire Games in Perth, and over 127,000 cups at the Rome Olympics, 1960… Drink delicious 'Ovaltine' every day; it's good for athletes – good for you [capitalisation in original].[47]

These aspects of the AAA's profile became more professionalised from April 1966, when the AAA's contract with the marketing agency Voice of Sport began.[48] This led to more publication advertising – for 1966-67, athletes were being advised on how Yardley products could help them 'to shave a minute off [their] record', and were being exhorted to 'Come alive!' as the 'Pepsi generation' in a cartoon advertisement based on pole vaulting[49] – and to the use of a sponsor's name on a specific race, the Pepsi Cola 5,000 metres at the 1969 AAA championships.[50] However, the role of advertising remained problematic, particularly for television coverage on the non-commercial BBC: and the Byers Committee into the development of athletics, whose report was published in 1968, called for an overhaul of the rules on advertising, some of which were seen as 'unbelievably stupid'.[51] This came a year after Barry Willis, the AAA's Honorary Secretary, had admitted that the sport was 'losing money fast' and that the AAA felt 'bankruptcy' to be a 'very real threat',[52] and two years before the AAA had to sell its investments.[53]

The AAA's fortunes and status began to improve after this low point: and by the late 1970s, when the amateur status debate was coming to an end, it was a far more professional and commercially-oriented organisation than it had been even 15 years earlier. Different indicators of this change include the Bagenal Harvey Organisation's appointment as the AAA's 'promotion consultants' from 1971;[54] Ford's sponsorship of indoor meetings for £6,000 in 1972;[55] and the acceptance in 1976 of sponsor's names on competitor's numbers at events, with competitors who objected to this being allowed to 'fold the card' to hide the name, but not to mutilate the card.[56] This period – during which the rules on amateur status, and the administrative framework for British athletics, were frequently under examination – was thus one in which the trend towards commercialism and professionalism was being consolidated. This was fundamental to the subsequent development of the sport after 1981.

The poor financial situation, then, caused by the expense of the sport, the costs of maintaining facilities that were under-utilised, and the decline in paying spectators, had a major impact on the sport's administrators by the early 1970s. Throughout the 1950s and 1960s, the growing relationship with the commercial world seems to have been essentially unplanned: the use of *The News of the World* was based on historical and personal links, and the employment of an agency from only 1965 shows that the AAA started courting commerce pragmatically. What is also clear is that the trends, while recognised as necessary by most, were not universally welcomed; and some contributions to the debates stressed the need for all involved to keep the sport's voluntary and amateur traditions alive. As Willis put it in his annual report for 1966–67, while sponsorship and government grants might be helping to improve training and infrastructure, they could not cover the costs of maintaining a thriving culture throughout the sport's 'broad-based pyramid':

> All who benefit from the organisation of athletics must face up to paying more in return.... We cannot hope to sit back and have all our financial problems solved for us. Only by making greater efforts to help ourselves, can we prove that we are worthy of greater assistance.[57]

The permission given to anti-commercial dissenters to hide the sponsor's name on their numbers is also evidence of the compromises that were being made between old and new views of athletics. While some welcomed the opportunities that the diversification of income offered, as in Jack Crump's description of *The News of the World*'s 'invaluable sponsorship', the period from 1945 until the 1970s was clearly a transitional one for athletics administrators.[58] The economic context forced experimentation in areas that were out of keeping with their traditional cultural view of the sport.

When we place this economic crisis in the context of debates going on about national sporting decline throughout the 1950s and 1960s, we can see how the apparent failing health of athletics became tied up with the wider issue of national prestige. The tone for this debate was set not just in media coverage and popular discourse, where it continues to thrive, but also in the influential critique of sport published by a group of University of Birmingham educationalists in 1956. This call for an overhaul of the amateur culture that underpinned British sport, including pleas for structured government involvement and for clubs and administrations to diversify into commercial activities, explicitly drew attention to the 'world which regards success in sport as an index of national vitality and national prestige'.[59] The growth of international competition in the post-war period, and the attendant growth of pressure on sportsmen and women to perform well, had a significant impact on British sporting culture as a whole. These influences were felt in many sports, and fed into the development of more professional management cultures, a greater emphasis on training and coaching, and an increasing willingness to use non-British models and resources.[60]

However, while administrators were forced to experiment in some areas, there was one area in which this period saw very little movement: the model of amateurism that athletes had to match to become and remain eligible. Despite the increasingly professional commercial and administrative structures which were beginning to bring extra funding into the sport, and despite the AAA's acceptance of a Pepsi Cola and Harvey Bagenal culture, athletes themselves remained constrained by older views. The amateur definition remained central to the AAA's agenda: and on the occasions when it was discussed, the entrenched views of its defenders made it very hard for any compromises to be made. It is to these restrictions, and the problems that arose in the sport because of them in the changing context of the post-war period, that we should now turn.

The Application of the Amateur Rules

The issue of the amateur definition was raised very early on in our period, when the IAAF – which shared some key personnel with the AAA, including Exeter as president and Ernest Holt as honorary secretary – discussed broken time payments at its 1946 congress. The Federation established a committee to investigate the issue, which aimed to report in 1948.[61] Broken time payments, which covered wages lost by the individual missing work for sport, had always been a problematic feature for sports which aimed to remain amateur, but which also wished to encourage and exploit talented sportsmen and women who could not take paid leave from the work in order to compete. As Richard Holt notes in relation to rugby in the late nineteenth century, a refusal to give such compensation meant that a governing body was 'effectively excluding manual workers from the better teams'.[62] They were thus a controlling mechanism based on the social identity of a sport's administrators, and the place of sport as a recreation within their world view. The IAAF's raising of the issue was a recognition of the high profile that the first post-war Olympics would have, and the problems that many competitors would face in travelling and competing so soon after the war. It was not intended to open all competition up to this form of payment, only the Olympics, international matches, and such meetings as world and European championships. In his role as the AAA's Honorary Secretary, Ernest Holt noted that the whole issue of amateur status was 'perhaps the most outstanding problem' that the IAAF, and thus its British members, was facing; and the AAA duly instituted its own sub-committee of the General Committee to explore the issue.[63]

The IAAF's committee reported in January 1948. Its recommendations were discussed by all national governing bodies, and provided a framework on amateur status that was to last until 1981. The assumption that amateurism was a more morally superior basis for sport than professionalism remained strong, as exemplified by the first clause: 'An Amateur is one who practises and competes ONLY for the love of sport' [capitalisation in original]. The regulations covered a wide range of activities which rendered an athlete ineligible, including betting on an event, selling or pawning prizes, making any money from an event, receiving 'compensation for using the goods or apparatus of any firm, manufacturer or agent', using his or her name in any advertisement, and writing on athletics, unless he or she was a professional journalist. However, there was a significant development over broken time. The clause is worth quoting at length, as it is indicative of the compromises made in order to accommodate athletes short of actually agreeing to pay them. After starting with a refutation of the broken time principle – 'An amateur may not directly or indirectly accept payment for any loss of time, salary or wages in attending, or training for any athletic competition' – the clause went on:

> however, it will be permitted and not be considered as a violation of the amateur rule, for an athlete who is the SOLE support of his family, i.e. wife, children, mother or father, to be reimbursed by his National Association or Federation through his employer for loss of time, salary or wages during his absence after one day, when competing in Olympic Games, European ... Championships and official International Matches between Members of the I.A.A.F. [capitalisation in original].[64]

However, the AAA chose not to accept this dilution, and requesting or receiving reimbursement for broken time remained an offence. So, as the international body was beginning to alter the inherited line on amateurism, the AAA continued over the next three decades to maintain and enforce its tight regulations. Examples of this show how deeply entrenched the assumptions about the purity of amateurism and the dangers of professionalism really were, and how the amateur rules gave the AAA great control over athletes' freedoms in a number of areas, including work, advertising and writing. Moreover, the actual enforcement and maintenance of regulations were underpinned by frequent statements on the superiority of amateurism over any form of professionalism. Two examples of this are worth noting in detail as evidence of the predominant ideologies held by amateur administrators, and of how the idea of the amateur fitted into their world views.

In the Annual Report for 1953, Ernest Clynes, the AAA's Honorary Secretary, stressed how the AAA was:

> not only concerned with champions but with the average young man who wishes merely to participate in a healthy outdoor

recreation, to build up a fit body and mind, in the friendly company of other athletes. Too much emphasis cannot be given to the essential fact that amateur athletics is primarily and always a recreation. This is the foundation on which the Association has been built.[65]

A fuller defence came in Exeter's detailed speech as President, 'The fundamental difference between Amateurism and Professionalism', to the Association's Annual General Meeting on 15 March 1959. Its wider significance is shown by the fact that it was printed and circulated with the minutes, a rare treatment for any particular speech. He offered a candid view of the professional as one who 'quite honourably decides that sport shall be the trade which he is going to follow to earn his daily bread', and who has to maintain a certain standard of performance in order to please the crowds on whom his income depends. He compared this to the amateurs, particularly the ordinary club athletes:

> It is immaterial to them if one person or ten thousand come to see them perform, and they enjoy too the thrill of the competition and the good fellowship which they find in Club [sic] life…and…all this without any thought of financial reward or their livelihood depending on it.

He stressed that 'this type of approach to competition and club life develops not only healthy and happy people, but also the characteristics which the community needs for good citizens'. This theme recurs in his emphasis on athletics for the amateur being 'a happy recreation…which…develops some finer sides of the individual's character'.[66] The regulations, and their enforcement, cannot be divorced from the ideologies that this rhetoric illustrates.

Control over athletes' work was enforced to ensure that no individual was gaining advantage through a job which allowed them effectively to train on more than an amateur basis. This came under the laws' restrictions on athletes engaging in, assisting in, and teaching athletics 'for pecuniary consideration', or 'exploiting' their 'athletic ability for profit'.[67] The concern was also based on the practice employed by individuals and clubs in many sports whereby purely nominal jobs were created either within clubs or through patron's companies for talented individuals, who were thereby enabled to train full-time while legally holding a non-sporting job. In order to limit athletes' opportunities for this, we can see the AAA, particularly in the 1940s and 1950s, often ruling on the legitimacy of certain occupations. For example, in May 1946, the AAA ruled that if an athlete took up employment at a Butlin's holiday camp in order to organise sports activities while also training, then he would 'lose his amateur status'.[68] A month earlier, the amateur definition sub-committee recommended that any full-time physical education teacher could remain an amateur, but that he would lose his status if he ran private lessons;[69] while any athlete employed as a hospital masseur was also safe.[70]

However, it is clear that there were some abuses to this system through structures of patronage: while full evidence of this is difficult to pin down for obvious reasons, a taster of such patronage is evident, for example, in Philip Noel-Baker's 1950 correspondence with Angus Scott, a hurdler and 400 metre runner. Noel-Baker, who competed in the 800 metres and 1500 metres at the 1912 and 1920 Olympics, winning the silver in the 1500 at Antwerp, had combined his political career with a continued involvement in athletics, particularly through the Achilles Club. At the time of this intervention, he was Minister of Fuel and Power in Attlee's Labour government. Scott, who had been a member of Great Britain's victorious 4 x 400 metre relay team at that year's European championships in Brussels, worked for a company with which Noel-Baker had family connections. After praising his performances, Noel-Baker asked:

> But what I really wanted to say was this: how are the training facilities in Peterborough? Will Baker Perkins make adequate arrangements for you to be able to train? Is there anything you would like me to say to my nephew, Ivor, the Chairman? I will, in any case, be writing to him very soon, and I feel sure that he will want to do anything I suggest.[71]

Noel-Baker was also involved in the 1958 case cited by Jeremy Crump, using his contacts in the coal industry to gain broken time payments for shot putter Arthur Rowe.[72] So, while the official view was that an athletes' job should be distinct from their sport, and that broken time, special facilities, or other advantages were abuses of these rules, there is evidence of some within the athletics establishment finding ways around the restrictions.

As well as athletes' employment, advertising was another area in which the AAA applied tight controls. In 1950, the Amateur Status

Sub-Committee addressed advertising in response to some questions on the application of the clause of the amateur definition which made an athlete 'receiving money or any other consideration for allowing his name as an athlete to be used for advertising purposes in connection with any commodity' an offence.[73] The Sub-Committee ruled that advertising was out of bounds for individual athletes 'under any circumstances whatever', and that while an athlete could sell the rights to an athletic 'device or commodity' he had invented or developed, he could not have his name attached to it. Moreover, an athlete could work as a salesman only if 'it [was] his normal occupation'.[74] The same sub-committee's claim in 1951 that the use of active athletes' names in advertising was 'not in the best interest of amateur athletics' consolidated this view.[75] An example of this being applied came in April 1953, when McDonald Bailey was suspended by the AAA's Southern Committee after his name appeared in an advertisement for Lillywhites 'Comet' starting blocks. Bailey was a high profile name. The bronze medallist in the 100 metres at the Helsinki Olympics in 1952, his domestic fame rested on his performances in the AAA championships, where he won the 100 yards and 220 yards double seven times between 1946 and 1953.[76] The offending advertisement, placed in the programme of the Oxford v Cambridge match in March, claimed that the blocks were 'made to the requirements of E. McDonald Bailey, Ltd.' and were 'similar to the type used in the Olympic Games 1952'.[77] McDonald Bailey was reinstated on appeal: his argument that 'he had not agreed to his name to appear *as an athlete* in the advertisement' [emphasis in original] was upheld.[78] This case not only showed up how the rules could be evaded – in this case, by the use of Bailey's company's name rather than his own name – but also how keen the Association was to enforce its restrictions. The juxtaposition of these restrictions on individuals in the sport's 'best interests' with the fact that the AAA was by this time receiving sponsorship from *The News of the World* shows up some of the contradictions and double standards involved: while athletes could not capitalise on their personal prestige or the image of the sport, the AAA could capitalise on its organisational prestige and the image of the sport. This is a good illustration of how the defence of amateurism must be seen, at least partially, in social terms rather than purely sporting ones.

Allied to this form of control was the AAA's enforcement of the prohibition on active athletes writing, lecturing or broadcasting on athletics for payment without permission. Again, this specific restriction was tied to the wider assumption that athletes should not capitalise on their fame, and that fees from writing and broadcasting could be a thinly-disguised form of professionalism. The AAA overhauled this regulation, and instituted a procedure for athletes to seek permission, through the Permission to Write, Broadcast and Lecture Committee, set up by the General Committee in February 1952.[79] The Committee's report in May laid down six 'broad principles' that should govern any decision, specifically designed to stop any athlete from gaining nominal employment as a journalist, and to limit the opportunities of athletes cashing in on their fame. For example, in order to control ghost-writing, they reserved the right to question an athlete's capability of writing, and stressed that newspapers carrying articles by athletes should be 'moderate' in their references to that athlete's 'distinctions'. They also wanted to prevent the payment of 'exaggerated fees [which] indicate that more value is attached to the athletic reputation of the athlete-author than to the actual contributions', and barred athletes from writing on events in which they were taking part.[80] In short, the AAA recognised that athletes wanted to write and broadcast, and that media organs were willing to pay, but attempted to keep the process as moderate and controlled as possible. The General Committee accepted these recommendations, and gave the Permission Committee the powers to grant permission and investigate abuses. The Committee duly managed this process, granting permission in many cases. In May 1953, for example, Norris McWhirter and Ross McWhirter were given exemptions from having to apply, as both were journalists, while Bannister was given permission to write a 'medical publication' on the 'physiological and psychological aspects of athletics',[81] and Christopher Chataway gained permission to broadcast in 1955.[82] Others were unsuccessful, including middle-distance runner F. Peter Higgins in May 1952,[83] and hurdler Peter Hildreth in December 1957.[84] Overall, the law on writing, and its enforcement through the AAA's committees, ensured that the Association retained a degree of control over athletes' earning potential, and over the views they were able to express in public. This control was perceived by many athletes as a deliberate form of censorship, a view put very strongly by Pirie on his retirement from amateur athletics:

Every British amateur athlete wears an invisible gag. He dare not break into print, even if he could get his views printed, because he would be branded as a professional. Only if he gets express permission to earn some of his heavy expenses by writing or broadcasting can he do so. And you may be sure he will not get permission if officialdom suspects that his views are not safe and conventional.[85]

These are examples of some of the ways in which the AAA exercised control over individual athletes. Other methods existed, including the work of the Athletes To and From Abroad Committee, which controlled the competition programmes of elite athletes. Moreover, there is also evidence of individual acts of what we could call either patronage or philanthropy from administrators towards athletes of smaller means. As with the cases of job opportunities cited above, Noel-Baker figures in this aspect of the sport's history. In December 1947, for example, he offered to pay for miler Sidney Wooderson to see an osteopath for his ankle injury, although Wooderson recovered without this.[86] Noel-Baker did pay for Cambridge University miler Peter Robinson's osteopathy treatment in October 1953, patronage he described to Robinson as his own 'contribution to the welfare of the C.U.A.C. [Cambridge University Athletics Club] and the defeat of Oxford'.[87] This particular act of kindness should be seen in the context of Noel-Baker's earlier request to Robinson to act as a pace setter in Roger Bannister's unsuccessful attempt at the four minute mile at White City in May 1953:

> It would be a glorious achievement for Britain and the Achilles [Club] if Roger could get near the four minute mile, and anybody who helps him will have a place in athletic history.[88]

Although Robinson was unable to oblige, the incident provides an interesting example of the networks and power relationships that existed within athletics, alongside the more formal mechanisms of control.[89]

In the light of these controls, we can now build on Pirie's comment quoted above and consider athletes' views of the amateur rules, and of the structures that underpinned them. The apparent anomalies that existed between the rules and leading athletes' needs and demands helped to create a conflict between athletes and administrators. In the

British context, the 'growing assertiveness of leading athletes' that Jeremy Crump describes was a significant factor in forcing the changes that came in the late 1970s and early 1980s.[90]

Elite Athletes' Occupational Culture

There were a number of general contexts for the development of this more assertive culture, and it is worth noting these before we look at some selected issues. One was demographic. In the post-war period, the sport began to attract more people from lower middle and working class backgrounds than in previous periods, with the relative improvement in opportunities and resources (particularly through the armed forces, and educational institutions after 1944), and the increased popularity of and accessibility to the Olympic Games and other major tournaments through media coverage, bringing in new people. While university athletes continued to dominate in the 1950s, more top class athletes were from less privileged backgrounds. While athletes' memoirs must be treated with caution, many are candid on their roots. We can note, for example, Derek Ibbotson, whose 'family was not well off';[91] Alan Pascoe, 'a grammar-school boy-elect, still living in a council house and about as typical a kid from a lower middle-class background as you could ever meet';[92] Geoff Capes, the son of a casual agricultural labourer, who recalled his family's economic status as being 'good enough' on occasion, 'but in winter times were tough';[93] Dorothy Hyman, the daughter of a Yorkshire miner, whose first competitive races were at Monk Bretton colliery's gala day;[94] Mary Rand (née Bignal), the daughter of a self-employed chimney sweep and window cleaner;[95] and Brendan Foster, from a Roman Catholic family in County Durham, whose father worked in the local authority's rating office, who grew up 'with this underlying feeling that you were never likely to get the breaks because you lived in a place where fortune so often turned a blind eye', and who 'found it difficult to identify with people whose fathers had two or three cars' when he got to Sussex University in 1966.[96] When we take these backgrounds into consideration, we can see one of the reasons for the conflict that developed in British athletics. Even avoiding simplistic class-based reductionism, we can see that the life experiences of many of the athletic elite of the 1950s, 1960s, and 1970s were very different from those of their predecessors; and that the opportunities that many of these individuals encountered through welfarist educational policies, which took many of them to grammar schools, teacher training colleges and universities, created a culture of expectation and aspiration very different from that of athletics administrators.

When this general context is allied to the more specifically sporting one mentioned above, that of the growth of international competition and the attendant rise in pressure to succeed, we can see another reason for the conflict in athletics. All of the top British athletes breaking through in the 1950s and after were aware that notions of national prestige were resting on them, and that they were having to compete against people who were effectively professionals. The state-sponsored systems of the USSR and the USA, predominantly military and university based respectively, created an imbalance: and many British athletes felt that they were being constrained from reaching the top internationally by this anomaly. This aspect also manifested itself in more tangible terms in many athletes' discussions of the problems facing the sport in the UK, as they felt that they should be able to earn a living from the sport to which they were dedicating themselves.

These issues were argued with great force by Pirie in his memoirs, published in 1961, after a very successful ten-year career. While his own history of conflict with the athletics establishment must be remembered when using his writing, the text provides a good example of the ideological and cultural gulf between active athletes in the post-war period and what he called the 'elderly dictators of British athletics' whose code of amateurism was based on 'the Old School Tie and the Old Pals Act'.[97] He argued that there was a need to 'bridge the mental and physical gap between British athletic attitudes and world standards', and that this bridging could come through more scientific training, state investment, an overhaul of the sport's administration, and through some form of payment for athletes so that they could make 'a reasonable living free of humiliating patronage'.[98] As we shall see, these themes recur frequently in other athletes' writing on the sport, often underpinned by the athletes' perception of a cultural – and, indeed, generational – gap between administrators and active participants: as Steve Ovett put it, by the 1970s,

> the grateful, touching-forelock era towards the administrators ... was fading. The pre-war order of things which carried on into the fifties was not really acceptable to young people living in the more materialistic world of the seventies.[99]

With these contexts, and some evidence of the ideological fault lines, in place, let us move on to consider some of the ways in which athletes asserted themselves against Pirie's 'elderly dictators'. Methods varied, but a number of themes emerge.

One way in which this assertiveness was exercised was through pressure from athletes for an overhaul of the way in which athletics was run. This was not just about the amateur rule as such, although many of the athletes involved combined agitation for organisational reform with their attempts to win the right to make money from the sport. In 1958, Hildreth and Derek Johnson formed the International Athletes Club (IAC) as a forum for British international athletes, 'in effect...a collective body', with the aim of gaining greater representation for athletes on the AAA and BAAB's decision-making structures.[100] This came after problems of team management at the 1956 Olympic Games, and the AAA's subsequent rejection of the idea from athletes for the team captain to be an elected individual with genuine responsibility.[101] The IAC applied pressure to the AAA at various times, with some successes and some failures. In April 1959, for example, the IAC's bid to have the restrictions on writing for pay dropped was rejected by the AAA, although their simultaneous request for the IAC to gain selection rights for the international athletes' places on the Athletes Advisory Committee was granted.[102] In October 1963, the IAC attempted to negotiate some share of television interview fees from the AAA, which led to a compromise whereby the AAA allowed part of the fees to go to the club, association or charity of individual athletes' choice.[103] The IAC's failure here led to some athletes, including Robbie Brightwell, the athletics team captain for the following year's Tokyo Olympics, to refuse to give television interviews. This affair caused a major breach between some of the athletes and the administrators, particularly Jack Crump, the BAAB's Honorary Secretary, who had been a frequent target of athletes' criticism for his aloof stance.[104]

Further pressure for administrative change, this time far more wide-reaching, came in the early 1970s. In 1971, at the end of the European Championship in Helsinki, team captains Alan Pascoe and Pat Lowe organised a meeting through which athletes expressed criticism of team management systems. Despite Pascoe's efforts to keep the criticism constructive, he later claimed that he ended up feeling as if the administrators viewed him as a combination of 'Che Guevara, Arthur Scargill and Tariq Ali' and 'the Wat Tyler of the track'.[105] In the following September, with backing from the Sports Council, Pascoe, David Hemery, Les Piggott and Lynn Davies, all of whom had held the Great Britain men's team captaincy, wrote an open letter to the Sports Council, the BAAB, 'and all those interested in the future of British athletics'. In it, they listed a series of charges against the administration, including 'inefficiency and internal strife', 'centralization of power', a 'lack of communication', 'poor public relations and ineffectual publicity', a 'lack of systematic support for athletes' training programmes', and the 'squandering of sponsors' goodwill'. They concluded, in a way that shows a clear awareness of how the international context of the sport had changed faster than its management, 'in light of the increasing complexity of international sport, it is evident that the current part-time amateur establishment is no longer equal to the task'. They called for a 'complete revision' of the administration, to include a professional director of athletics, a professional co-ordinator for international events, and a selection board appointed by the Sports Council in order to destroy the 'system of self-perpetuation'.[106] This 'cry for reform' was followed up by a meeting between the BAAB and Hemery, Pascoe and Pat Cropper in November: and while no immediate action was taken, the conflict signalled the seriousness with which the whole issue of administration was being taken by this time.[107]

These examples of open confrontation were proof of the gulf that existed between athletes and administrators. Some athletes' published views of the administrators illustrate the depth and intensity of feeling, from Ibbotson's gentle suggestion that all administrators should retire at the age of 55, through to Pirie's more blatant chapter entitled: 'The elderly dictators of British athletics: these men must go'.[108] One of the most vitriolic in this context has been Geoff Capes, through his ghost-writer Neil Wilson: from the opening shot in the 'Foreword', claiming that the book 'owes its existence to the sport's administration – to those officials who could never accept that athletes have minds of their own and wish to speak them', through to his machine gun blast of 'What is necessary is a "St Valentine Day's [*sic*] massacre" of the old school, the Black Hand Gang... Let them work for their knighthoods on the Sports Council' – the message is blunt.[109]

Another interesting way in which athletes attempted to assert themselves was over the issue of the amateur rule itself. One of the anomalies in the early post-war period was that while active athletes were prohibited from the range of activities covered above, there were no regulatory restrictions on officials. For example, officials were able to write, broadcast and lecture for pay without having to gain permission; while the apparent and perceived differences in their lifestyles while abroad with teams, in such areas as travel arrangements, accommodation, and entertainments, suggested to many athletes that double standards were applying. This was formally addressed at the AAA's 1957 AGM, when Phil Gale successfully proposed a motion calling for the rephrasing of the amateur definition so that it applied to officials.[110] This change was duly made by the dropping of the word 'athlete' from the laws.[111] However, inconsistencies and abuses survived, at least according to athletes: Ibbotson's criticisms of Jack Crump's conflict of interests over writing and managing, Hyman's general criticisms of double-standards, and Capes' indictment of officials' abuses make this clear.[112] Capes' charges against unnamed officials, including taking their families on international trips on expenses, having better accommodation and transport than athletes, and taking contraband through customs – sometimes hidden in athletes' luggage – do not paint a favourable picture: and while we must remember Pascoe's warning here that athletes can be 'notorious moaners,' we should also recall Capes' career in the police force.[113]

A third way in which we can see the gulf between athletes and administrators is in certain athletes' abuse of the amateur laws. Obviously, evidence for this is difficult both to find and to measure: it necessarily leaves few records, and has clearly been the subject of much anecdotal exaggeration. However, the consensus that emerges from athletes' memoirs is that illegal payments were the worst-kept secret of the sport. Ibbotson's tone suggests this:

> Do amateur athletes get paid for running? Of course, some of them do! This is known to leading officials, but they do not take action as it cannot be proved. Suspicions and rumours do not constitute evidence and I have no intention of sparking off a witch-hunt.[114]

Davies was more under-stated but just as open in his note on whether or not 'Britain's top athletes' strictly adhered to the laws on amateurism: 'Some do; some don't'; while Capes was perfectly candid about 'what we loosely call "expenses"'.[115] Clearly, many individuals were prepared to take illegal cash payments from meeting promoters throughout the pre-1981 period and it is clear that one of the motivations behind the reforms of 1981 was the widely recognised need to regulate what was a highly developed part of sport's black economy. The level of the abuse is perhaps indicated by Mel Watman's acknowledgement of it in the 1981 edition of his *Encyclopaedia of Track and Field Athletics*, a genre of historiography that rarely courts controversy. In the brief entry on 'professional athletics', he noted how the USA's International Track Association's professional circuit had closed down in 1976:

> In view of the increasingly lucrative pickings to be made 'under the counter' in so-called amateur competition, the organisation had been unable to recruit...topliners. In the words of one big star approached: 'I just can't afford to turn professional!'[116]

Some athletes admitted to their abuses at the time as a way of publicising what they saw as an unfair system, in which they were out of pocket after representing their country. Pirie did this in 1961 by writing an article in the *People* in which he claimed that he had been paid to run in a number of events: but the AAA's investigation was unable to prove his claims, leaving them with a compromise punishment of refusing his expenses claim for one meeting as they believed that he had been ineligible at the time.[117] Others waited until writing their memoirs before confessing to their abuses, including pentathlete Mary Peters. Her account is a good example of the genre, as it stresses that it was the rules being out of date, and the administrators – in this case, the IOC, but the general culture of amateurism was also being indicted – being unable to recognise this, that forced otherwise honest athletes into dishonesty. After the 1962 Commonwealth Games, and alongside her teaching career, she started working at a Belfast gymnasium as 'the dog's-body factotum' whose duties included clerical work and 'some health instruction'.

> I was now, under the quite ludicrous law laid down by the millionaires and noblemen of the International Olympic Committee, a professional. Within their terms of reference I was a cheat throughout the remainder of my athletic career... I was 'investigated' several times and on each occasion had no compunction at all about telling the first lie that came into my head.

She noted that she was losing money by competing, and pointed out the anomaly that had she been giving health instruction in a school or in the armed forces, 'I would have been regarded as a true-blue amateur': 'If you wanted to make money in the late 1950's or early 1960's the last thing you became was a churchmouse or an Olympic competitor.'[118] Others admitted to receiving broken time payments from their employers, including Hyman from her job at the National Coal Board which was 'virtually created for me', and Rand from her work in the Guinness brewery post room.[119]

Taken together, these themes show that there was an increasingly professional occupational culture among elite athletes by the 1970s, linked both to their socio-economic background, and to their recognition of the fact that success in the 1960s and beyond had to be based upon disciplined and scientific training, which did not come for free. They also show that the generation coming to maturity from the 1950s onwards did not all subscribe to the Exeter view of amateurism, and had different assumptions and expectations; and that many of them were not prepared to tolerate an administration that they found paternalistic, amateur (in a derogatory sense), and interfering, and were prepared to criticise where they saw fit. If we combine these attitudes with the athletics organisations' movement towards a more professional and commercial culture, we can see that by the early 1980s, the climate in the UK was right for the major changes that took place: and while the rewriting of the amateur rules came from the IAAF, it must be noted that the AAA began to debate 'a more modern and generally accepted attitude towards amateurism' in December 1979.[120] Their emergency general meeting on the issue, held on 28 February 1981, showed that there was still resistance to the sport going open but that some form of accommodation with professionalism was, in the words of Dr. E. Illingworth of the Northern Counties Athletic Association, 'part of an inevitable trend'.[121]

Conclusion

The themes and evidence explored in this essay have illustrated some of the ways in which the amateur rules were defined, approached, defended and abused in the period between 1945 and the IAAF's acceptance of limited professionalism in 1981. Since then, the sport has changed in many ways, a history narrated by Downes and Mackay.[122] The growth of subventions, trust funds, appearance fees and marketing have created an elite who can make significant amounts of money from the sport and its related commercial sector: and the beginnings of an occupational culture that we saw from the 1950s has developed into a fully professional culture, in which all leading athletes have agents, contracts, endorsement deals and media profiles. Some of the beneficiaries of these changes have bemoaned the gigantism that this has engendered: javelin thrower Tessa Sanderson, for example, claimed that 'fat appearance money not only blunts appetite...but it also leads to a distortion of values'.[123] Others have openly criticised the possible abuses of the trust fund systems: distance runner David Moorcroft, for example, noted that the general nature of some of the 'training expenses' allowed to be taken from trust funds during the athlete's active career included transport and accommodation, 'so presumably you could buy a Rolls-Royce and Buckingham Palace if you felt like it'.[124] However, despite these and other voices of caution in the early days of the trust fund period, there is no doubt that the changes made in the early 1980s helped to reconstruct elite British athletes as relatively free agents in a global sporting industry. The sport's administration is also more streamlined and professional than it was in the pre-1980 period: although financial disaster killed off the first experiment in a truly national organisation – the BAF – its successor, UK Athletics (formed in 1999), has started in its attempt to run the sport in its 'new era'. Its first President was one of the rebels of 1972, David Hemery, who was voted in by the clubs; its stated aim to 'co-ordinate and support rather than intervene and control', and its pledge 'that all appointments will be based on competence and skills', are indicative of the revolution that has occurred in the management of British athletics over the post-war period.[125] As this piece has shown, amateurism has not just been about money, but also about approach.

However, it would be wrong to end this essay without noting two issues. First, the ways in which the athletics establishment and the media have reacted to the increasing use of performance enhancing drugs in athletics shows that while the socio-economic means of control over athletes may have declined, other channels have been found. Drugs, in some ways, can be seen to have replaced professionalism as the perceived evil that is corrupting a once pure sport. This area of the sport requires further socio-historical research so that it can be placed fully in context: but we can see connections between the earlier condemnations of payment and gambling and the more recent condemnations of drug use. This has been most evident in British athletics in the case of middle-distance runner Diane Modahl, who was tested positive for testosterone in 1994, and whose successful legal challenge of this result effectively bankrupted the BAF. More recently, Linford Christie, the UK's most successful sprinter of the post-war period, tested positive for banned substances: at the time of writing, this case is under investigation. There are clearly differences in the discourses over these two forms of abuse, particularly the way in which drug use is widely condemned in elite athletes' own public pronouncements, whereas some form of regulated professionalism was generally welcomed. This is best seen in Moorcroft's chapter on 'Drugs, doping and dollars', where he points to the perceived anomalies in a sport where he could be banned for taking either drugs or extra payments:

> Although I can say with a clear conscience that I have never, and would never take drugs to improve my performance, I would have to think very hard about saying that I had never received money under the table for competing in certain athletics meetings.[126]

However, despite some athletes' condemnation of drugs' effects on athletics and athletes, the evidence of usage suggests that many do not share these compunctions: and the athletics establishment's structures of detection, investigation and punishment must be seen in the perspective of its history of controlling athletes.

A second issue to note in conclusion is that amateurism is still a significant factor in British athletics, despite the money, the trust funds, the television contracts, and the undoubted corruption that has gone with it, explored by Downes and Mackay.[127] At club level, and even at the level of unaffiliated individuals who enjoy athletic sports, the traditions of voluntarism and amateurism are thriving. Here, as in the grassroots of all sports, participants pay to take part, and give their time and resources to manage, coach and administer. Interest in the sport has grown, helped in part by the burgeoning of marathons and shorter mass runs, and by the change in popular perceptions about these events which has made them more accessible to women, runners of all ages and abilities, and to wheelchair athletes. By seeing this in its context as an appropriate sport for an era in which equality of opportunity is a social priority and cultural assumption, we can understand how such voluntarism and amateurism can continue. However, this side of athletics cannot be divorced from the high profile elite sport, which, with its emphasis on individualism, laissez-faire economics, meritocratic advancement, and all the trappings of post-industrial marketing culture, is also appropriate for its era. Taking these two distinct but related strands together, we can see in post-war athletics an excellent case study in how sports history needs to be attuned not just to apparently straightforward contexts in which sporting practices took place. To describe athletics since 1981 as, for example, Thatcherite would tell only part of the story, as would any labelling of it as a sport still based on Victorian notions of voluntarism and self-help. It is the historian's role to see the two together, to recognise the relationship between grass roots and elite, and to explore ways in which apparently alternative cultures can survive alongside each other.

ACKNOWLEDGEMENTS

The author wishes to express his gratitude to the staff of the University of Birmingham's Special Collections Department and the Churchill Archives Centre, Cambridge. The material from Philip Noel-Baker's papers is quoted with the permission of the Master and Fellows of Churchill College, Cambridge.

NOTES

1. Carl Lewis and Jeffrey Marx, *Inside Track: My Professional Life in Amateur Athletics* (London: Pelham, 1990) pp.204–5.
2. See 'The Unofficial Denise Lewis Homepage', http://come.to/denise_lewis. Accessed Jul. 1999.
3. Rob Draper, 'The girl most likely to…', *Total Sport*, Sept. 1997. Copy in 'The Unofficial Denise Lewis Homepage', http://come.to/denise_lewis. Accessed Jul. 1999.
4. Harold Abrahams, 'Sport, Professionalism and the Olympics', text of address given to the South Place Ethical Society, 27 Mar. 1977. University of Birmingham Special Collections Department (hereafter UBSCD), NCAL XXV.H27.
5. Quoted in Richard Liston, 'Hungry for Gold', *Pride*, Aug. 1998. Copy in 'The Unofficial Denise Lewis Homepage', http://come.to/denise_lewis. Accessed Jul. 1999
6. For a good brief introduction to pedestrianism and its legacy, see Eric MacIntyre, 'Pedestrianism to the Trust Fund: athletics in its historical and social contexts', in

Amateurs and Professionals in Post-War British Sport

J.A. Mangan and R.B. Small (eds.), *Sport, Culture and Society: International Historical and Sociological Perspectives* (London: Spon, 1986), pp.124-8.

7. For a description of professional pedestrianism in the 1960s, see Geoffrey Nicholson, *The Professionals* (London: Andre Deutsch, 1964), chapter 9.

8. The best overall history of British athletics is Jeremy Crump, 'Athletics', in Tony Mason (ed.), *Sport in Britain: A Social History* (Cambridge: Cambridge University Press, 1989), pp.44–77. Bibliographical guides of value here include Richard Cox, *Sport in Britain: A Bibliography of Historical Publications 1800-1988* (Manchester: Manchester University Press, 1991), especially pp.29-30; and Peter Lovesey and Tom McNab, *A Guide to British Track and Field Literature, 1275-1968* (London: Athletics Arena, 1969). For the AAA, see Peter Lovesey, *The Official Centenary History of the Amateur Athletic Association* (Enfield: Guinness, 1979); Mike Farrell, 'The History of the AAA', in Heather Thomas (ed.), *The AAA Runner's Guide* (revised edition, London: Willow, 1987), pp.7–11.

9. For a general survey of these issues, see Martin Polley, *Moving the Goalposts: A History of Sport and Society since 1945* (London: Routledge, 1998), pp.114–27.

10. The Marquess of Exeter, 'The Fundamental Difference between Amateurism and Professionalism', AAA Annual General Meeting, 15 Mar. 1959. UBSCD, ACC 1998/6.

11. Letter from Christopher Brasher to the AAA General Committee, read at meeting on 15 Mar. 1986. AAA General Committee minutes, 15 Mar. 1986. UBSCD, ACC 1998/6.

12. Stan Greenberg, *The Guinness Book of Olympics Facts and Feats* (Enfield: Guinness, 1996), pp.78–101, 172–90.

13. Neil Macfarlane with Michael Herd, *Sport and Politics: a world divided* (London: Willow, 1986), p.169. See also Crump, 'Athletics', pp.48–50.

14. Macfarlane with Herd, *Sport and Politics*, p.169.

15. Tony Mason, 'Foreword', in Richard Cox, *Index to Sporting Manuscripts in the U.K.* (Frodsham: Sports History Publishing, 1995), p.vi.

16. For a brief overview, see Steve Hewett, 'Papers of the Amateur Athletic Association', University of Birmingham Information Services, *Research Libraries Bulletin*, No. 6 (1998), p.14.

17. Tony Mason, *Association Football and English Society, 1863-1915* (Hassocks: Harvester, 1980); Wray Vamplew, *The Turf: a social and economic history of horse racing* (London: Allen Lane, 1976); Eric Halladay, *Rowing in England: a social history* (Manchester: Manchester University Press, 1990).

18. Crump, 'Athletics'.

19. Richard Holt, *Sport and the British: a modern history* (Oxford: Oxford University Press, 1989), p.2.

20. For the former, see for example, Tony Ward's survey of the 1980s, *Athletics: the golden decade* (London: Queen Anne Press, 1991). Quantitative surveys and event-based histories include L. Blackman, *Athletic Records in the Twentieth Century* (London: Book Guild, 1988); P. Matthews, *Track and Field Athletics: the records* (Enfield: Guinness, 1986); Mel Watman, *History of British Athletics* (London: Robert Hale, 1968); Robert Quercetani, *A World History of Track and Field Athletics, 1864-1964* (London: Oxford University Press, 1964).

21. Lovesey, *Official Centenary History*.

22. J. A. Mangan, 'Series editor's foreword', in Nicholas Fishwick, *English Football and*

110

Society, 1910-1950 (Manchester: Manchester University Press, 1989), p.vi.
23. Steven Downes and Duncan Mackay, *Running Scared: how athletics lost its innocence* (Edinburgh: Mainstream, 1996). See especially pp.11–16 for the authors' view of the sport's cleaner past.
24. David Miller, *Sebastian Coe: born to run* (London: Pavilion, 1992), p.139.
25. Miller, *Sebastian Coe*, p.138.
26. Downes and Mackay, *Running Scared*; Ward, *Athletics*.
27. Crump, 'Athletics', p.49
28. See Halladay, *Rowing in England*, pp.67–101.
29. Amateur Athletic Association, *Rules for Competitions under A.A.A. Laws* (London: Amateur Athletic Association, 1946), pp.55–8.
30. Amateur Athletic Association, *Rules for Competitions under A.A.A. Laws* (London, Amateur Athletic Association, 1948), pp.44, 45.
31. Crump, 'Athletics', pp.52–3
32. Peter Radford, 'George Wilson', in James Huntingdon-Whiteley, compiler, *The Book of British Sporting Heroes* (London: National Portrait Gallery Publications, 1998), p.231.
33. Lovesey, *Official Centenary History*, p.16.
34. Lovesey, *Official Centenary History*, p.92.
35. See Polley, *Moving the Goalposts*, pp.70–1
36. Lovesey, *Official Centenary History*, p.103.
37. Crump, 'Athletics', p.48.
38. Lovesey, *Official Centenary History*, p.103
39. See Theodore Cook (ed.), *The Fourth Olympiad, being the Official report of the Olympic Games of 1908 celebrated in London* (London: British Olympic Association, 1909), p.71; Martin Polley, 'Great Britain and the Olympic Games, 1896–1908', in C.C. Eldridge (ed.), *Empire, Politics and Popular Culture: Essays in Eighteenth and Nineteenth Century British History* (Lampeter: Trivium, 1989), p.106.
40. Lovesey, *Official Centenary History*, p.122. For a general discussion of sponsorship in post-war British sport, see Polley, *Moving the Goalposts*, pp.67–84.
41. AAA, *Annual Report, 1952*, p.13. UBSCD, NCAL VI.A6.
42. AAA, General Committee, 2 Oct. 1954. UBSCD, NCAL XVIII.G7.
43. AAA General Committee, 1 Oct. 1955. UBSCD, NCAL XVIII.G7.
44. Lovesey, *Official Centenary History*, p.126
45. AAA, General Committee, 22 May 1965. UBSCD, NCAL XVIII.G7.
46. AAA, General Committee, 15 Apr. 1961. UBSCD, NCAL XVIII.G7.
47. AAA, *Rules for Competition under A.A.A. Laws* (London: AAA, 1964), inside front cover.
48. AAA, General Committee, 22 May 1965. UBSCD, NCAL XVIII.G7.
49. AAA, *Rules for Competition under A.A.A. Laws* (London: AAA, 1967), p.50, inside back cover.
50. AAA, General Committee, 2 Dec. 1967, 15 Feb. 1969. UBSCD, NCAL XVIII.G7.
51. *Report of the Committee of Enquiry into the Development of Athletics under the direction of the Amateur Athletic Association and the British Amateur Athletics Board*, 1968, p.32. See also Lovesey, *Official Centenary History*, pp.131–2, 134–5, 149–50.
52. AAA, *Annual Report, 1966-67*. UBSCD, NCAL VI.A6.
53. AAA, Finance and General Purposes Committee, 9 Oct. 1970. UBSCD, ACC 1998/6.

54. AAA, Finance and General Purposes Committee, 16 Oct. 1971. UBSCD, ACC 1998/6.
55. AAA, General Committee, 26 Feb. 1972. UBSCD, ACC 1998/6.
56. AAA, Rules, Revisions and Records Committee, 6 Nov. 1976. UBSCD, ACC 1998/6.
57. AAA, *Annual Report, 1966–67*. UBSCD, NCAL VI.A6.
58. Jack Crump, *Running Round the World* (London: Hale, 1966), p.191
59. Physical Education Department, University of Birmingham, *Britain in the World of Sport: An examination of the factors involved in participation in competitive international sport* (S.l.: Physical Education Association for Great Britain and Northern Ireland, 1956), p.13. See also Polley, *Moving the Goalposts*, pp.18–19.
60. For a general discussion of this issue, see Polley, *Moving the Goalposts*, pp.41–53.
61. E.J. Holt, 'AAA: Report for the year ended 31st December 1946'. UBSCD, NCAL XVIII.G7.
62. Holt, *Sport and the British*, p.105.
63. E.J. Holt, 'AAA: Report for the year ended 31st December 1946'. UBSCD, NCAL XVIII.G7.
64. IAAF, 'Recommendations of the Amateur Status Commission', 1948; received by AAA General Committee, 7 Feb. 1948. UBSCD, NCAL. XVIII.G7.
65. E.H.L. Clynes, 'Annual Report, 1953'. UBSCD, NCAL VI.A6.
66. Lord Exeter, 'The fundamental difference between Amateurism and Professionalism', AAA Annual General Meeting, 15 Mar. 1959. UBSCD, ACC 1998/6.
67. AAA, *Rules for Competition under A.A.A. Laws* (London: AAA, 1946), p.55.
68. AAA, General Committee, 4 May 1946. UBSCD, NCAL.XVIII.G7.
69. Ibid.
70. AAA, General Committee, 6 Apr. 1946. UBSCD, NCAL. XVIII.G7.
71. Phillip Noel-Baker to Angus Scott, 6 Oct. 1950. Churchill Archives Centre, Cambridge (hereafter CAC), NBKR 6/2/2.
72. Crump, 'Athletics', p.55.
73. AAA, *Rules for Competition under A.A.A. Laws* (London: AAA, 1948), p.45.
74. AAA, General Committee, 4 Feb. 1950. UBSCD, NCAL. XVIII.G7.
75. AAA, General Committee, 5 May 1951. UBSCD, NCAL.XVIII.G7.
76. Lovesey, *Official Centenary History*, pp.179–80.
77. AAA Southern Committee press notice, 25 Apr. 1953. Copy in AAA General Committee, 2 May 1953. UBSCD, NCAL. XVIII.G7.
78. AAA, Appeals Committee report, in General Committee, 2 May 1953. UBSCD, NCAL. XVIII.G7.
79. AAA General Committee, 2 Feb. 1952. UBSCD, NCAL.XVIII.G7
80. Report of the Permission to Write, Broadcast, Lecture Committee, undated; AAA General Committee 3 May 1952. UBSCD, NCAL.XVIII.G7.
81. AAA General Committee, 2 May 1953. UBSCD, NCAL.XVIII.G7.
82. AAA General Committee, 1 Oct. 1955. UBSCD, NCAL XVIII.G7.
83. AAA General Committee, 3 May 1952. UBSCD, NCAL XVIII.G7.
84. AAA General Committee, 7 Dec. 1957. UBSCD, NCAL XVIII.G7.
85. Gordon Pirie, *Running Wild* (London: Allen, 1961), p.10.
86. Philip Noel-Baker to Jack Crump, 8 Dec. 1947; Sidney Wooderson to Philip Noel-Baker, 16 Dec. 1947. CAC, NBKR 6/3/1.
87. Philip Noel-Baker to Peter Robinson, 16 Oct. 1953. CAC, NBKR 6/12/3.

88. Philip Noel-Baker to Peter Robinson, 14 May 1953. CAC, NBKR 6/12/3.
89. Philip Noel-Baker to Roger Bannister, 19 May 1953. CAC, NBKR 6/12/3.
90. Crump, 'Athletics', p.55.
91. Derek Ibbotson (as told by Terry O'Connor), *Four-minute Smiler: The Derek Ibbotson story* (London: Stanley Paul, 1960) p.38.
92. Alan Pascoe with Alan Hubbard, *Pascoe: The Story of an Athlete* (London: Stanley Paul, 1979), p.17.
93. Geoff Capes with Neil Wilson, *Big Shot: An Autobiography* (London: Stanley Paul, 1981), p.13.
94. Dorothy Hyman, *Sprint to Fame* (London: Stanley Paul, 1964). pp.16–18.
95. Mary Rand, *Mary, Mary: An Autobiography* (London: Hodder & Stoughton, 1969), p.17.
96. Brendan Foster and Cliff Temple, *Brendan Foster* (London: Heinemann, 1978) pp.7–8, 23.
97. Pirie, *Running Wild*, p.12.
98. Pirie, *Running Wild*, pp.11–13.
99. Steve Ovett with John Rodda, *Ovett: An Autobiography* (London: Grafton, 1985), p.223.
100. Crump, 'Athletics', p.54; see also Pirie, *Running Wild*, pp.41–2.
101. Crump, 'Athletics', p.54; AAA, General Committee, 7 Dec. 1957. UBSCD, NCAL XVIII.G7,
102. AAA, General Committee, 25 Apr. 1959. UBSCD, NCAL XVIII.G7.
103. AAA, General Committee, 6 Oct. 1963. UBSCD, NCAL XVIII.G7,
104. Crump, 'Athletics', p.54. For Jack Crump's account of this affair see *Running Round the World*, pp.235–47.
105. Pascoe with Hubbard, *Pascoe*, pp.45, 48.
106. Copy in Harold Abrahams' papers. UBSCD, NCAL XXV.H27.
107. Pascoe with Hubbard, *Pascoe*, p.47; see also Lovesey, *Official Centenary History*, pp.149–50.
108. Ibbotson, *Four-minute Smiler*, p.139; Pirie, *Running Wild*, chapter 5.
109. Capes with Wilson, *Big Shot*, pp.6, 71–2.
110. AAA, AGM, 16 Mar. 1957. UBSCD, NCAL XVIII.G7.
111. AAA, General Committee, 1 Feb. 1958. UBSCD, NCAL XVIII.G7; AAA, AGM, 15 Mar. 1958. UBSCD, NCAL XVIII.G7.
112. Ibbotson, *Four-minute Smiler*, pp.139–40; Hyman, *Sprint to Fame*, pp.119–20; Capes with Wilson, *Big Shot*, pp.66–72.
113. Capes with Wilson, *Big Shot*, pp.66–8; Pascoe with Hubbard, *Pascoe*, p.47.
114. Ibbotson, *Four-minute Smiler*, p.141.
115. Lynn Davies, *Winner Stakes All* (London: Pelham, 1970), p.89; Capes with Wilson, *Big Shot*, p.115.
116. Mel Watman, *Encyclopaedia of Track and Field Athletics* (fifth edition, London: Robert Hale, 1981), p.144.
117. AAA, General Committee, 28 Oct. 1961, 2 Dec. 1961. UBSCD, NCAL XVIII.G7.
118. Mary Peters with Ian Wooldridge, *Mary P.: Autobiography* (London: Stanley Paul, 1974), pp.33–4.
119. Hyman, *Sprint to Fame*, pp.118–19; Rand, *Mary, Mary*, p.42.
120. AAA, General Committee, 1 Dec. 1979. UBSCD, ACC 1998/6.
121. AAA, EGM, 28 Feb. 1981. UBSCD, ACC 1998/6.

122. Downes and Mackay, *Running Scared*.
123. Tessa Sanderson with Leon Hickman, *Tessa: My Life in Athletics* (London: Willow, 1986), p.170.
124. David Moorcroft, and Cliff Temple, *Running Commentary: An Autobiography* (London: Stanley Paul, 1984) p.145.
125. Introduction to UK Athletics, http://www.ukathletics.org/about/default/html, accessed Jul. 1999.
126. Moorcroft and Temple, *Running Commentary*, p.144. For some other recent elite athletes' comments on drug use, see for example, Sanderson with Hickman, *Tessa*, pp.159–65; Sally Gunnell and Christopher Priest, *Running Tall* (London: Bloomsbury, 1994), pp.94-102; Miller, *Sebastian Coe*, pp.204-5; Roger Black with Mike Rowbottom, *How Long's the Course? My Autobiography* (revised edition, London: Andre Deutsch, 1999), pp.78-88.
127. Downes and Mackay, *Running Scared*.

Still Crazy after All Those Years: Continuity in a Changing Labour Market for Professional Jockeys

WRAY VAMPLEW

Lanfranco Dettori is not like other men: he travels over 200,000 miles a year in search of work; he weighs merely 115 pounds; he is a millionaire. 'Frankie' Dettori is a jockey. Here his experiences are used to explore the working life of the professional jockey, at both the elite and journeyman level, and within the two branches of the industry, flat and jump racing.[1] It will be shown that, despite changes in the labour market, there has been a significant degree of continuity in a profession with a 250-year history.[2]

Supply and Demand

The demand for jockeys is a derived one, stemming from the amount of racing taking place. In essence the opportunities for any one jockey are dependent upon the number of race days, the number of concurrent race meetings, the number of races on each card, and the number of horses entered in each race. Rarely, until very recently, have there been more than one or two meetings a day; normally no more than six or seven races feature on the card; and typically fields have been in the range of eight to twelve runners.[3] Turning to the supply side, at the start of their respective seasons in 1995 there were around 350 registered flat jockeys, about 230 of them apprentices,[4] and some 330 licensed professional National Hunt jockeys, roughly 200 of them conditional riders, the jumping equivalent of apprentices. Although today there are four to seven race meetings a day in summer and 300 more fixtures than ten years ago, the market situation is still one of a vast oversupply of labour. At times, as shown below, this has been aggravated by incursions from foreign riders and by gender changes in the profession.

When his mount *Lammtarra* won the *Prix de l'Arc de Triomphe* at Longchamp in 1995, Dettori noted that the British national anthem was played to salute the success of a horse bred in the United States, trained and owned by Dubaians and ridden by an Italian, an indication of how globalised racing had become.[5] In 1990 the top ten jockeys in the British championship presented literally a league of nations, featuring three Irishmen, two Scots, two Welshmen, an American, a South African and, of course, one Italian. Yet the regular international movement of jockeys is no modern phenomenon. It dates back well into the nineteenth century, coinciding with the development of railway networks in Britain and Europe.[6] British jockeys took advantage of the absence of Sunday racing in Britain to ride in France and Belgium. It is equally clear from the *Racing Calendar* that European riders, French jockeys in particular, came to England to participate in classic and other elite races, usually on mounts from European stables.

In the late nineteenth century there was an American invasion of the British turf as racing faced increased political hostility in the United States. In 1900 five of the top ten riders came from America including the champion, Lester Reiff, and in the next six years the Derby, the blue riband of the British turf, was won five times by the Americans. These men not only won a large number of races, they also were victorious in a high proportion of the races in which they had mounts: in 1900 Danny Maher, Johnny Reiff and 'Skeets' Martin topped 20 per cent, Lester Reiff gained 26 per cent, and Tod Sloan almost 27 per cent.[7] Since then there has been a constant flow of talented foreign riders, especially from Australia, including the 'Boy Wonder', Frank Wootton, champion jockey in 1909 at only 15 years of age, Frank Bullock, 'Brownie' Carslake, Edgar Britt, Rae Johnstone, four times champion 'Scobie' Breasley, George Moore, Bill Williamson and Ron Hutchinson, all of whom made their mark in British racing. More recently Steve Cauthen came from the United States to be champion three times in the 1980s and Michael Roberts from South Africa to top the table in 1992. These were high-class imports whose presence drastically reduced opportunities for domestic riders. These developments have not been matched in National Hunt racing, the

Irish excepted, mainly because the earnings have not warranted it and also because jump racing is not such a major sport elsewhere in the world.

When Alex Greaves won the 1991 Lincoln Handicap, Frankie Dettori finished in third place, two-and-a-quarter lengths behind her mount *Amenable*. Nineteenth-century jockeys faced no such competition from female riders. Victorian propriety did not even allow women to openly own horses. Equestrian events have traditionally been one of the few sports in which men and women compete on equal terms; but not in racing.[8] In Britain the Jockey Club, for centuries a male fortress, did not allow women to race on the flat until 1972, compete against male amateurs until 1974, or against male professionals until 1976, when forced to do so by the Sex Discrimination Act. Opposition to women riders came from several quarters: conservative administrators who raised the economic smokescreen of the costs of providing separate changing facilities; chivalrous traditionalists who feared for the safety of women riders, especially over the jumps; and many male jockeys, particularly the journeymen, who openly argued that women would be dangerous as they did not have the strength to control fractious horses but covertly feared more competition in an already oversupplied labour market.[9] Arguments against the introduction of women jockeys were often patronising, rarely substantiated, and eventually overruled. Yet the removal of gender barriers has been more apparent than real. Although women have ridden winners in Britain, they have not, with the exception of Alex Greaves, yet emerged as a major threat to their male counterparts. Owners and trainers are still reluctant to employ female jockeys who thus are caught in a vicious circle of non-development: without rides they cannot demonstrate their ability to win but without a winning record they cannot get the opportunities. This applies to the aspiring male rider as well, but, with women, it is a prejudice to be overcome, not merely a rational comparison with the best male jockeys. Writing in the mid-1980s, leading northern jockey Eddie Hide claimed that those women who were successful had generally relied on relatives to provide sufficient rides for them to gain experience and develop their skill.[10] The great majority of Greaves's mounts come from Yorkshire trainer, David Nicholls, who is also her husband. In 1998 Sophia Mitchell remained the only professional female jump jockey. That season she had 137 rides but only four winners, though she did not attribute this relative lack of success to gender, pointing out that 'there are a lot of jockeys worse off than me'.[11]

In the stables, however, from where future jockeys might emerge, lasses are taking over from lads and recent stable staff training courses at both the British Racing School and the Northern Racing College have intakes dominated by females.[12] Replacing stablelads with stablehands has proven economically viable as well as politically correct. Trainers appreciate – and exploit – female workers who love horses and are prepared to work long hours at menial tasks for little money simply to be with them. It is generally acknowledged that in some respects girls make better grooms than boys as they are considered quieter and more reliable. Trainers also find them less militant. Susan Gallier, who worked as a stablehand in the 1980s in both France and Britain, felt that the girls received preferential treatment as they were paid the same rate as the boys but were rarely asked to deal with a rampant colt or to unblock a stinking drain. That said, boys were also more likely to be called on to ride trial gallops, an aspect of the job which provides valuable experience for the budding jockey. This is because many trainers adhere to the view that the very qualities which make women such good exercise riders – lightness and gentleness of touch – work against them as jockeys where full control of mounts is vital.[13]

One thing which flat-race jockeys can be thankful for is that they face no competition from amateur riders. Apart from novelty events, there are now no opportunities for amateurs to race against their paid counterparts on the flat. There are rare examples of successful amateurs in the nineteenth century such as 'Squire' Abington, but few amateurs were prepared to sacrifice the good life sufficiently to ride at flat-race weights. On the other hand leading amateurs did win the National Hunt jockeys championship, the last being Harry Brown in 1919. Today amateurs can only compete against professionals over jumps if they have been awarded a permit as being competent to do so.[14] Nevertheless there are sufficient of them to reduce riding opportunities for the professionals. Of these many are genuine amateurs who have no inclination to turn professional, but for some it is a stepping stone towards professionalism. The Jockey Club has recognised this and now requires owners to pay them the equivalent of a riding fee when they employ an amateur who has had 75 rides in races open to professionals. They also suggest to successful amateurs

118

that they consider turning professional, as they did to Peter Scudamore in 1979, who then went on to become joint champion National Hunt jockey in 1981–82.[15]

Weight Watching

During his winter holiday Dettori's weight balloons out to 9 stones 2 lbs, but at the start of the racing season in March he rides at 8 stones 5 lbs which, even with the lightest of saddles, necessitates turning the scales at 8 stones 3 lbs. To lose 13 pounds is not easy, especially from a fit and already fairly scrawny frame. That riding weight then has to be maintained for six to seven months if mounts are to be secured on a regular basis. Dettori has tried most options open to weightwatchers including an American drug, Lasix, which brought about a five pound reduction in a matter of hours but had violent side-effects.[16] Like most elite jockeys he has a sauna at home which can be supplemented by a similar facility available at many racecourses to sweat off a vital pound or two just before a race. Records kept by Eddie Hide show that he sweated off an average of 18 stones a season.[17] The primary method of weight control is diet, which, according to Dettori, has 'become the most compelling factor in my life'.[18] Ex-champions Lester Piggott and Pat Eddery chose to eat very little, especially after they 'had conquered the hunger of the first few months'; they 'got used to having to go without', the former using cigars, the latter cigarettes to help suppress the appetite.[19]

Fortunately for modern jockeys they no longer have to rely simply on doing what their forefathers did. When Michael Turner became Chief Medical Adviser to the Jockey Club in the early 1990s one of his early decisions was to treat jockeys as professional athletes and offer them scientific advice on nutrition and weight control. Over the past five years jockeys have also resorted more to the gym to help them lose weight and keep fit.[20] In contrast the nineteenth century jockey relied on eating very little and a regimen of long walks in heavy clothes, Turkish baths and purgatives. Fred Archer, the champion jockey for 13 consecutive seasons from 1874 to 1886, once had to lose 12 pounds in less than a week, an occasion on which yet again he resorted to 'Archer's Mixture', a devastating laxative developed for him by Dr. J.R. Wright, a Newmarket physician. George Barrett was known to eat well then stick his fingers down his throat.[21] Such practices have not ceased.

Ex-champion jockey turned commentator, Willie Carson, notes that 'bulimia is not a secret in the weighing room'.[22] Steve Cauthen, who rode a stone under his natural weight, exhibited bulimic behaviour and Walter Swinburn, who returned to racing following a horrific accident in Hong Kong which put him out for six months, has admitted to a 'persistent eating disorder' which forced him to take another 'temporary' retirement.[23]

Almost by definition there is no such person as a fat jockey: if riders cannot make the weight then they do not have a job. Moreover there is always the temptation to try and get an extra pound off so as to increase the chances of employment. Modern jockeys use a combination of diuretics, laxatives, rubber suits, saran wraps, pre-race saunas and, despite Turner's advice, virtual starvation via appetite suppressants and self-discipline. Continued efforts by jockeys to keep their weight artificially low is dangerous to their health. Although Eddie Hide, who used to go running wrapped in sweaters and a mackintosh, found 'life more relaxing and easier once saunas became available', sauna-induced dehydration and long periods of inadequate nutrition reduce the ability to concentrate, affect the body's thermostatic qualities and blood flows, and deplete liver glycogen – all of which can lead to accidents and serious illness.[24] Leading flat rider, John Reid, was hospitalised by kidney stones caused by chronic dehydration.[25]

Certainly, wasting contributed to the early deaths of Victorian riders Tom French, John Charlton and Tom Chalenor, all of them Classic winners; John Wells, twice champion jockey; Archer himself; and in the early twentieth century, both three times champions, Danny Maher and Australian Brownie Carslake.[26] Over time the Jockey Club has raised the minimum weight to its present level of 7 stones 10 lbs in contrast to the 4 stones of 1850 and 5 stones 7 lbs of 1875. In the nineteenth century this was done to protect horses and owners rather than jockeys. Too little weight implied insufficient strength to control a fractious mount which might have led to accidents or to erratic running straight in a tight finish, both of which could have serious financial consequences for those who owned valuable horseflesh. More recently the legislation has recognised that, even for jockeys, average body weights have risen.

In the early nineteenth century, prior to minimum weight legislation, owners sometimes resorted to child riders. The official weight of little Kitchener when he won the Chester Cup in 1844 was a feather (nominally four stone), but his actual body weight has been alleged as 2 stone 12 lbs. Such low weights imply very little strength and if a horse proved troublesome there was little that the diminutive rider could do. Fifteen-year-old George Fordham weighed only 3 stone 12 lbs when he won the 1851 Cambridgeshire but his horse ran on into Newmarket before he could pull it up. Five years later, in the Goodwood Stakes, *Chevy Chase* could not be controlled by his jockey, a little boy named Hearden, and he brought down seven other horses and put two jockeys in hospital for several weeks.[27] Although the days of the 'infant phenomenon' were legislated away, child riders continued well into the twentieth century before the minimum age was set at 15 in the 1960s (16 today). Eddie Hide was 13 when he had his first official ride in 1950; Lester Piggott rode his first winner at Haydock Park in 1948 aged only 12; and Josh Gifford broke his maiden at ten.[28] It is worth noting that Hide, weighing just over four stones, found it difficult to control his mount which collided with the rails.

The whole system is artificial. At the elite level some sports now resemble freak shows with seven-foot basketball players and 300-pound American footballers. Yet these athletes are not compelled to be so tall or so large: theoretically, and sometimes in practice, there is still room in these sports for the deviant, normal-sized player. In horseracing such a person has no place; at least not on horseback. Why jockeys have to be so small is not clear. In the mid eighteenth century nine stones seems to have been a minimum in racing for normal thoroughbreds.[29] The emergence of lighter weights probably owes something to gambling owners – and most of them were – realising that they gave an advantage in a race as well as lessening the risk that a valuable thoroughbred would break down. Such weights contradict the oft-used nineteenth century rationale for horse-racing as a racecourse test producing horses from which quality army remounts could be (half) bred. Put simply, army officers rarely weigh less than eight stones. There is more logic to the argument if applied to National Hunt racing where, perhaps because of its origins in the hunting field, average weights carried were normally two to three stone higher than on the flat. However, paradoxically only flat-racing qualified for the Sovereign's Plates, where racing was subsidised for such military breeding purposes. Yet even modern jump jockeys have weight problems. Current champion, Tony McCoy, rides about two stones under his normal weight and lives on 'a near starvation diet'. Striking a balance between sufficient strength and reduced weight is a continuing problem.[30] Jockeys' weights are illogical, artificially imposed, and dangerous to health, but they are unlikely to change as there are too many vested interests, including most existing jockeys who fear even more competition in the labour market if weight levels were raised significantly.

Industrial Injuries

Dettori has ridden in only one National Hunt event, an invitation hurdle race at Chepstow between flat and jump jockeys, in which he confesses he was 'terrified'.[31] And rightly so: Jockey Club figures show that a fall can be expected every 14 rides over jumps and hurdles and an injury every 80.[32] Imagine the state of mind of a jockey who has not fallen for 20 rides knowing that one is almost inevitable in the very near future. But at least a jump jockey knows that most falls happen when his horse meets obstacles deliberately placed in its path and can be mentally prepared to take action. Flat-racing has no such advance warning system and when a horse slips over at 35–40 miles per hour, often in the midst of other half-ton creatures, the consequences can be severe.[33] However, not all accidents occur during the race itself. The conclusions of local stewards' inquiries were published in the *Racing Calendar* from the late 1950s to the late 1960s and an examination of those for 1969 shows that, while 60 falls occurred during the race, a further 17 took place in the parade ring, 35 on the way to the start, 44 at the starting gate and a further 12 after the race had finished.[34] So much can go wrong: a non-exhaustive review of accidents in flat-racing in 1958 revealed that jockeys were injured by horses rearing in the parade ring, charging the starting gate, bolting, crossing legs, breaking blood vessels, running out at bends, and striking the heels of another runner; as well as being pulled off by the starting gate and falling off because of a saddle slipping.[35] Although the domination of rides by the leading jockeys increases their chances of injury, it is the journeymen who have to ride the bad horses, of which, to quote Guy Lewis, one such rider, there are 'bad useless and bad horrible', the latter a dangerous mount. Yet the rides have to be taken: they might encourage the trainer to put you on a good horse and 'even if he doesn't, it's that fee in your pocket'.[36] It has ever been the case. In contrast leading jump riders with more rides available can afford 'to refuse the cash and be fit for a winner tomorrow'.[37]

All workers run the risk of industrial injury though for most the risk is minimal. For jockeys, however, serious injury at work is not a possibility or even a probability: it is inevitable. Every leading jockey, whether flat or National Hunt, has suffered serious injury during their careers. One survey of 700 jockeys found that they aggregated over 1000 fractures, mainly limbs.[38] John Francome, seven times National Hunt champion jockey, calculated that in 15 seasons he lost 460 days through injury.[39] Terry Biddlecombe, champion National Hunt jockey on three occasions in the 1960s, broke a shoulder-blade six times, his wrists five times, bones in his left hand five times, his left collar-bone, elbow, forearm and ankle once each, as well as cracking two vertebrae, dislocating his right ankle, breaking a rib, and chipping a bone in his shin; not to mention over 100 cases of concussion.[40] In Biddlecombe's day a jockey could have a terrible fall but, if showing no signs of distress, be allowed to ride in the next race. Now Jockey Club regulations enforce a compulsory suspension of up to 21 days where concussion has occurred. This has come too late to prevent 'punch drunkenness' among several retired National Hunt riders.[41] Since 1980 there have been seven deaths on the British turf, five of them in National Hunt racing.[42] Although comparative calculations are difficult because of inadequate measures of participation, it has been suggested that jump racing ranks below only mountaineering and aerial sports in risk of fatality.[43] Champion jump jockey Tony McCoy puts it succinctly: 'Any time you walk to your car at the end of the day: that's not a bad day.'[44] So far Dettori's worst injury has been a broken elbow which put him out of racing for four months; but he is still only in his mid-twenties.[45]

Riding work is a way of becoming acquainted with the idiosyncrasies of the horses of particular trainers. For many mounts, however, jockeys have little or no knowledge of the animal which they are to pilot, an extreme example of this being Eddie Hide's 1973 Derby-winning ride on *Morston*, a horse which he had never seen until he entered the paddock. Since horses vary in temperament such ignorance is potentially dangerous, particularly as 'charm and placidity are not the qualities that win races'.[46] Thoroughbred racehorses are highly strung animals, inclined at the best of times to be fractious, especially when young. Inexperienced horses too can be dangerous but the 'schooling' of horses, particularly over hurdles and jumps, has never been a major priority in Britain. However, following the inquiry into the death of Richard Davis, who was crushed under an inexperienced horse which simply failed to rise at the first fence, the Jockey Club have insisted that unreliable jumpers are banned from the racetrack.[47] Fortunately Jockey Club minimum weight legislation and the coming of compulsory education put paid to that other dangerous youth, the child rider. Regulations on the licensing of amateur riders from 1879 also ensured that only 'gentlemen' of certain ability were allowed to compete against professionals, though, as with child riders, the rationale was to protect valuable horseflesh not the bones of riders.[48] Jockeys have also developed their own risk-minimisation procedures. Particularly in National Hunt racing they will use the dressing room and 'the mill' at the start to discuss their plans through the first obstacles so as to avoid calamity in early traffic. During the race, information on positions and gaps is readily exchanged: as Grand National winner Carl Llewellyn has pointed out, 'The more people are aware of everything in the race, the better.'[49]

Until well into the twentieth century little safety equipment was available to protect the rider. In 1923 crash helmets for jump jockeys became compulsory following the death of Captain Bennet at Wolverhampton but this was only for racing and was not enforced for training gallops until the 1970s.[50] Body protectors too are now also mandatory. Jimmy Thompson, along with Lester Piggott, was a prime mover in the introduction of goggles, though not until after he had lost an eye in an accident at Newcastle.[51] As late as 1980 a majority of jockeys thought 'that the safety precautions provided for them were laughable', but much has been done in the past decade or so to lessen the risk of injury from course layout and construction.[52] Turns have been made less stiff, heights of fences and hurdles have been regulated, and the jumps themselves redesigned to encourage horses to take off correctly.[53] To its credit the Jockey Club discontinued all-weather jumping on the grounds of safety in 1994 and, two years later, outlawed chase or hurdle racing on any going officially described as 'hard'. Since 1984 the Levy Board has increased its grants to replace concrete posts with plastic ones and to introduce light plastic running rails at fences and hurdles.[54]

Not until the mid-twentieth century was an insurance scheme established to look after the interests of professional jockeys.[55] Up to that point distressed riders had to appeal to the trustees of various funds for assistance. The nineteenth century had seen the Bentinck Benevolent and Rous Memorial Funds both set up to honour distinguished turf administrators. In 1923 the Jockey Club inaugurated the Jockeys' Accident Fund, but it was stressed that this was not an insurance scheme and that, despite its nomenclature, no jockey had a right to draw upon it. Jump jockeys had recourse to nothing but individual charity until the Rendlesham Benevolent Fund of 1902 made some provision for jockeys killed or injured while riding in National Hunt races. It was open only to licensed professionals and payment was entirely at the discretion of the management committee. After the First World War this was reinforced by the National Hunt Accident Fund which paid £1,000 in instances of death and £3 a week for 26 weeks for temporary disablement. The fund was initially financed by half of the jockeys' licence fees with supplementation after the 1920s from the Racecourse Betting Control Board (later the Horserace Betting Levy Board).[56] During the 1963–64 jumping season riders Tim Brookshaw and Paddy Farrell both broke their backs and a public appeal raised nearly £48,000 for them. Another £6,000 came in after the appeal had been closed and this was used as the basis for the Injured National Hunt Jockeys' Fund. In 1971 this was renamed the Injured Jockeys' Fund to incorporate flat-race jockeys, though, as might be anticipated, the demands on its resources have tended to be dominated by those who ride over hedges and hurdles. As a registered charity the Fund is dependent on public goodwill. By the mid 1990s the pay-out to jockeys, most of whom had had to quit racing because of their injuries, totaled £3.4 million with a further £2.3 million outstanding in cheap loans.[57]

The Fund is not designed to cope with short-term injuries. For this there is the Professional Riders Insurance Scheme which has emerged out of the Racehorse Owners Compensation Fund. It is financed by a mandatory levy on owners of 13 per cent on all riding fees. This raises about half a million pounds per annum of which about half is spent on weekly compensation for temporary injuries and most of the rest on premiums to insure all professional jockeys against death or career-ending injuries. The temporary weekly benefits are paid on a sliding scale dependent upon the number of rides the jockey had the previous season, ranging from £100 plus sickness benefit for less than 75 mounts to £1,033 at the top level. However, what is being compensated for is the loss of riding fees not the share of prize money lost and thus some jockeys also subscribe to private insurance schemes, though premiums are not cheap and cover is limited. Although Lester Piggott, who retired in 1995, accepted that during his long career there had been 'massive advances in racecourse safety', as well as better equipment and improved medical guidelines, he still maintained that riding 'remains a very dangerous and potentially lethal business'.[58] Serious injuries today are at an all-time high and, in early 1997, a record 31 jockeys were being paid weekly compensation under the Professional Riders Insurance Scheme.[59] In earlier days, with no such source of compensatory income, many of them might have been tempted to continue to ride whilst injured.

Trains and Boats and Planes … and Cars

In 1995, when both Frankie Dettori and his challenger for the championship, Jason Weaver, had more than 1000 rides in the United Kingdom, they travelled some 200,000 miles.[60] The vocation of jockeys is significantly different from most occupations in that the main place of work changes almost daily. Few race meetings last more than three days and most are single day affairs. In the pre-railway era riders had to travel to meetings by coach, on horseback, or even walking with their racing saddles tied to their waist. The coming of the railway eased travel problems but most top jockeys took advantage of the new mode of transport not to relax but to increase their workload and earnings. Tommy Loates, for one, travelled 2000 miles and rode 33 times in 17 days in 1889, including successive days at Derby, Paris and Nottingham. Indeed, increasingly during the late nineteenth century, leading jockeys took advantage of changes in race dates following the emergence of enclosed suburban courses to race in Britain on a Saturday and in France the next day. From the 1840s full racing results, including the names of every rider in every race, are available in the *Racing Calendar* and this allows the tracing of individual work patterns. Nat Flatman, champion jockey in 1849, when the railway network was relatively undeveloped, raced on only 75 days of the season, but by 1899, Sammy Loates, the leading rider in that season, was able to manage 179 days. Estimates of the respective distances travelled are 4,270 and 10,770 miles.[61]

Two major points can be made about workloads of the modern jockey. First, the vast majority of riders would prefer it to be heavier. The top few jockeys monopolise the mounts available leaving the bulk of riders to join the demoralising and stressful struggle for the few remaining opportunities. Given that Dettori and other elite riders have a ride in most races at the meetings they attend, for the majority of jockeys there is more money to be earned in riding work and schooling horses than in race-riding.[62] Second, to the initial travel convenience offered by the railway can be added that of the automobile, plane and helicopter, all of which have enabled top riders to race more frequently than in the past, often including both afternoon and evening meetings on the same day within their itinerary.[63] Generally a professional jockey may have to cover between 50,000 and 60,000 miles annually in Britain alone. As current champion Kieren Fallon puts it, 'All you do is live in the car and drive to racing.' Driving long distances is a routine part of a jockey's life, though motorways and ring roads have eased the hassle and, according to Eddie Hide, have helped halve journey times between the 1950s and the late 1980s.[64] Nevertheless Dettori is of the opinion that 'the motorways…have finished off more jockeys than anything else', not in the sense of road fatalities and injuries – though this is surprising given the manic, certainly risky driving, which comes through in all jockey biographies – but because the journeyman jockey has 'to flog halfway across the country to ride a useless horse with no possibility of winning'.[65] The elite can afford to employ a chauffeur; the rest have to drive themselves or arrange lifts with colleagues. For the elite there is also air travel. As early as 1946 Tommy Weston flew 1000 miles in a week to ride at York, Newmarket, Salisbury, Liverpool and Goodwood.[66] Today most leading jockeys have their own planes enabling them to leave home later, arrive fresher and get back earlier. Thanks to air travel most top flat-race jockeys also race for lucrative prizes on the continent most Sundays (thus freeing up Sunday rides at home for lesser jockeys). Flying has also allowed jockeys to race overseas both during the close season – though this also occurred in the days when seafaring was required – and for short spells or even just one meeting in Europe, America or Asia. In 1995, in addition to his United Kingdom rides, Frankie Dettori had mounts in France, Germany, Italy, the United States, Australia, Dubai and Hong Kong. As the money in overseas racing has increased, winter contracts have provided quality jockeys with well-paid holidays. Only a minority of riders, however, can pursue this avenue, and it is one that is not so readily available to National Hunt riders because of the geographically restricted nature of that branch of the sport.

Earnings and Emulation

When Dettori first came to England in 1985 at the age of 14 to work at the Newmarket stables of Luca Cumani, he was paid £12 a week plus board.[67] Now he earns a six figure sum because, like other top jockeys, he has the ability to make that split-second decision during a race which means the difference between winning and losing, between success and failure, between a horse being worth a few million or a few hundred thousand.[68] It is difficult to find accurate information on earnings but some estimates can be made on the basis of the basic riding fee and the percentage of the prize money which placed jockeys receive. Even without the presents from grateful owners and backers, and retainers to secure the services of the best performers, it is clear that, as in the nineteenth century, there is an earnings pyramid with rewards reflecting the skewed distribution of mounts and even more so that of winning rides. In his first week back after serious injury Dettori won races worth over £400,000 from which he would receive his 4.5 per cent.[69] Dettori also has a handsome retainer from the Dubai-based Godolphin training establishment. Along with perhaps four or five others he makes an exceptional living from propelling half a ton of horseflesh faster than most of his rivals. Eddie Hide, writing in 1988, accepted that the very top jockeys were probably millionaires.[70] Next come the two dozen or so who can ride perhaps 20 winners a season. They are followed by 'a large band of men who struggle to make ends meet', who earn relatively little and obtain most of their income from riding work rather than races.[71]

The money to be earned from jump and hurdle racing bears little comparison with that available on the flat. The basic riding fee is higher but the level of prize money is substantially lower and always has been. As on the flat a few outstanding individuals dominate the earnings pyramid. Champion jockey Tony McCoy paid his agent £17,000 in 1998 which suggests earnings of just under £200,000.[72] Richard Dunwoody, champion in 1993 and 1994, may earn around the same. In contrast Guy Lewis, who, in 1996, had 88 rides and only two winners all season, made a financial loss after travel expenses, valet and agent fees, and equipment costs.[73] One estimate is that 250 rides and 20 winners are now required to show a profit at the end of the season, a figure attained by around 30 jockeys. Dunwoody reckons 'only five or six of us make a good living' and overall 'very few jump jockeys make more than a very basic living'.[74]

Then there is the matter of psychic income from the applause of the crowd and the plaudits of the media. Dettori was not the first jockey to achieve 'superstar' status. Fred Archer, the long-legged 'Tinman', who won over a third of his 8,004 races, including 21 classics, has that honour. Town criers announced his arrival; 'Stevengraphs' of his image had record sales; special trains brought adoring crowds to his wedding; and Newmarket virtually closed on the day of his funeral.[75] Nevertheless Dettori inhabits a much more media-aware world in which he is used by racing to promote the sport not only to the initiated but also by appearances on pop music programmes and in other non-racing venues. His behaviour has broken the mould and taken some of the stuffy insularity out of English racing. Until Frankie's era riders rarely exhibited excitement, emotion, or even enthusiasm for their job. Dettori's trademark flying leap from winning mounts, fractured English, and charismatic flamboyance have endeared him to the racing public. Yet even stars can crash to earth, both literally and metaphorically. In September 1996, to the delight of Ascot fans, Dettori galloped into turf history as the first jockey to win all seven races on the card. A season later he looked ridiculous when dumped by his mount *Sea Wave* as it left the starting stalls in the Prix Neil at Longchamp, and he also felt the sting of public criticism in 1998 when his riding tactics cost *Swain* victory in the Breeders' Cup.[76] But the crowd and punters talking through their pockets do not pay the jockey's wages. The rider is more concerned with the reaction of owners and trainers. There is a racing aphorism that good jockeys lose fewer races that they should have won than do other riders. This is appreciated by trainers such as Henry Cecil who stood by Kieren Fallon after his poor performance on *Bosra Sham* in the 1997 Eclipse Stakes. Fallon went on to become champion jockey. A general loss of form is more worrying than a momentary lapse in judgement. Adrian Maguire, number one National Hunt rider for the Jackdaws Castle stable, was forced to resign his position and go freelance in 1998 when owners put pressure on trainer David Nicholson to replace him with Richard Johnson who had ridden twice as many winners.[77]

In racing success breeds success and it is often easier to remain at the top than to get there. Owners wish to have a fashionable jockey on board their animals so if he – or increasingly his agent – is a good judge of horseflesh more winning rides will come his way. One notable change over the past two decades, and particularly in the 1990s, has been the emergence of the jockey's agent, first used in Britain by Willie Carson. Lester Piggott, renowned for 'jocking off' other riders from animals he fancied in big races, finally succumbed and employed Anna Ludlow, a Newmarket businesswoman, as his agent. Today even some apprentices, no longer subject to the restrictions of the old indenture contract, have agents.[78] Prior to this development a top jockey could spend as much time on the phone trying to secure rides as on the horses themselves. One can only wonder at how barely literate Fred Archer managed to arrange his 667 rides in 1885. The use of agents who offer trainers their complete client list obviously reduces the opportunities for spare mounts for the lesser riders. In the nineteenth century a retainer from an owner guaranteed rides, but, over time, stable retainers from public trainers were seen as more attractive as they were less reliant on the whims of one particular owner. However a retainer does mean that a jockey has to accept all mounts supplied, good or bad, and many riders view going freelance as a chance to be more selective, though it has a downside in that he 'must try to keep all his contacts sweet so that none of his sources of mounts dries up'.[79] Here the agent can usefully shoulder the burden. What agents do not do, however, is to remove the need for the ambitious jockey to study form, to watch races in which he does not have a ride, and to replay videos in the evenings so that he is aware of the potential opposition in his next races. This also enables him to learn the assets and characteristics of his own mounts: is it a horse which needs 'covering up' during a race; does it run better on hard or soft ground; does it have finishing speed? For the aspiring jockey the key is getting a chance to ride in a race. As Dettori puts it, 'Ability, natural light weight, temperament, and the right attitude to work are helpful but do not guarantee success. You also need opportunity.'[80] It may come from the misfortune of others, unable to ride through injury, or due to successful networking, but it has to be seized. In particular winning a televised race can get a rider noticed and set his mobile phone ringing.

Money and fame tempt many to try but few turtles reach the sea. Director of the British Racing School, Rory MacDonald, estimates that nine out of ten budding apprentices fail to become full professional jockeys.[81] Little has changed since 1900 when of the 187 registered apprentices only 75 became jockeys and a mere 23 (12 per cent) continued as such for more than three years.[82] As they receive weight allowances in recognition of their inexperience, outstanding apprentices and conditional riders can do well. In 1923 Charlie Elliott was champion whilst still an apprentice, as was Elijah Wheatly 18 years before him. But under the scheme operating since 1991, the allowance is reduced progressively, disappearing after the total of winners reaches 85. Losing one's 'claim' to an allowance is a major rite of passage after which the young rider has to compete on ability alone. Even a leading apprentice has no guarantee of future success. Lester Piggott, Pat Eddery and Dettori himself all went on to become champion jockeys, but who recalls David Coates or Richard Dicey, joint champion apprentices in 1968?

Both historically and contemporarily, most elite jockeys have come from families associated with racing. Dettori's father, Gianfranco, was champion jockey in Italy 13 times. Journeymen National Hunt riders too generally have had equestrian backgrounds. Nevertheless, particularly in flat racing, there is room for the uninitiated. Steve Donoghue, winner of six Derbies, ran away from a Warrington wire works at the beginning of the century; victor in five classics, Geoff Lewis came to racing from being a pageboy at a London hotel; and leading apprentice Royston Ffrench had never ridden before he attended the British Racing School. That said, those with families associated with the sport have the advantage of early training and later support by relatives who know the industry.

Successful jockeys have to possess many skills, including being smart out of the stalls, balance on the horse, rapport with their mounts, judgement of pace, the ability to look behind while keeping a horse running straight, using the whip both left and right-handed and being able to transfer it from one to the other if necessary during a hard finish. Some stables, especially those with ex-jockeys on the staff, taught apprentices how to race ride. Indeed where an apprenticeship promised the trainer half the boy's earnings it was in his interest to do so. Men such as Frenchie Nicholson, Sam Armstrong, and Major Sneyd, a first rate but hard teacher, from whose Sparsholt stables brothers Doug and Eph Smith and Joe Mercer graduated, earned a reputation as well as an income from their ability to produce good, young riders. Other trainers, perhaps the majority, saw apprentices as simply cheap stable labour.[83] Until two decades ago apprentices were indentured to a trainer with whom they had to stay until they completed their articles. Today they have the freedom to switch stables, though, at the insistence of the Jockey Club, they are not allowed to race ride for the remainder of the season unless both trainers agree. This is rarely implemented. The old apprentice system has now gone, along with what many believed to be overharsh discipline, but, with nothing to tie an apprentice to the stable, the incentive to pass on advice and give young riders a chance has been weakened.[84] Indeed, most apprentices are now virtually freelance riders and, though many trainers no longer take half their earnings, they no longer pay half their expenses.

Based on a perception that the traditional system of training – if indeed it could warrant such a designation – was failing to produce riders capable of matching the foreign jockeys coming to ply their trade in Britain, an enquiry by John Marriage QC in the early 1980s recommended the establishment of an apprentice training school. The British Racing School at Newmarket and, to a lesser extent, the Northern Racing College at Rossington Hall near Bawtry, took on this task. The Northern Racing College, however, has always given priority to training stable staff and recently the British Racing School also has gone down this track with other courses being offered to apprentices in which they are taught the essentials required before riding in public and how to improve their race and work riding. When the apprentices lose their seven-pound allowance they are given a three-day intermediate course dealing not so much with riding as with career management, money matters, interview techniques, fitness and diet.

But that is the extent of teaching and training available. Once apprentices become fully-fledged jockeys they are on their own; all further skills acquisition is very much a matter of 'independent learning'. As leading northern rider Eddie Hide put it, good jockeys 'keep learning'. To some extent this involved tips from admired senior riders: Edgar Britt taught him to hold the reins shorter on a tight track and Frankie Durr to catch hold of the mane in the starting stalls to give the horse full freedom when it jumped out.[85] Otherwise it was down to experience. Racing itself was the best way to appreciate that different tracks required different skills: that Brighton's long, uphill finish was a different proposition to the sharp, ill-cambered final bend and short run-in at Catterick; that Chester's sharp left-hand bends do not suit big horses; and that the steep and perilous descent to Tattenham Corner at Epsom can cause tired horses to drop back and impede other runners.

As this suggests, many skills were acquired or refined simply via 'learning by doing'. At times, however, new skills had to be developed

132

as a matter of urgency. In 1965 the introduction of starting stalls in flat-racing meant that the experience of jockeys who knew how different starters operated the gate and had the ability to manoeuvre horses ready for the off was rendered redundant virtually overnight. Now what had to be learned was the art of keeping horses ready for the opening of the stalls and being prepared to go instantly from a standing start. In the late 1980s the introduction of all-weather tracks on which a smooth run was all-important necessitated the development of new tactics. Some riders grasped the essentials more quickly than others and it was on such tracks at Wolverhampton, and particularly Southwell, that Alex Greaves established herself as 'Queen of the Sands'. More recently furore has erupted over new restrictions placed on the use of whips. Jockeys propel their mounts mainly by physical effort and skill, using legs, hands and heels, sometimes their voice, but the only material aid permitted is the whip. Recently the Jockey Club, under the pressure of public opinion, has taken exception to 'excessive' use of this implement and it has taken many riders some time to come to terms with what is now required.[86] Yet having to adjust to innovation is nothing new. In the late nineteenth century a whole new style of riding had to be learned when the American invasion threatened the livelihood of British jockeys. The Americans were masters of their craft but the key factor was that they brought a different style with them. Crouching along the horse's neck, they rode with the saddle pushed forward, reins and stirrups shortened, and knees bent. This not only provided a better weight distribution on the horse, it also offered less wind resistance. For a while there was a possibility that the American jockeys would dominate British racing, but then many local riders adopted the American style and were able to compete more effectively.[87]

Power Relationships

In 1996 when Dettori won the 2000 Guineas, he was fined £500 for his flying leap from the saddle, performed illegally before his horse had left the track; he was also suspended for eight days for excessive use of the whip.[88] The Jockey Club has never been in awe of leading riders. When in 1901 suspicion of corruption fell on champion jockey Lester Reiff the Jockey Club simply told him not to bother to reapply for his licence. In the 1920s, Derby-winning jockey Charlie Smirke was banned *sine die* (in actuality five years) for not trying at the start of a two-year-old plate. More recently record-breaking National Hunt champion Tony McCoy received five suspensions totalling 33 days for excessive use of the whip and was sent to the British Racing School to learn how to modify his technique. Although its role in the running of racing has been diluted in the past decade, the Jockey Club still remains the paramount disciplinary authority in the sport. These days jockeys may be represented by solicitors when brought before the Portman Square stewards, but in the past even natural justice had no place in that establishment. Until very recently the stewards retained the right to refuse a licence to any jockey without having to specify a reason. Even in 1999, amidst allegations of race-fixing, there has been debate about the legal and moral authority of the Club in forcing jockeys to pay for racing's discomfiture by suspending riders who had been arrested but not charged, let alone convicted. Suspension for riding offences is more common than in Archer's era, especially since the introduction of the patrol camera in the 1960s, and, more recently, of a totting-up system under which, once 12 days have been accumulated under one head of offences, another 14 days ban is automatic. In contrast to Archer who, despite his aggressive riding, received only 14 days suspension in his whole career, the modern top jockey expects at least a compulsory fortnight's holiday almost every season.[89] Additionally, fines have been levied on jockeys for a variety of offences. On the more positive side, it was the Jockey Club which took steps in the nineteenth century to protect the income of riders by insisting that riding fees were deposited by owners with the clerk of the course before a race took place; and in 1969 it determined that jockeys should receive a guaranteed percentage of prize money which was paid to them via Weatherby's, the Club's administrative arm.

Nevertheless the attitude of the Jockey Club towards riders remained almost feudal well into the twentieth century. A television documentary in 1982 revealed that the stewards at York treated senior jockeys such as Willie Carson and Eddie Hide like errant schoolboys, demanding that they stand to attention while being questioned and insisting on being called 'Sir' by the riders but addressing them by their surnames. The resultant outcry led to the Club adopting the courtesy of calling jockeys 'Mister'.[90] Until the past two decades or so, the Jockey Club has showed little inclination to bring ex-jockeys into the regulatory arena. The application form for the position of Stewards' Secretary in the 1970s asked candidates to supply their 'rank and regiment' and, when Eddie Hide applied for the position in the mid 1980s, the successful applicant was the one individual with virtually no racing experience, though he was a former household cavalry officer.[91] More recently several retired jockeys have been employed by the Club as inspectors and safety officials.

Jockeys are involved in several other power relationships within the sport. Apprentices, like stable lads, have been subject historically to the almost absolute power of the trainer. More recently that power has been curtailed by the development of trade unionism within the stables and, so some trainers argue, by the indentured apprenticeship becoming defunct. That said, many trainers and owners still believe in a master and servant relationship. Dettori may be a millionaire, but he still tips his cap to the owner of his mount and calls him 'Sir' when he enters the saddling enclosure, a symbolic reminder of the power relationship between employer and employee. Anthropologist Kate Fox has argued that the body language indicates that this is a vestigial gesture rather than an expression of genuine deference, particularly since syndicalisation has to a degree democratised ownership. Be that as it may, jockeys Francome and Hide both attest that 'tact' and 'diplomacy' are vital components of success and that 'chatting up' owners and trainers 'can be the most important part of the job'.[92] Owners do not like to acknowledge that they have purchased a dud and would rather blame the jockey than his mount.[93] According to Jeff King, rider of over 700 National Hunt winners, loyalty by owners to the jockeys they employ 'is not one of this sport's most obvious qualities'.[94] Hence the occurrence of what Derby-winner Bill Rickaby describes as 'the series of sackings which plague almost every jockey's career' and what Michael Caulfield, executive manager of the Jockeys Association, labels a working life of confidence-sapping mental abuse.[95] More recently the friction between owner and rider has surfaced on the issue of sponsorship. The Jockeys Association has secured sponsorship for its members to be displayed on their breeches and polo neck, but the Racehorse Owners Association has insisted on individual owners having a veto which could deprive riders of an extra £10 a mount.[96]

Although jockeys are in competition for mounts, wins and prize-money, and 'jocking off' has become more prevalent since agents began to do the scrambling for rides, inside the weighing room, a jockeys' sanctuary from which all others are excluded, the atmosphere resembles that of a team sport.[97] Mutual support, trust and good fellowship abound within a group bonded by the risk and excitement of their occupation. Francome says that it is the possibility of being injured that creates the 'wonderful camaraderie amongst jump jockeys'. It is a rare professional sport where in 1982 a potential champion (John Francome) simply refused further rides once he had equalled the total of the existing leading rider (Peter Scudamore), who had been sidelined for the season with a broken arm when 20 wins ahead.[98] Nevertheless it was not until the 1960s that this solidarity manifested itself in organisational form, most particularly in the founding of the Jockeys Association in 1969 via an amalgamation of the northern and southern sections of the Flat Race Jockeys Association and the Professional National Hunt Jockeys Association, all of which had developed a few years earlier. The Association has concerned itself with matters of racecourse facilities and safety and also operates a pension fund, savings plans and insurance services. Although it negotiates with the Racehorse Owners Association on riding fees, in many respects it is more of a guild than a union, with a prime aim of maintaining the highest standards of integrity among its members. When confrontations have occurred they have been flashpoint combinations of riders rather than premeditated strikes, as when jockeys refused to race at Beverley in 1989 and at Haydock in 1996 because of what they judged to be dangerous conditions.[99] Despite, or perhaps because of, its lack of militancy, jockeys do not have representation on the British Horseracing Board, unlike the owners and the racecourse operators.

Corruptive Influences

No mention of racing scandal is associated with the Dettori name. He has been accused of losing through misjudgement and overconfidence but never by deliberately stopping a horse. Although Detorri says that he has never been asked to pull a horse in this country, there is no doubt that a subculture of corruption has long existed in racing.[100] Because of its connection with gambling, horse racing has always been subject to corrupt influences. Knowing that a jockey will not be trying to win on a particular horse gives a gambler an advantage in the betting markets. Most jockeys understood that in an overcrowded labour market riding to orders was crucial to their future employment prospects: and those orders were not always to win.[101] Neither the extent of corruption in racing nor the degree of involvement of jockeys can be quantified. Malpractice certainly occurs. Racing writer Danny Hall acknowledges that 'no-one with the remotest connection to the turf believes that racing is scrupulously clean', but few accept that up to 30 per cent of races are fixed, as was alleged by the disillusioned and dispirited Lewes trainer, Roger Hoad.[102] Owner Stan Hay notes that 'racing may have its problems, but its stables are nowhere near as dirty as some of those in other areas of public life...none of us can pretend that racing is completely clean, but nor is it as bent as some other sports wracked by drugs and gambling scams. Nor indeed is it any more corrupt than the financial services industry, whose various disgraces over the last decade far outstrip anything that racing has so far produced.'[103] All that can be asserted is that, for some riders, losing is a more certain way to make money than trying to win. Even those jockeys anxious to create a positive image for their sport do not deny that corruption occurs, though they take pains to stress that elite jockeys are not involved.[104] Jockeys would be fools to risk riding doped horses – the game is dangerous enough anyway – but making sure that a horse does not feature in a finish is still relatively easy even with the race patrol cameras and Jockey Club regulations on riding out. This may not be at the behest of gamblers but simply riding to orders so as to deceive the handicapper. Nevertheless Guy Lewis notes that 'it's an open secret in the weighing room that some jockeys have close associations with big punters'.[105] If this became less of a secret their careers might be at risk: at one stage in his career John Francome was suspended by the Jockey Club for six weeks as his relationship with bookmaker, John Banks, was seen as being damaging to the interests of racing.[106]

In 1992 Dettori had his license to ride withdrawn by the Hong Kong racing authorities after he had been caught in possession of cocaine.[107] This use of drugs seems to have been an indiscretion of youth rather than related to his occupation. For other jockeys, however, drug and alcohol abuse is a product of a stressful life. Few would argue with Dettori's claim that 'being a jockey is a pressure job, and when things don't go well, you take your losers home'.[108] No one is immune. In the year he was champion Doug Smith once went over 100 rides without a winner. Nevertheless a good rider with plenty of rides can expect most losing streaks to end relatively quickly; a lesser rider might have to wait some time, all the while having his confidence sap away.

John Reid, a leading rider, talks of getting 'grumpy' with his family.[109] Graham Thorner, National Hunt champion rider in 1971, reckoned 'The worst thing about the job was the periods of depression when I couldn't ride a winner.'[110] Moreover, every time jockeys race they are subject to public and employer appraisal; they are constantly watching their weight; and they anticipate injury each time they get on a horse. No wonder so many jockeys appear to have used alcohol to escape reality. Apocryphal stories abound for the nineteenth century. Jem Snowden is said to have turned up a week late for Chester races; Charles Marlow to have lost a two-horse race for the 1850 Doncaster Cup on the odds-on favourite through lack of sobriety; and, after a morning at the brandy bottle, Bill Scott is alleged to have been so drunk at the Derby of 1846 that he did not realise that the race had started.[111] In the modern era both Walter Swinburn and Steve Cauthen have acknowledged having drinking problems. National Hunt riders, with notable exceptions, such as teetotallers Tony McCoy, Jonjo O'Neill and John Francome, see drinking as part of the social life associated with their sport, and regard it as a means of winding down. Whether the stress or culture of their working lives contributed to jockeys resorting to alcohol more than other workers remains conjectural in the light of current research.[112]

The effects of alcohol are often aggravated by the lack of food. Nutrition expert Professor Michael Lean suggests that 'alcoholism is a probable effect of being starved'.[113] Allegedly both Cauthen and Swinburn were bulimic. Yet, although the idea of a drunk or drugged jockey aboard a horse is a frightening one, the Jockey Club took no action on this issue until October 1994 when, at the instigation of Michael Turner, their new chief medical adviser, a protocol was developed for the testing of riders for banned substances. These included marijuana, cocaine, amphetamines and alcohol, the threshold for the latter initially being set at the drink-driving limit but later reduced to half that level.[114] Although some 600 tests have revealed no alcohol abuse, one apprentice and two conditional riders have been suspended for recreational drug use, though it should be noted that amphetamines, the banned substance in two of the cases, speed up the metabolism and can be used for weight loss.[115]

Retirement

In his autobiography Dettori remarks on riding alongside the incomparable Lester Piggott when the latter was approaching his sixtieth birthday and almost 50 years in the saddle. Willie Carson was in his mid-fifties when he had his last ride as, in earlier decades, were Scobie Breasley, Frankie Durr, Charlie Smirke and Gordon Richards. Clearly experience counts in Britain's 'horses for courses' situation. Retirement comes earlier over the sticks. By the age of 30 the elder statesman stage has been reached. John Francome called it a day at 32 after a fall too many at Chepstow in 1985, and eight-times champion Peter Scudamore did likewise at 34. When Simon McNeil retired in 1998 aged 42 he was the oldest jump jockey around.[116] Lack of rides ends most jockeys' careers: loss of nerve, injuries and weight problems the rest. Some never made the grade: others could no longer sustain their performance. Most jockeys try to remain connected with racing. Jonathan Haynes, condemned to a wheelchair by a fall at Southwell, explained that 'racing is all I know'.[117]

Yet it must be noted that most of the skills which they possess are specific to the racing industry and not easily transferable to other occupations. Some move on to become trainers though they find business sense as vital as horse sense if they are to be successful. Others, particularly the failed apprentices, return to the stables where, unlike the market for jockeys, there is always a labour shortage, becoming work riders or stable hands hoping to supplement their income by 'doing a good horse' or perhaps rising to become a senior lad earning around £6 a hour.[118] For the articulate and successful there are media opportunities. Others have secured positions as clerks of courses, racecourse inspectors, agents and valets. For the younger ones today there is the Jockeys Employment and Training Scheme initiated by the Jockeys Association to provide some of the basic skills required to secure employment when they finally opt out. Talk of retirement used to be taboo in the changing room but times have changed and career advice and training are now more accepted.[119]

Piggott finally retired aged 59. Dettori, at 27, can look ahead to a long and prosperous career. Nevertheless his millionaire status has not been easily earned. Although his income is far higher than most jockeys, Dettori is less unique when it comes to the problems faced by professional riders. Like other jockeys he has to watch his weight carefully; his work site is constantly changing necessitating significant travel; he faces appraisal of his work performance by both the public and his employer every time he goes out to ride; and almost each season he can expect to be sidelined by injury and suspension. Indeed jockeys are extraordinary sportspersons. They contrast with other professionals uniquely in terms of their physique, age, gender and the danger of their occupation. In what other occupation are participants expected to peak mentally and physically five or six times a day – even more if there are evening meetings – for six and increasingly seven days a week, risk serious injury every time they go to work, and all the time restrict themselves to a diet designed to keep their weight well below the norm? Yet, like Dettori, most of them still believe that 'it is a wonderful game'.[120] They share his view that 'racing is my life, it is everything. It is my good times, my bad times, my happiness, my sadness, everything.'[121]

ACKNOWLEDGEMENTS

I am grateful for help towards the research costs of this paper from the Wellcome and Leverhulme Trusts and for comments received at various conferences and seminars at which earlier versions were presented. Especial thanks are due to Michael Turner, Chief Medical Adviser to the Jockey Club; Rory MacDonald, Director of the British Racing School; Jim Gale, Director of the Northern Racing College; Michael Caulfield, Executive Manager of the Jockeys Association of Great Britain; Dede Scott Brown, Curator of York Racing Museum; and fellow researchers John Tolson, Joyce Kay and Iris Middleton.

NOTES

1. The starkest contrast can be gained from a reading of Frankie Dettori, *A Year in the Life of Frankie Dettori* (London: Mandarin, 1997) and Sean Magee and Guy Lewis, *To Win Just Once: The Life of the Journeyman Jump Jockey* (London: Headline, 1997).

2. For basic histories of flat and National Hunt racing see Wray Vamplew, *The Turf* (London: Allen Lane, 1975); also Roger Munting, *Hedges and Hurdles* (London: J.A. Allen, 1987). More recent developments can be found in John Tyrell, *Running Racing: The Jockey Club Years since 1950* (London: Quiller, 1997). Unless otherwise specified, information on jockeys in general is mainly derived from annual editions of the *Racing Calendar*, the official organ of the racing authorities, *Ruff's Guide*, and similar commercial publications, with supplementary information from the racing press.

3. On occasions, particularly at major holiday times, there could be up to 12 meetings held on the same day, providing more mounts for the ordinary jockey. National

Hunt meetings are more likely to be called off because of adverse weather conditions but, in the last decade, some financial compensation has been offered through that branch of the sport becoming an all year round affair. Nevertheless a long freeze can be disastrous for the journeyman jockey without a retainer who relies on a few rides to pay the mortgage.

4. Young riders learning their trade while formally tied to a trainer and able to claim a weight allowance because they have ridden insufficient winners.

5. Dettori, *Year in the Life*, p.63.

6. John Tolson and Wray Vamplew, 'Derailed: Railways and Horseracing Revisited', *The Sports Historian*, Vol.18, No.2 (1998), pp.41–3.

7. Wray Vamplew, 'The American Invasion of the British Turf: A Study of Sporting Technological Transfer', paper presented at the 11th ISCPES Congress, Leuven, 1998.

8. For a survey see Wray Vamplew and Joyce Kay, 'Horse Racing', in Karen Christiansen and David Levinson (eds.), *World Encyclopedia of Women in Sport* (forthcoming).

9. C. Ramsden, *Ladies in Racing* (London: Stanley Paul, 1973), p.156.

10. Edward Hide, *Nothing to Hide* (London: MacDonald, 1989), p.121.

11. Sarah Potter, 'Chasing the right kind of break', *The Times*, 5 June 1998.

12. Marcus Armytage, 'Girl jockeys preparing for takeover', *The Daily Telegraph*, 8 Mar. 1997.

13. Susan Gallier, *One of the Lads* (London: Stanley Paul, 1988), pp.43–4.

14. Munting, *Hedges and Hurdles*, p.135.

15. Alan Lee, *Jump Jockeys* (London: Ward Lock, 1980), p.69.

16. Dettori, *Year in the Life*, p.75.

17. Hide, *Nothing to Hide*, p.229.

18. Dettori, *Year in the Life*, p.73.

19. Lester Piggott, *Lester* (London: Partridge, 1995), p.16; Pat Eddery, *To Be a Champion* (London: Coronet, 1993), p.11.

20. Richard Evans, 'Dunwoody a non-runner in retirement stakes', *The Daily Telegraph*, 22 Mar. 1999.

21. E. Spencer, *The Great Game* (London: 1900), p.128.

22. Bob McGowan, 'Top jockey's great race to beat eating disorder', *The Daily Express*, 27 Mar. 1997. Although there is a substantial medical literature on athletes and eating disorders the bulk of it pertains to female sports participants, with nothing specifically on the problems faced by jockeys.

23. Jamie Reid, 'Cool, clear Walter', *The Guardian*, 5 June 1998.

24. Hide, *Nothing to Hide*, pp.50, 67; Gavin Evans, 'Medical Cabinet', *The Guardian*, 15 May 1998.

25. Jocelyn Targett, 'Slim Chance', *The Sunday Telegraph Magazine*, 29 Nov. 1998.

26. Michael Tanner and Gerry Cranham, *Great Jockeys of the Flat* (London: Guinness, 1992), pp.71, 129.

27. J. Kent, *The Racing Life of Lord George Cavendish Bentinck* (London: 1892), p.122; Tanner and Cranham, *Great Jockeys*, p.64; Sir John Astley, *Fifty Years of My Life* (London: 1895), p.176.

28. Hide, *Nothing to Hide*, pp.25–7; Piggott, *Lester*, p.11; Geoffrey Nicholson, *The Professionals* (London: Sportsman's Book Club, 1966), p.207.

29. Information supplied by Iris Middleton from her research on horse-racing in

141

eighteenth-century Yorkshire.

30. Tony McCoy and Claude Duval, *The Real McCoy* (London: Hodder and Stoughton, 1998), p.4.

31. Dettori, *Year in the Life,* p.94.

32. Based on information supplied by Dr. Michael Turner. A further breakdown suggests a fall every eight mounts over fences and every 27 over hurdles. In contrast, on the flat, there is a fall only every 300 rides.

33. Hence the ratio between injuries and falls is 1:2.3 compared to 1:1.57 in National Hunt.

34. The underestimation of accidents in National Hunt racing will be much smaller as jump horses are generally older, more experienced, and hence less fractious. Moreover, starting stalls, a cause of many accidents, have yet to be introduced in jump racing.

35. *Racing Calendar* (1958).

36. Magee and Lewis, *To Win Just Once,* pp.130, 151.

37. Steve Smith-Eccles, *Turf Account* (London: Queen Anne Press, 1987), p.12.

38. Cited in Evans, 'Medical Cabinet'.

39. John Francome, *Born Lucky* (London: Pelham, 1985), p.75.

40. Tim Fitzgeorge-Parker, *Steeplechase Jockeys: The Great Ones* (London: Pelham, 1971), pp.58–9.

41. John Oaksey, 'Image taking a hammering', *The Daily Telegraph,* 20 Feb. 1998; Robert Philip, 'Therapist harnesses horse power to help the wounded', *The Daily Telegraph,* 2 Feb. 1998.

42. G. Rock, 'Silent tributes paid to memory of Davis', *The Observer,* 21 July 1996.

43. Magee and Lewis, *To Win Just Once,* p.28.

44. David Walsh, 'Fall Guys', *Inside Sport,* Dec. 1997, p.92.

45. Dettori, *Year in the Life,* p.130.

46. Simon Barnes, *Horsesweat and Tears* (London: Heinemann Kinswood, 1988), p.20.

47. J.A. McGrath, 'Bad jumpers to face bans under safety proposals', *The Daily Telegraph,* 12 Dec. 1996.

48. In 1961 permits were introduced into National Hunt racing with Class A being required for races open only to amateurs and Class B for all steeplechase and jump races.

49. Dudley Doust, *Sports Beat* (London: Hodder and Stoughton, 1992), p.89; Chris Madigan, 'Turf Life', *Total Sport,* No.37, Jan. 1999, p.66.

50. Munting, *Hedges and Hurdles,* p.151.

51. Hide, *Nothing to Hide,* p.21.

52. Lee, *Jump Jockeys,* p.156.

53. Sean Magee, *The Channel Four Book of Racing* (London: Hamlyn, 1995), p.38.

54. Munting, *Hedges and Hurdles,* p.143; John Oaksey, 'Early learning essential to improve safety', *The Daily Telegraph,* 11 Apr. 1997; J. Garnsey, 'Injured jockey blasts Jockey Club policy', *Daily Express,* 20 Sept. 1996.

55. The Workmen's Compensation Act of 1897 did not apply to jockeys on several counts: many earned more than £250 a year; they worked on premises not under the control or management of their employer; and most were casually employed for a purpose not directly connected with their patron's trade or business. See D.J. Hanes, 'The First British Workmen's Compensation Act 1897' (London: 1968), p.103; A. Wilson and H. Levy, *Workmen's Compensation* (London: 1939), pp.101–2.

56. Munting, *Hedges and Hurdles,* pp.132–3, 142.
57. Anne Alcock, *They're Off: The Story of the First Girl Jump Jockeys* (London: J.A. Allen, 1978), pp.58–9; *One Fall Can End a Jockey's Career* (Newmarket: Injured Jockeys Fund, 1996).
58. Piggott, *Lester*, pp.214–15.
59. John Oaksey, 'Counting cost of top jockeys on injured list', *The Daily Telegraph*, 28 Feb. 1997.
60. Dettori, *Year in the Life,* p.92.
61. Tolson and Vamplew, 'Derailed', pp.42–3.
62. Madigan, 'Turf Life', p.63.
63. On 4 July 1981 Paul Cook rode the winner of the 2.45 at Sandown, the 5.00 at Bath, and the 7.50 at Nottingham. See Tanner and Cranham, *Great Jockeys*, p.222.
64. Magee, *Channel Four Book of Racing*, p.115; Sue Mott, 'Fallon keeps tight rein', *The Daily Telegraph*, 30 May 1998; Hide, *Nothing to Hide*, p.34.
65. Dettori, *Year in the Life,* p.85; Magee and Lewis, *To Win Just Once*, p.12.
66. Tommy Weston, *My Racing Life* (London: Hutchinson, 1952), p.179.
67. Dettori, *Year in the Life,* p.14.
68. When Pat Eddery's mount, *El Gran Senor*, failed by a short head in the 1984 Derby its stud value fell from $80 million to $30 million in a matter of seconds. Reid, 'Cool, clear Walter', p.10.
69. Dettori, *Year in the Life,* p.186.
70. Hide, *Nothing to Hide*, p.205.
71. Hide, *Nothing to Hide*, p.205; Dettori, *Year in the Life,* p.30.
72. Charlie Brooks, 'Agent is the central source of information', *The Daily Telegraph*, 1 Feb. 1999.
73. Magee and Lewis, *To Win Just Once*, p.218.
74. Robert Philip, 'Dunwoody at forefront of a revolution', *The Daily Telegraph*, 15 Mar. 1999; Giles Smith, 'Dunwoody still down but no longer riding for a fall', *The Daily Telegraph*, 31 Oct. 1998; Magee and Lewis, *To Win Just Once*, p.36.
75. Tanner and Cranham, *Great Jockeys,* pp.78, 105; E.M. Humphris, *The Life of Fred Archer* (London: 1923), p.76; John Welcome, *Fred Archer: A Complete Story* (London: Lambourn, 1990), pp.158–9.
76. Sue Mott, 'Under the whip', *The Daily Telegraph*, 9 Jan. 1999.
77. Brough Scott, 'How Maguire suffered in the battle of Jackdaws Castle', *The Sunday Telegraph*, 3 Jan. 1999.
78. Piggott, *Lester*, p.277.
79. Jonjo O'Neill, *Jonjo* (London: Stanley Paul, 1985), p.82.
80. Dettori, *Year in the Life,* p.30.
81. Interviewed by the author, 18 Mar. 1999.
82. Calculated from data in the *Racing Calendar*.
83. Doug Smith, *Five Times Champion* (London: Pelham, 1968), pp.24–5, 38–9; Richard Baerlein, *Joe Mercer: The Pictorial Biography* (London: MacDonald, 1987), p.21; Nicholson, *Professionals*, pp.206–8; Francome, *Born Lucky*, p.27.
84. Weston, *My Racing Life*, p.13; Hide, *Nothing to Hide*, pp.238–9.
85. Hide, *Nothing to Hide*, pp.60, 80.
86. Richard Evans, 'Whip ban to carry more sting', *The Times*, 12 Jan. 1999.
87. Vamplew, 'Technological Transfer'. Eighty years later, as an apprentice, Dettori spent two winters in America learning the even more streamlined 'flatback' riding

143

style. See J. Karter, *Frankie Dettori: The Illustrated Biography* (London: Headline, 1995), p.29.

88. Dettori, *Year in the Life,* p.120.
89. Tanner and Cranham, *Great Jockeys,* p.12.
90. Hide, *Nothing to Hide,* p.243; Francome, *Born Lucky,* p.86.
91. Hide, *Nothing to Hide*, pp.8–9.
92. Kate Fox, *The Racing Tribe* (Oxford: Social Issues Research Centre, 1997), p.16; Francome, *Born Lucky*, p.42; Hide, *Nothing to Hide*, p.237; Lee, *Jump Jockeys*, p.57.
93. Smith-Eccles, *Turf Account*, p.46.
94. Lee, *Jump Jockeys*, p.116.
95. Smith-Eccles, *Turf Account*, p.46; Lee, *Jump Jockeys*, p.116; Bill Rickaby, *First to Finish* (London: Souvenir Press, 1969), p.16; Caulfield interviewed by the author, 2 June 1999.
96. Chris McGrath, 'Savill stalls on jockeys logos', *The Times*, 15 Dec. 1998.
97. Fox, *Racing Tribe*, p.32.
98. Francome, *Born Lucky*, pp.72, 108–10.
99. 'Jockey Club Rules under the Microscope', *Daily Express*, 20 Feb. 1997.
100. Helena de Bertodano, 'Life after the Ascot seven', *The Sunday Telegraph*, 11 May 1997.
101. This is brought out quite clearly for the inter-war years in Weston, *My Racing Life*, p.26. See also Robert Philip's interview with National Hunt rider, Dave Dick, 'Aintree anti-hero savouring the lucky life of ups and downs', *The Daily Telegraph*, 25 Mar. 1996.
102. *Daily Express*, 28 Feb. 1998; Richard Evans, 'Hoad risks disciplinary charges', *The Times*, 19 February 1998.
103. Stan Hay, 'Odds and Sods', *The Independent*, 19 Jan. 1998.
104. For example see Francome, *Born Lucky*, p.127; for a slightly different view see Lee, *Jump Jockeys*, p.91.
105. Magee and Lewis, *To Win Just Once*, p.127.
106. Francome, *Born Lucky*, p.16.
107. Dettori, *Year in the Life,* p.35.
108. Dettori, *Year in the Life,* p.2.
109. Targett, 'Slim Chance'.
110. Quoted in Lee, *Jump Jockeys*, p.51.
111. Vamplew, *The Turf*, p.164; Tanner and Cranham, *Great Jockeys*, p.55. For allegations of alcoholism see Roger Mortimer, Richard Onslow and Peter Willett, *Biographical Encyclopedia of British Flat Racing* (London: MacDonald and Janes, 1978), pp.174, 219; Frances Collingwood, 'The Tragedy of Thomas Loates', *The British Racehorse*, Oct. 1967, pp.427–8; Tanner and Cranham, *Great Jockeys,* p.116.
112. Reid, 'Cool, clear Walter', p.10; James Lawton, 'A lifetime of agony', *Express Sport*, 18 January 1998; Lee, *Jump Jockeys*, p.11. Michael Caulfield, executive manager of the Jockeys Association, suggests that the real alcohol problem among jockeys emerges post retirement as income, status and self-esteem all decline. Caulfield interviewed by the author, 2 June 1999.
113. Targett, 'Slim Chance'.
114. *The Jockey Club Protocol and Rules for the Testing of Riders for banned Substances* (London: Jockey Club, August 1994).
115. Letter from Michael Turner, chief medical adviser to the Jockey Club, to the author,

25 Mar. 1999; 'Drugs ban costs Walsh young jockeys' title', *Daily Express*, 15 May 1997; 'McCarthy is first jockey to fail test', *The Guardian*, 10 Oct. 1995.

116. Marcus Armytage, 'Old stager McNeil is making a fresh start', *The Daily Telegraph*, 28 Nov. 1998.
117. Lee, *Jump Jockeys*, p.159.
118. Gallier, *One of the Lads*, p.55; Tony Stafford, 'Taxing time for lowly-paid stable staff', *The Daily Telegraph*, 2 Feb. 1999.
119. Fox, *Racing Tribe*, p.33.
120. Brough Scott, 'Dettori in Seventh Heaven', *The Sunday Telegraph*, 29 Sept. 1996.
121. De Bertodano, 'Life after the Ascot seven'.

Civil War in England:
The Clubs, the RFU, and
the Impact of Professionalism
on Rugby Union, 1995–99

ADRIAN SMITH

The decision of the International Rugby Board (IB) in August 1995 to abandon an increasingly flimsy pretence that rugby union remained an amateur sport was taken in light of a global shift towards an open game. A key role in this change is played by satellite television in facilitating club-based professional rugby in the British Isles, especially in England, and this creates tension within the domestic game, as well as in relations with rival nations in the southern hemisphere. The balance of power between the English Rugby Football Union (RFU) and the most senior sides has swung heavily in favour of an elite of no more than a dozen clubs, of which paradoxically only a handful operate from a genuinely stable commercial base. How have clubs survived – or not – at a key moment when professionalism has forced previously protected, often deeply conservative, institutions to acknowledge the uncompromising forces for change which have determined the nature of mass spectator sport at the end of the twentieth century? After four years of ceaseless wrangling and ill will – of euphoria, followed rapidly by disenchantment, but also cautious optimism – how successfully has English rugby coped with the previously alien notion of playing for cash as well as cachet? How has the regulatory body handled a visible erosion of its authority: the RFU coming face-to-face with a new generation of ambitious high-profile owners, managers/coaches, and players, all of them indifferent to the attitudes and assumptions that have moulded English rugby for well over a hundred years? At grassroots have the same amateur values survived intact – assuming of course that they existed in the first place – or has rugby union experienced changes so profound that they impact upon every level of the game?

The Roots of the Open Game – The Early 1990s

In May 1995, on the eve of the third World Cup, most clubs in the then Courage League Division One paid scant attention to the anticipated arrival of professional rugby.[1] Even the better-known clubs rarely paid their first XV players anything more than travel expenses, the size of the club determining just how generous such 'expenses' could be. Gate revenue was complemented by bar-takings and sales from scarves and replica shirts revenue, and star players were expected to seek a financial return on their talent via country not club. Most senior clubs, therefore, were financially secure, even if their business strategy and management structure were rooted in amateurism and voluntarism. Committee members, some of whom would be running their own small businesses, were wary but by no means unaware of the commercial revolution taking place in the repackaging and marketing of mass spectator sports.

The social composition, preoccupations, attitudes and aspirations of committee members running senior clubs was not that dissimilar from those of fellow enthusiasts fulfilling similar functions within much more modest operations up and down the country. The RFU reflected this grass-roots homogeneity, albeit with an in-built hierarchy of elected officials, based upon wealth, social status, playing record, age, and place of residence (ideally southern). At the centre of this conservative and increasingly outmoded institution there did exist a paid bureaucracy attuned to the need for change, particularly in the light of what was happening to rugby union beyond the British Isles – and to rugby league – as rugby's governing bodies across the globe rushed to emulate football's enthusiastic embrace of satellite television. The presence of these professional administrators within an ostensibly amateur and voluntary organisation like the RFU suggests that its reactionary reputation was never wholly justified – even if charges of financial incompetence certainly were.

Although the knockout competition dates back to 1971, an English club championship dates only from 1987, its arrival hastened by *The*

Daily Telegraph's unofficial league table of the major English sides' performances across a season. The undiminished interest in the Five Nations Championship, the clear link between league and national performance in Scotland and Wales, and England's modest expectations in the forthcoming inaugural World Cup – let alone the commercial potential – together encouraged the RFU to negotiate a £1.6 million deal with Courage. The brewing conglomerate's sponsorship lasted a decade, by which time the RFU negotiators and consultants were eager to exploit the value of their product to the maximum. From the beginning of the 1990s financial institutions were keen to raise their profiles and update their images through sponsorship of mass spectator sports, witness the important role of Endsleigh Insurance and the Nationwide Building Society in enabling the Football League to survive a breakaway Premier League in 1992. Shifting commercial priorities and fresh marketing strategies were further confirmed in April 1997 when the Allied Dunbar financial services group agreed to sponsor the 24 clubs in the RFU's top two divisions for the next three seasons to the tune of £7.5 million. The renamed Premiership One clubs received £500,000 and Premiership Two half as much, with Twickenham endeavouring to reassure smaller clubs that further cash would trickle downwards. As Ian Malin has pointed out, the deal was highly symbolic in that the Courage League's pyramid structure embraced all 1,169 clubs. Allied Dunbar was only interested in the clubs featured on Sky Sports and represented by EPRUC (English Professional Rugby Union Clubs, now effectively superseded by the powerful elite umbrella organisation EFDR (English First Division Rugby)). All other leagues and clubs had to secure sponsors wherever they could, thus ending the principle of a seamless game and the ideal that all clubs, from the great to the humble, were in this together.[2]

As far back as 1989 the Welsh RFU's official historian, Gareth Williams, acknowledged that 'the development of sponsorship has accelerated the drive to overt professionalism': too many players were now enjoying executive responsibility within the private sector not to appreciate international rugby's commercial potential and to recognise that they were marketable assets in their own right.[3] The first generation to enjoy global recognition, based upon the great Welsh sides of the 1970s, had rarely sought to make serious money out of their achievement, preferring to pursue their chosen careers in education, medicine, local government, and so on. No matter how highly regarded as a player and as a person, anyone deriving a financial reward for past effort was 'guilty' of professionalism.[4] A ghosted biography, a place in the commentary box, or a column in the *Western Mail* meant no further involvement in the game at any level, whether in coaching or administration. By the end of the 1980s most leading players judged such draconian restrictive practice intolerable and increasingly unenforceable, not least if challenged in court.

Faced with the emergence of genuine media personalities like Will Carling and Jeremy Guscott – and growing evidence that the home-based 1991 World Cup would be the biggest sporting event in Britain since 1966 – more enlightened elements within the RFU recognised that players could not be penalised for taking PR jobs, where their principal value to employers was instant customer recognition. Carling and his Scottish counterpart, Gavin Hastings, became *de facto* public relations companies in their own right. Their role model was the self-employed, product-endorsing rugby personality commonplace in New Zealand and South Africa for a generation. The 1991 World Cup was crucial in terms of the Home Nations' relations with television but also with regard to loosening the restrictions upon technically amateur players' ability to make money out of the game. In Britain 13.6 million viewers saw Australia beat England in the final at Twickenham, still not a television audience comparable to that secured by the football team *en route* to the World Cup semi-final a year earlier, but enough to make Rob Andrew almost as famous as Paul Gascoigne.[5]

Nevertheless, the overwhelming majority of the England squad that dominated the Five Nations Championship between the second and the third World Cup continued to hold down 'real' jobs, in one case seeing unemployment as the only means of adequately preparing for South Africa '95. The RFU's strict adherence to Bylaw 4 of its constitution, which forbade direct or indirect payment or other material reward for taking part in the game, precluded instances of major companies bankrolling whole teams; as openly occurred in Italy, or less publicly in France with its notorious reputation since the 1930s for turning a blind eye to payments in cash or kind.[6] Yet the RFU had no objection to major players being employed by clubs as 'rugby development officers', or being paid vastly inflated 'expenses', a practice especially prevalent in Wales. The WRU tolerated, and if anything tacitly encouraged, 'shamateurism', in order to stop key players accepting generous contracts to move north and play rugby league. Wales's 1991 World Cup defeat by Western Samoa at home in Cardiff confirmed for key young players like Scott Gibbs that they had little to lose by turning professional, particularly given the success and earning power of Jonathan Davies since switching codes.[7] All such players were banned for life from involvement in rugby union and were *persona non grata* – in theory, if by the 1990s, rarely in practice – at Welsh, or indeed any other rugby union grounds. Scott Gibbs thus had good reason for going public on Welsh 'shamateurism':

> It grates me that I am called a prostitute while players and officials keep on covering up what's going on in union. Every player in Wales knows that when you play on a Saturday, if you win you can get a few quid. Players get the cash after the game.[8]

Carling's unashamed millionaire status ('Every penny I make is down to who I am and what I have achieved in the game'), and lawyer/hooker Brian Moore's success in negotiating a squad pool for the 1995 World Cup worth around £11,000 per player, highlighted just how unfair and inequitable was the treatment meted out to anyone, however junior, who sampled rugby league.[9] As late as 1994 the RFU was attracting opprobrium for punishment of two young prospects who had occasionally played *amateur* rugby league.[10]

'Shamateurism' in the British Isles, and especially in Wales, had been further exposed by the controversy surrounding rebel tours to South Africa in the 1980s. Players (and WRU officials) received up to £30,000 each for participating in the 1989 centenary 'Tests'. The controversy that engulfed the WRU led to a purging of the old guard, and the emergence of barrister Vernon Pugh as a major figure in the International Rugby Board's embrace of professionalism. Pugh's official inquiry into recruitment of the 'international XV' prompted the RFU to interview three current England players, none of whom were suspended from the game.[11] None of the 1989 'tourists' or the members of the previous year's 'Crawshay's Welsh' side, were banned by their home unions, if only because such action would have been challenged in the courts. The 1986 'New Zealand Cavaliers' included current All Blacks, all of whom were generously remunerated for defying the Gleneagles Agreement and the 1985 legal judgement that touring South Africa would not 'promote or foster and develop the game in this country [NZ]'.[12] The then South African Rugby Board –

after 1992 absorbed into the new and ostensibly non-racial South African Rugby Football Union (SARFU) – simply ignored the credo that rugby union was an amateur sport. If it could remain a full voting member of the IB throughout the years of sporting isolation from the rest of the world, and even secure the Board's permission to invite individual players to tour, then there was scant prospect of expulsion over a simple matter like asking the England back row to name their price.

By the time South Africa officially returned to international rugby, in 1992, SARFU was not simply turning a blind eye to professionalism, but actively encouraging it. Taking the white man's game into the townships would always be a secondary consideration. The real priority was to focus on 1995: in front of their own die-hard (for which read white) supporters the 'Boks would prove that, despite isolation since 1981, they had always been the *real* world champions. Present or future Springboks had to be committed to their game full-time, so that by the time of the third World Cup anyone representing his province in the Currie Cup could anticipate an income of around £3,000 a month. Captain Francois Pienaar was a great ambassador for South Africa rugby, particularly on the 1994 tour of Wales, Scotland and Ireland, but he was rumoured to be earning around £200,000 a year. Pienaar's main task was to focus attention away from the success of notorious racists like Transvaal's Louis Luyt in regaining control of SARFU.[13]

A combination of Springbok salaries and a long history of All Black promotional work meant that neither New Zealand nor Australia was averse to setting up trust funds. These in theory protected their players' amateur status (as with Olympic athletes), but in practice offered lucrative contracts based upon the number of appearances at national and/or financial level. Revenue from the game plus sponsors' donations provided income for both countries' trust funds, of which predictably New Zealand's was by far the largest. It needed to be, because in the spring of 1995 Rupert Murdoch's News Corporation (News Corp) launched its bid to secure sole TV rights to coverage of rugby league in Australia and in Europe, where an £87 million deal over five years was intended to fund a Super League. A massive influx of money into the game would establish rugby league as the predominant sport across the whole of Australia (superseding Australian Rules Football, and further ghettoising rugby union on the eastern seaboard). At the same time the summer-based European Super League would revive interest in France and London, and forge a new and glamorous image for a sport that had repeatedly failed to break out of its northern, working-class bastion.[14] Murdoch's millions meant not just more opportunities for Welsh 'mercenaries' but a genuine incentive to hard men from Down Under to switch codes; ageing All Blacks now had cause for genuine soul-searching (more so for [white] *pakeha* than Maori, the latter often preferring to play rugby league anyway). Between the announcement of News Corp's global investment in rugby league and the launch of the 1995 World Cup a month later, it was reported that 11 All Blacks now felt the money on offer was sufficient to sacrifice the prestige, privileges, perks, and above all the substantial income, accrued by the last generation of 'amateurs' to wear the silver fern.[15]

The Global Impact of Satellite Television

Television is of course the key to understanding why, in Paris on 27 August 1995, the International Rugby Board – including two English representatives – made its surprise announcement that:

> Rugby will become an open game and there will be no prohibition on payments or the provision of other material benefit to any person involved in the game. It was also agreed that (1) payment might be made at any level of participation; (2) there should be no pay ceiling imposed by the council; (3) payment for results is not prohibited.[16]

Twenty IB representatives, covering 67 different unions, indicated that, exactly 100 years after the creation of the Northern Union – from 1922 the Rugby League – the penalties for playing both codes had been abolished. The opportunity for professional players to negotiate both league and union contracts was acknowledged, but with hindsight what is striking is the failure to appreciate the speed with which change would take place. Vernon Pugh, chair of the IB working party on amateurism, appreciated the full implications of his recommendations being endorsed. Yet Tony Hallett, the RFU's newly-elected secretary and soon to be in the vanguard of reform in English rugby, speculated on modest rewards for leading club players 'within two or three seasons'.[17] It was television, as well as genuine embarrassment at the hypocrisy of 'shamateurism' and its detrimental impact on a sport which still claimed a unique set of ethics and values, which forced the IB to act – and it was television which ensured that the momentum for change was maintained over the ensuing months and years. When an RFU commission recommended in the spring of 1996 that professional rugby in England would have to be club-based it was not simply accepting the inevitable. The report saw Premiership One as an added attraction to international rugby the next time Twickenham began talks with rival broadcasters.[18]

Whannel's claim, that the 'rise of television turned sport into a whole new cultural form, with extensive marketing potential', is especially pertinent to rugby and TV in the 1990s.[19] News Corp's apparent success in securing monopoly rights to rugby league placed enormous pressures on the leading members of the IB, particularly Australia and New Zealand. The latter felt genuinely threatened at the very moment when TV coverage of South Africa '95 was confirming rugby union as a major world sport. Murdoch's determination to talk tough, and insist that the game adapt to meet the particular demands of satellite broadcasting, was reinforced by the knowledge that terrestrial television companies had managed to secure and retain coverage of the first three World Cups, and had successfully demonstrated the game's enormous commercial potential. Furthermore, Sky experienced serious problems in reporting matches in South Africa, even having its accreditation temporarily withdrawn after complaints from ITV. The latter's attempts to hijack coverage of international rugby from the BBC were largely unsuccessful, other than during the 1991 and 1995 tournaments. ITV Sports' hope that full coverage of the matches in South Africa would later reap benefits at home lasted less than a year – in June 1996 the RFU all but abandoned terrestrial television. Exactly 12 months earlier the home unions of South Africa, Australia and New Zealand had accepted that the only way to ensure the future prosperity of rugby union in the southern hemisphere was to stop antagonising Rupert Murdoch and do a deal with him.[20]

On 23 June 1995, the eve of the World Cup final, it was reported that News Corp had paid US$550 million for ten years exclusive rights to rugby in South Africa and Australasia. Not only had Murdoch's negotiators secured a bargain (£250,000 per match between teams from the three most powerful rugby nations in the world), but it could also flex its financial muscle to determine the nature and size of future competitions in the southern hemisphere. The downside might be an exhausting schedule of Tri-nation clashes, but a real plus was the Super 12 regional competition, with its massive impact on how the modern game is played.[21]

The early success of Super 12, with the onus on exciting and positive play, both to win the game *and* to win new audiences, clearly influenced the less hidebound members of the RFU Council. The slick and glitzy approach of Sky Sports, its overall audience rising on the back of live Premiership football, appealed to the body set up by the top two division clubs as an early response to the arrival of open rugby, which technically did not arrive in England until 6 May 1996: the advent of EPRUC (English Professional Rugby Union Clubs) confirmed professionalism. EPRUC's members, especially the Division One clubs, felt BSkyB offered a genuine opportunity to raise the profile of club rugby once current contracts were substantially renegotiated and matches became a regular feature of Sky Sports' winter schedules. BBC coverage, via *Rugby Special,* had generated little revenue for the clubs, and anyway there was general dissatisfaction with the programme's Sunday teatime scheduling and low audience of 1.4 million. Contracting *Rugby Special* out to an independent production company had greatly improved presentation and content, but ultimately to no avail.[22] Both EPRUC and the RFU's TV and Media Committee looked enviously at the deal cut with News Corp by the Tri-nations *and* at the success of the Premier League in securing a £670 million contract extension with BSkyB the same month that English rugby officially went open.

Talks began on 24 May 1996 and a Heads of Agreement was signed by the RFU's treasurer and its secretary, Tony Hallett, chief negotiator and arch-moderniser. BSkyB acquired sole rights to broadcast live for the next five years all internationals, club and representative games in England. The price of £87.5 million dwarfed the £27 million previously paid by the BBC for the three-year contract due to end in 1997. £22.5 million was set aside for the senior clubs. The RFU would service and reduce its £34 million debt incurred in rebuilding Twickenham, fund its sizeable infrastructure, and cascade around £60 million down to the 1,980 clubs and 3,000 affiliated schools. Hallett insisted that 'there will be more rugby on television than ever', while also conceding that the RFU had to sign given its ongoing costs and the size of its bank loan.[23]

Controversy surrounding Twickenham's embrace of BSkyB arose because the deal was unilateral, and not part of a jointly negotiated package with the three other Home Nations (France having always – as England now pointed out – negotiated independently). The 'Celtic nations' objected strenuously, at one point threatening to expel England from the Five Nations. Encouragement for England's initiative came from the pro-Murdoch Tri-nations, who had little respect for the tradition and domestic popularity of the Five Nations Championship, let alone the standard of rugby. Modernisers below the Equator envisaged a new world order in which England and France would play mostly southern hemisphere sides: the extended tour would gradually give way to individual fixtures, facilitated by the speed of modern jet travel.[24] This vision of the future horrified not only the Scots, Welsh and Irish, but also the bulk of the RFU membership (the EPRUC clubs constituting merely 0.01 per cent of the constituent body, given the union's pyramid structure). Loyalty to the basic concept of public service broadcasting, with 'free' access for all, ensured that most club and county representatives in England openly endorsed the Celtic view that Twickenham had a moral if not a legal obligation to perpetuate the status quo. In addition they feared that Hallett and his negotiating team had waived the RFU's right to veto any future move by BSkyB to introduce pay-per-view for major fixtures, as was already happening in satellite broadcasting of other sports, notably boxing. Will Carling for once found himself in the unusual position of supporting the 'old farts', arguing that it was terrestrial and not satellite television which had popularised rugby since 1991 – a view subsequently rubbished by his one time fly-half turned Sky Sports commentator Stuart Barnes. A compromise agreement was finally hammered out with Wales, Scotland and Ireland, involving compensation of up to £50 million over five years and an assurance that the RFU would not negotiate the next deal unilaterally. The other three ruling bodies then negotiated separate deals with the BBC and ITV/S4C, having initially rejected substantial offers from BSkyB on principle, because they were significantly less than what England had secured (and still largely retained 15 months later). Beneath the veneer of ultimate compromise, the RFU stood firm. It had a legal obligation to respect its agreement with BSkyB; and could not afford to renege. Twickenham also knew that the other members of the Five Nations Committee – especially the cash-strapped Welsh Rugby Union – feared England's absence would greatly diminish the reputation and revenue-raising potential of the Championship.[25]

A key figure in persuading the WRU to accept the seemingly inevitable was Cliff Brittle, elected chair of the RFU Management Board in January 1996 and initially the most vocal opponent of the Sky deal. Having been deliberately excluded from the negotiating team, Brittle complained that 'democracy no longer prevails within the RFU'. He assiduously courted popularity at grassroots level, with great success. Yet, once Brittle had privately conceded that Twickenham's financial situation necessitated a cash influx, which only Murdoch could provide, he was the ideal ambassador to placate the Welsh and thus hasten compromise.[26] A self-made millionaire, Brittle was a traditionalist, but in this particular instance also a realist. In the ensuing months he retained his carefully cultivated populist image as the defender of rugby's most basic values, and of an amateur ethos which Twickenham bureaucrats and money-gambling senior clubs were allegedly all too eager to abandon. Brittle's power base constituted those players, referees, and above all committeemen across the country who resented the power of the EPRUC clubs, and the speed with which the game was adjusting to the pressures and demands of commercialism. Brittle believed the grassroots game had given him a mandate. Often isolated in committees, and loathed by bureaucrats like Hallett, let alone the broadsheets' younger correspondents, Cliff Brittle is nevertheless difficult to feel sympathy for. Without doubt he was a destructive force within English rugby union. He thrived on the civil war waging within the RFU between January 1996 and July 1998, that month's AGM marking the point at which a majority of delegates had finally had enough. By virtue of the power he enjoyed as chair of the Management Board (constrained only by the full RFU Council and the President), the goodwill towards him in the shires, and the prestige of his staunchest supporters, Brittle could be outflanked but never ignored.[27] Ironically, Brittle shared his status as a tax exile with the man he despised for supposedly introducing the very worst aspects of professionalism into a previously decent and honourable game – the millionaire property developer who had restored Newcastle United to its former glories, Sir John Hall.

Only two months after the IB's August 1995 announcement Sir John Hall had offered Rob Andrew £750,000 over five years to lift

Newcastle Gosforth from the bottom of Courage Division Two to the championship title. By May 1998 Hall's chequebook and an uncompromising if rarely attractive style of play had secured 'Newcastle Falcons' the greatest prize in English club rugby; an achievement applauded by few beyond Gateshead's equivalent of the 'Toon Army'. The circumstances in which England's quarter-final hero and three team-mates had left Wasps, and Hall's eagerness to maximise the revenue potential of his club and of EPRUC, attracted widespread criticism throughout much of the game and in the non-Murdoch press, notably *The Daily Telegraph*. Hall recognised that a capacity crowd of 6,000 would not fund record-breaking transfer fees and the inflated wage bills he and Rob Andrew saw as necessary for instant success. Television was therefore crucial. Furthermore, high-spending broadcasters would only be interested in club rugby – whether English, or British, or ideally European – if assured that star names would be playing. Top players could not be unavailable because they were resting between internationals, or away training with the national squad. Nor could they be injured, as a result of summer tours having prevented rest and recuperation after a hard season.[28]

Hall was a role model for less high-profile businessmen who in succeeding months persuaded membership-based clubs to convert to company status (Leicester being almost the sole exception at the highest level). The first generation of millionaire rugby club owners came from a variety of backgrounds and was rarely soaked in the game. One exception was Nigel Wray, the executive chairman of an immensely profitable property investment company who, shortly after Sir John Hall was approached by Newcastle Gosforth, invested £2 million in Saracens and offered £500,000 of shares for sale. Saracens, for so long the poor relations of Home Counties rugby, soon said goodbye to north London and established fresh roots in the unlikeliest of settings, Vicarage Road, home of Watford FC.[29]

Hall's agenda became that of EPRUC and then EFDR: television revenue was a priority, closely followed by any other initiatives to market the club and its players as products. Not surprisingly, the Premier League offered a model for marketing a product with a clear and widely recognised identity, witness fast growing sales for rugby replica shirts, and Bath Rugby Club's football-style high-street shop.[30] The new business ethic meant that – as well-rewarded *employees* – each player was contractually obliged to place the requirements of his club above the interest of his country, even if he had signed a complementary contract with his home union. This was a legal convention unique to the British Isles, and contrasted starkly with the southern hemisphere where top players retained only the loosest contractual links with their home clubs. Football devotee Hall infuriated traditionalists like Brittle by his insistence on subverting the time-honoured tradition that an international cap was an honour for the club as well as the player. Although Hall was the most vocal in maintaining that club loyalty was paramount, other owners – like fellow football director Chris Wright, who in August 1996 merged Wasps and Queens Park Rangers, rarely demurred. Nor, with qualifications, did young players in the vanguard of professionalism, such as Wasps and future England captain, Lawrence Dallaglio.[31]

The First Two Years of Professional Rugby

The early part of rugby's first fully professional season, 1996–97, was blighted by a tiresome dispute between EPRUC and the RFU over availability of England players for pre-Christmas fixtures and squad sessions. As a gesture of solidarity to their clubs and to EPRUC all but one of the national squad boycotted training. The senior clubs threatened, by no means for the last time, to split from the RFU and negotiate a separate TV deal, the more ambitious envisaging the Heineken European Cup as the prelude to a European Super League, until BSkyB made clear that its first duty was to the RFU.[32] EPRUC, aware of its poor public image and paucity of allies, agreed in February 1997 that players would always be released for international duty. It set up with the RFU under Tony Hallet a liaison body, English Rugby Partnership, an initiative seen by Brittle and his supporters as a further betrayal of coarse rugby. The club versus country issue continued to diminish English rugby, climaxing in the furore surrounding the absence of 15 first-choice players from England's disastrous 1998 summer tour.[33] Brittle used the controversy to generate even greater hostility towards the senior clubs, and to support his call for a radical restructuring of English rugby: the power of his Management Board would be enhanced at the expense of the Council. Factionalism and recrimination within the RFU was endemic, poisoning relations between senior players and coach Clive Woodward. The latter, a rather maverick figure, was popularly regarded as being pro-Brittle and in favour of RFU rather than club contracts. Common sense prevailed when the RFU Council and President bypassed Brittle and initiated talks with English First Division Rugby, EPRUC's tough-talking successor. EFDR clearly had the ear of Allied Dunbar: witness the latter's promotion of the Premiership clubs' 'English Rugby Charter', a document conciliatory towards the RFU but insistent that:

> In contrast to the game in the Southern Hemisphere English rugby has developed around the club. This will continue to be the basis for the development of the game. Over the next three years the clubs intend to establish themselves as an independent organisation under the auspices of the RFU as its regulatory body, to further promote the interest of professional club rugby in England. It is the objective of the clubs to directly negotiate and control all club media and sponsorship rights once current contracts have expired.[34]

Fresh initiatives in Europe – the Heineken Cup being boycotted in 1998–99 because of dissatisfaction over organisation and TV proceeds – and the future potential for digital satellite transmission of every Premiership fixture, meant a genuine prospect of EFDR breaking away from the RFU. Northampton's owner, Keith Barwell, insisted in March 1998 that the continued presence of Cliff Brittle within the RFU management structure justified an immediate split. When Barwell insisted that Northampton's internationals would not be touring that summer, EFDR formally complained to the European Commission that the RFU was abusing its authority and engaging in non-competitive practices. Brittle's Management Board had chosen to withhold Tetley's Bitter Cup gate receipts unless the boycott of the Heineken European Cup was lifted, an inflammatory decision reversed by the RFU Council when it invited EFDR to resume negotiations. Not only were more enlightened elements within the RFU alarmed by the prospect of a 'Premier League' style split, and the consequent threat to control of the national side, but they were equally horrified by the antics of Brittle and Fran Cotton. The latter advocated: reducing the influence of the clubs within the RFU; reviving divisional competition as a prerequisite for international recognition; and most contentious of all, the contracting of players to 'Club England' and their then being leased out to the clubs.[35]

The RFU Council's peace initiative meant Brittle's isolation,

Cotton's resignation as his vice-chairman, and the Mayfair Agreement of 8 May 1998. The RFU endeavoured to address the senior clubs' concerns over issues such as fixtures congestion, two 14-club divisions, and the recruitment of non-EU players. EFDR agreed not to endorse unsanctioned cross-border competition, and promised that Five Nation players would be released for up to eight matches in the 1998–99 season. The clubs' guarantee to make leading players available for England duty helped placate an IB irate over an allegedly cavalier attitude to overseas tours.[36] Predictably Brittle and the Reform Group railed against the Mayfair Agreement. Nevertheless final confirmation that peace had broken out between the clubs and the RFU, *and* within the RFU, was the unexpectedly large vote at the July 1998 AGM to reject a man now seen by many former supporters as obstructive and obstreperous. Brittle's successor, Brian Blaister, attracted sufficient votes to claim a genuine mandate to work with the clubs on the long road to financial stability and ultimate self-sufficiency. Still reeling from England's disastrous summer tour, RFU representatives voted for peace and stability, not rancour and retribution.[37] The initial phase of professional rugby in England was over.

The Mayfair Agreement of May 1998 was crucial in taking the heat out of the club versus country dispute: the notion that players could be contracted to 'Club England' was deemed naïve and inappropriate, and the argument that rugby's future lay in more internationals quietly dropped. The clubs had been adamant that a congested fixture list meant reduced gate receipts and increased injuries, while the RFU had come to accept that poor performances against supposedly weaker teams such as Argentina meant a half-empty Twickenham. The new consensus, reinforced by the departure of Cliff Brittle, came not a moment too soon. Clubs in the top two divisions faced a number of problems, which together constituted a genuine crisis for the game. Corporate sponsors, noting Sky Sports' modest viewing figures for coverage of Premiership One and even the Tetley's Bitter Cup, began to ask if club rugby could provide a level of exposure comparable to other sports. NEC were prepared to go public over their dissatisfaction with Harlequins.[38] In 1996 Harlequins had offered a long-standing association with wealth and the City. Not only were they London's most successful club but the home of England's most famous player. For NEC, with its reputation for hi-tech quality products, this was the perfect marriage. By 1998, with Carling gone and 'NEC Harlequins' floundering, divorce seemed imminent. If other major sponsors withdrew from contract re-negotiations, or greatly reduced the cash flow, then even the most successful sides would be in trouble. Luckily for Harlequins a run of good results in the autumn of 1998 at least temporarily placated their sponsors.

Clubs experienced difficulty in maximising use of their grounds. Many stadiums were in urgent need of refurbishment in order to bring them up to the post-Taylor Report standard of top football or rugby league grounds. Some senior clubs were leaseholders, most famously Bath. The Recreation Ground stands on land rented from the Council and holds only 8,000, hence Bath's intention to build its own stadium and attract more spectators. With limited space and facilities there is little that can be done with a medium-sized stadium other than to maximise gate receipts.[39] Thus Harlequins shared The Stoop with rugby league's London Broncos, and from September 1998 with newly-promoted London Scottish. The latter previously had no proper stadium, sharing the Athletic Ground with Richmond, a club which, like 'Newcastle Falcons', had secured a wealthy patron prepared to bring in the biggest names in order to achieve early success. Richmond then followed Saracen's example by decamping outside the capital and in the autumn of 1998–99 shared Reading FC's new Madejski Stadium. The club retained its old offices, but only the most devoted of Richmond fans would regularly travel so far west of London. Owner Ashley Levett's strategy was to hold on to club stalwarts but at the same time build up a new loyal following, such as Saracens had secured in Watford. Tradition and community values counted for little, and rugby union was following a trend already emerging in rugby league and ice hockey in England whereby teams (no longer genuine clubs) became American-style franchises not averse to relocation if market conditions dictated this to be the best option. Rugby clubs would have to follow the example of Premier League sides like Southampton and Coventry, each intending to compensate for limited gates by offering their product within purpose-built sports complexes where other consumer/leisure activities would be available. Yet, given rugby's limited potential and paltry investment capital, this meant absorption within a multi-leisure complex or property development enterprise. Until Saracens moved in with Watford FC the most successful and cost-effective instance of ground sharing was Wasps playing at QPR's Loftus Road on Sunday afternoon. Even so, despite intense efforts to promote the game in West London, and Wasp's long cup run in 1997–98, the average gate for league matches was only 5,834, a 1.9 per cent drop on the previous season. No wonder shares in QPR/Wasps' parent company slipped from £1 in January 1997 to 20p in May 1998, only one example of how the Stock Exchange has little confidence in rugby union as a lucrative long-term, let alone short-term, investment.[40]

In contrast, 1997–98 was a spectacularly successful season for London's one-time also-rans, Saracens. With a missionary fervour and endeavour Saracens sold rugby to Watford. Persuading the 1997 Super League winners' marketing director to switch codes and move south was an inspirational move by Wray, as crucial to Saracen's success off the pitch as the services of his imported stars were on it. There was a growing acceptance throughout the game that rugby union had an enormous amount to learn from the rival code about selling itself to a mass audience. Traditionalists may have loathed the noise, colour, and 'blokeish' behaviour now associated with Saracens, but the parallels are more with American spectator sports than the Super League, or even the Premier League. The emphasis on families and on persuading children that supporting a successful star-filled rugby union team is 'cool', highlighted the importance of the club's community programme. Saracens forged close links with junior clubs, and with local schools, and sold multiple tickets via a successful cash-back scheme.[41] By May 1998 Saracens had seen a 176 per cent increase in average attendance, finished second in the Premiership One, and won the Tetley's Bitter Cup.[42]

EFDR, Allied Dunbar and Sky all highlighted a 22.4 per cent rise in first division attendance in 1997–98, but the global figure was only 823,446, with a club average of 6,238 (Leicester's 12,589 compensating for 4 out of 12 teams attracting only around 3,600).[43] Thus even the very best of club rugby attracted far fewer spectators than the Football League or the RL Super League, let alone the Premier League. To appease unhappy sponsors and investors, EFDR pointed out that each club had only played 11 home fixtures (12 from 1998–99), hence the need to increase English rugby's presence in Europe via a new competition to replace the boycotted Heineken Trophy. Control over competition structure and negotiation of broadcasting rights needed to be invested away from European Rugby Cup Limited, an umbrella organisation of the Five Nations' ruling bodies. The assumption was that more fixtures, with glamorous continental opposition, would significantly boost gate receipts *and* increase exposure for major sponsors like NEC. To emphasise the urgency of a new club-controlled pro-European competition, the two pioneers who had invested most heavily since 1995 – Newcastle's Sir John Hall and Saracens' Nigel Wray – threatened to sell up if there was no early agreement over Europe. These threats could easily be dismissed as bluffs. But if Hall and Wray perceived a crisis, how did the chairmen of failing clubs feel?[44]

Because clubs were desperate for success, and because the new owners were prepared at first to bankroll them in some cases to the tune of millions of pounds, wages spiralled. The bubble seemed to burst in the summer of 1998, but some clubs were so desperate for success that they were still prepared to gamble large sums on presumed miracle workers, often from New Zealand. The assumption was that southern hemisphere credentials guaranteed success. The first season of professionalism had seen a £13 million deficit, while the second saw income relatively static but senior clubs still obliged to fulfil the terms of contracts offered to players and coaches in the first wave of euphoria following the arrival of the open game. All clubs, even those still trawling the Pacific Rim, had to cut their wage bills in advance of the 1998–99 season. Ageing or injured players faced transfer to less prestigious clubs, or a substantial reduction in wages. Few of the players who had returned from rugby league, and who in 1996–97 had made such an impact at club and international level, retained high profiles and high wages 18 months later.[45] The chances of Welsh players returning home looked slim with Cardiff and Swansea – possibly the only clubs in the Principality capable of remaining fully professional – in dispute with the WRU. Some Welsh Premier Division sides were either on the verge of bankruptcy or actually in the hands of the receivers.[46]

While Welsh rugby went into freefall in the spring and summer of 1998, an alarming number of English clubs began declaring players' contracts null and void. Premiership Two's weakest and most poorly supported clubs, Wakefield and Fylde, went bankrupt, preceded by Moseley and Blackheath.[47] All four clubs were ultimately rescued from receivership, and revived on a semi-professional basis. They were followed by two of English rugby's most illustrious clubs: Bristol went bankrupt in July 1998, rapidly followed by Coventry. With debts of over £2 million, both clubs had found inflated salaries no guarantee of success. Bristol had failed to avoid relegation from Premiership One, and Coventry had yet again missed out on promotion.[48] Quite simply neither club's principal local benefactor could afford to keep making interest-free loans with no hope of repayment. A club owner had to be *extremely* rich in order to subsidise the gap between income and expenditure. However, if clubs of the size and status of Bristol and Coventry could be refloated as new companies – with players employed on a part-time semi-professional basis, and with wages to match – then this suggested that within two years all but a select group of highly successful, well-endowed clubs would be organised along similar lines.[49] Ironically, despite its initial intention to operate on a slimmed-down basis, Bristol soon acquired a fresh benefactor, with the ambition, drive and, above all, the cash, to ensure a speedy return to the inner circle of EFDR.

The Elite Clubs' Survival Strategies, 1998–99

Three years into a five-year strategy plan Sir John Hall sold his company's 76 per cent controlling interest in Newcastle Falcons. The initial investment was set at £1 million, but by the time Hall sold the club in March 1999 total losses were heading towards £9 million. The experiment of playing at Gateshead had failed, and the average gate back at Kingston Park was around 3,500. It had cost over £1.25 million to win the championship in 1997–98, and most of the star names that had brought instant success to the North East had gone, either to trim the wage bill or because of personality clashes with Rob Andrew. Hall's frustration with his fellow proprietors, and more especially with the game's ruling bodies, had left him eager to pull out once the sale of Newcastle United to cable television company NTL was agreed in December 1998. Having already offloaded his ice hockey team, Hall had abandoned his grandiose plan for a Geordie version of Barcelona's multi-activity Sporting Club. Unlike Hall, Andrew believed that a smaller Premiership One and a relaunched European Cup would ensure TV income and sponsorship totalling around £1 million a year – 15 games and a 10,000 gate would guarantee viability. Disarmingly honest in acknowledging that very few clubs averaged crowds of 10,000, Andrew nevertheless convinced a couple of very rich rugby fans to invest £3 million. The size of his task in selling rugby union to a football-mad region, now also supporting a RL Super League side at Gateshead, was cruelly illustrated in May 1999 when the Falcons' supporters were vastly outnumbered by Wasps' in a Tetley's Bitter Cup final which for the first time in a decade saw Twickenham half full.[50]

The Falcons still flew, even if their principal backer's five-year plan, and insistence that 'I can only do things if I can see that there is a commercial viability', sounded eerily reminiscent of Sir John Hall in the autumn of 1995.[51] By June 1999 Richmond, the third oldest club in the world, had ceased to exist. Following Hall's example, in March 1999 Ashley Levett decided that his personal losses of £8 million could no longer be sustained, so he put the club in the hands of an administrator. With no one willing to find around £1.5 million simply to keep Richmond afloat, the club prepared for end of season bankruptcy by reducing staff and players to the bare minimum, and immediately halving an astonishingly high monthly wage bill of £230,000. It was scarcely surprising that the anticipated deficit for the 1998–99 season was £1.8 million, particularly when it cost £15,000 every time a match was staged at the Madejski Stadium. The move to Reading was a further demonstration of long-standing supporters' resentment at being taken for granted; perhaps Saracens' success at Watford was an exception rather than a model for other sides in search of a fresh fan base. Levett now implied that the move to the Majedski had taken place primarily to satisfy Oracle, Richmond's sponsors, but – like Hall – he held the RFU and the IB largely responsible for the club's demise.[52]

The reality of course was that Richmond's business projection had been ludicrously optimistic given that in the past the Athletic Ground had rarely reached its 2,500 capacity. Having vacated Hampshire for tax exile in Monaco, Levett appeared to have lost his business nous. He forgot that rugby in central southern England has neither a tradition nor a mass appeal: in normal circumstances clubs need to be both firmly rooted in the community and successful if they are going to attract capacity crowds. Even then, they can only survive if they acknowledge the need to control salary costs. Levett's – and thus Richmond's – fatal combination was local indifference, too many support staff, and an extremely large and overpaid first team squad. Like most of the Premiership Two sides the previous summer, most notably Bristol and Coventry, Richmond could have been spared, with the club relaunched as an entirely new company acceptable to EFDR.

What sealed Richmond's fate was that the very organisation it had helped found was now intent on reducing the size of Premiership One by discouraging potential investors. EFDR's chairman, Tom Walkinshaw, applied the business ethics and hard bargaining of Formula One to seal Richmond's fate. Having rejected an offer of £500,000 from EFDR to terminate the club's professional status, Richmond was then informed that its registration as a Premiership side would cease at the end of the 1998–99 season: because of impending bankruptcy EFDR would exercise its right to pay £1 for the name and then close the club down. Like Rob Andrew, Walkinshaw saw future profitability dependent upon a senior division of 12 not 14 clubs, with south-west London (now extending as far as Reading) supporting far too many top teams. Walkinshaw insisted the other EFDR clubs supported Gloucester's view that here was an ideal opportunity to slim down the league.[53]

EFDR renewed its offer of a £500,000 cash incentive to rationalise, encouraging a now buoyant London Irish to absorb Richmond *and* London Scottish. Unlike Richmond, the Scottish Exiles were weak off and on the pitch, but were never serious relegation contenders in early 1999 so long as West Hartlepool and Bedford continued to lose. London Scottish's secure Premiership One status, but exposed financial position, had led to one of the more bizarre developments in a bizarre season. In January 1999 the relaunched and revitalised Bristol, with Bob Dwyer proving why he coached the Wallabies to World Cup success in 1991, were clear leaders of Premiership Two. The club's millionaire backer since the previous summer, Malcolm Pearce, feared a fresh restructuring of the top division, which might deny Bristol automatic promotion. In the brave new world of professional rugby there was nothing to stop one club buying another, and so Bristol announced a bid to buy up London Scottish, with a view to taking over its Premiership One status in the event of being denied promotion. The reaction of London Scottish fans and committee members was predictable, and in the event Bristol secured only a 24.9 per cent stake, which was available for purchase the moment a return to Premiership One rugby became a reality. London Scottish was rapidly losing control of its own destiny, and thus in no serious position to resist EFDR's efforts to merge it with Richmond and London Irish. All that remained was to reassure the latter's members that London Irish was the dominant partner, and that playing at the Stoop would not erode the club's identity and cohesion. Walkinshaw, Andrew, Barwell, and the nine other surviving Premiership bosses had what they wanted: a smaller number of top clubs sharing out the same tranche of television income.[54] The two weakest sides remaining in the top division in the summer of 1999, Bedford and Sale, must have been aware that, irrespective of their playing record, they were prime candidates to be the next sacrificial lambs if a British League failed to materialise and Premiership One was to become an ultra-elite championship, as envisaged by the most powerful members of EFDR.[55] Sure enough, in June 1999 Worcester's multimillionaire backer, Cecil Duckworth, sought to buy out Sale. Worcester, having invested heavily in first-class training and playing facilities, and yet still missing out on promotion, saw Bristol's earlier initiative as a precedent for buying a place in Premiership One (plus the contracts of Sale's top players). The Lancashire club's directors, desperate to avoid bankruptcy, were prepared to face the wrath of the fans and drop down a division. However, both the RFU and EFDR vetoed the proposal, ostensibly because Sale was not actually insolvent.[56] Nevertheless, by the summer of 1999 rugby union was, like rugby league, clearly following the path of American-style franchising. A club's league status could be surrendered if the price was right, and in the direst of circumstances its very identity could disappear: history and tradition counted for naught if the books did not balance.

A complicating factor in the future composition of Premiership One was whether Swansea and Cardiff would ultimately seek entry. They saw themselves having more in common with the big English clubs than with the traditional powerhouses of the Valleys, notably Llanelli and Pontypridd. With morale in Welsh rugby at an all-time low after the national team's dismal season in 1997–98, and with a serious slump in attendances at club matches, Swansea and Cardiff announced that they would be leaving the Premier Division in order to play friendlies against all the English Premiership One sides: their 1998–99 fixtures would be the prelude to future league competition, and would attract bigger crowds because the standard of play would be better.[57] English encouragement of the two rebel clubs was evident by the ease with which all 56 fixtures were finalised, and the election to EFDR's management board of Gareth Davies, Cardiff's chief executive. Davies argued that the two largest clubs in Wales were heading for bankruptcy if they accepted the status quo, but this viewpoint cut no ice with the rest of the Premier Division or the WRU. The 1998–99 season in Wales was marked by an astonishing series of writs and counter-writs between the WRU and each of the breakaway clubs. The WRU tried to use financial as well as political muscle by withholding revenue and imposing large fines. Peace broke out in May 1999, and common sense prevailed: Swansea and Cardiff returned to the Premier Division on the understanding that they could join the Allied Dunbar League in the autumn of 2000 if by then a British League had failed to materialise. The claim that the standard of Welsh rugby was too low had been undermined by Wales's recent much improved form, culminating in a momentous defeat of England (and later South Africa), and by Llanelli and Pontypridd demonstrating that they were every bit as good if not better than Swansea and Cardiff. With legal costs mounting to levels that neither side could afford the WRU agreed to compromise at an emergency meeting called while a resolute Vernon Pugh was absent chairing the International Rugby Board. Pugh, on his return, echoed the view of the Premier Division clubs that the WRU had surrendered, and promptly announced he would not be seeking re-election to its general committee.[58]

The row in Wales looked set to continue, but Pugh's opposition was wholly consistent with that adopted by the IB throughout the preceding six months. The Board had placed heavy pressure on the WRU to implement sanctions against Cardiff and Swansea, and in January 1999 fined the RFU for ignoring the Anglo-Welsh club fixtures by withholding £60,000 from a development grant. Less than a month later Twickenham was hit by a further fine of £80,000, of which £50,000 was suspended for two years provided that 'the RFU conducts itself in an open and honest manner with the IB'. In its turn, the IB questioned whether concessions made by the RFU to EFDR under the Mayfair Agreement were permissible under the Board's rules, but more crucially, it claimed to have been 'deliberately misled and misinformed' over the recent conduct of English clubs.[59] The Board's disciplinary committee found the RFU guilty of offering *de facto* support to EFDR in its complaint to the European Commission that IB regulations were anti-competitive and a restraint of trade. The top English clubs still insisted that the IB was illegally restricting their commercial and marketing rights, and the European Commission privately signalled its support for their case. If EFDR's complaint was upheld in the European Court then the IB's Regulation 8, compelling clubs to release players for international duty in any circumstances, would have to be rewritten, given that in England the RFU had conceded the clubs' primacy of contract over players. Not only that, but under the terms of the Mayfair Agreement the RFU had agreed to pay clubs in lieu of a player's services.

Once the RFU had chosen to follow the Brian Blaister line of partnership with the clubs, rather than the Cliff Brittle/Fran Cotton alternative of confrontation, a clash with the IB was highly likely. Southern hemisphere members, committed to the Super 12 and national squad contracts, found it hard to understand why the top English clubs were so powerful as to force the RFU into a policy of pragmatism rather than coercion. The RFU, pointing out privately that none of the IB's disciplinary committee knew anything about European Union commercial and employment law, saw the Board as belatedly seeking to shore up its authority after decades of apparent indifference to 'shamateurism' in France and the Tri-nations.[60]

The undermining of regulatory bodies in the name of the free market is, of course, a consequence of global capitalism, with governments often complicit in destroying the authority of well-established, historically very powerful institutions. Thus, in January 1999 the Office of Fair Trading launched a legal challenge to the Premier League's right to negotiate television deals on behalf of all 20 clubs, arguing that this constituted a cartel. Ironically, at the same time those same 20 clubs were questioning the Football Association's composition, and even its right to remain the game's disciplinary and administrative body.[61] The big clubs' earlier bruising encounter with UEFA had seen the former European Cup transformed into the European Champions League in order to generate more income and spread it more widely. Professional rugby in England saw the aims, ambitions and profit-driven negotiating methods of the Premier League as pioneering an equally tough and uncompromising stance when dealing with a hostile IB and phlegmatic RFU.

A further incentive for EFDR to cut the size of Premiership One, while cultivating Cardiff and Swansea, was the prospect of a British League capable of attracting that elusive combination of big gates and generous television and sponsorship deals. Although the home unions (excluding Ireland) were keen to demonstrate serious intent, seeing such an initiative as a means of breaking the impasse over Europe, predictably it was EFDR that made the running.[62] To be more accurate, it was the bigger, more ambitious clubs which promoted an ultra-exclusive superleague – if necessary without the RFU's endorsement, and *ipso facto* the IB's approval. The home unions assumed that a British League would be precisely that, but EFDR saw it as the top English clubs plus the rebel Welsh sides. When the home unions' working party proposed in December 1998 two conferences – a powerful English-dominated East Division and a much weaker motley collection of clubs in the West Division – the idea was rejected. Of course it was not EFDR which turned down this American-style structure as the top ten English clubs were all in the elite East Division, with the weakest sides (including the two Exiles teams) shoehorned into the 'Celtic ghetto division'.[63] The proposal was so outrageous that it attracted widespread disapproval, and the credibility of the working party was further undermined when the RFU withdrew in protest at the IB's £100,000 fine for not taking action over the Anglo-Welsh friendlies.

The idea of a British League would not go away. The return of the two rebel clubs to the WRU fold, the restructuring of Scottish rugby so that Edinburgh Reivers and Glasgow Caledonian were genuine superclubs fielding the cream of the national squad, and the informal talks that continued against the backdrop of an unusually exciting Five Nations Championship, all suggested that a tri-nation league would ultimately arrive.[64] In the meantime the absence in 1998–99 of the English clubs, and the consequent withdrawal of Heineken's sponsorship, highlighted the need for the European Cup to be placed on a fresh footing – free of EFDR charges that its management was a 'Celtic cabal'. By early 1999, despite newspaper reports of big offers to southern hemisphere superstars not to return home after the World Cup, the cash woes of even the most stable and secure Premiership One sides were crystal clear.[65] The bait to entice the EFDR back into negotiations over Europe was a three-year £10 million deal with the management and marketing company, ISL. The new sponsor was only interested in a European Cup boasting the top Premiership sides, and by March 1999 ISL had got what it wanted: the top six at the end of the season would compete with their French counterparts and with 12 clubs from the rest of the now Six Nations. Each competing side would receive £750,000, and each of the remaining Premiership One clubs would bank half that sum – surely ample reward for agreeing to drop EFDR's submission to the European Commission. This was an astonishing climbdown by rugby's ruling bodies, even if the RFU had implicitly acknowledged the bargaining power of the top English clubs when signing the Mayfair Agreement the previous year. Yet still some owners, managers, and coaches were unhappy, pointing out that a top international in a successful club might be playing over 40 major games between the onset of the World Cup in October 1999 and the end of the season eight months later. Physically and mentally even the toughest, fittest, and most resilient professional would be drained by the time preparation began in June 2000 for a tour of Australia.[66]

Continued Celtic Tensions, 1999

Such was the price of success, with the 1999 World Cup highlighting the financial gulf between the stars and the journeymen of professional rugby. The latter spent the preceding summer renegotiating contracts with chief executives determined to slash salaries. Many found themselves seeking fresh employment, as their former squad had either been reduced to the bare minimum or – in the case of Richmond and London Scottish – wiped out altogether. In contrast, the England squad, in addition to regular club and country contracts, stood to earn £32,000 each, progressing to £90,000 if they actually won the World Cup. This might be twice what an England cricketer would have earned had his team actually made the Super Six and proceeded to victory at Lords in June 1999, but in footballing terms it was modest: in 1997–98 the average wage of the top Premier League players was £190,000. Before his resignation as England captain in the spring of 1999 it was estimated that Lawrence Dallaglio had earned around £275,000 over the preceding 12 months. Yet his counterpart in football, Alan Shearer, took home £2.8 million. Shearer was the eleventh wealthiest sportsman in the UK, and Dallaglio the hundredth, despite being the best paid rugby player.[67]

Assuming that he could survive drug allegations and continue to play for England, Dallaglio would remain a – perhaps *the* – major earner in English rugby, matched only by big names from the southern hemisphere enjoying lucrative short-term contracts in the wake of the World Cup. The trend to recruit foreign stars, and thus attract an AB market prepared to pay £20 for a stand seat (and up to £3 for a programme), meant a further squeeze on home-grown players. Not only would the opportunity to play first-team rugby be reduced, so too

171

would the financial reward. In the summer of 1999 those players not released from their contracts by cash-strapped clubs were often forced to go semi-professional, boosting their part-time salaries with win bonuses and first team appearance money. For such players absurdly inflated salaries of £50,000–£80,000 were a thing of the past. Clubs had to renegotiate the contracts of their stalwarts in order to fund the stars, especially after EFDR agreed in March 1999 to follow the example of rugby league and introduce a salary ceiling: stung into action by Richmond going into receivership, the Premiership sides agreed to keep their wage bills between £1 million and £1.5 million. The credibility of the agreement was almost immediately undermined by Northampton and Leicester publicly expressing dissent. The players' agents and the Professional Rugby Players Association all rejected the salary cap, the latter ironically charging EFDR with a 'restraint of trade' under EU law.[68] Certainly the aggressive recruitment of a revived and ambitious Bristol in the summer of 1999 suggested that the ceiling would be ignored by a club proprietor and benefactor intent on spending his way to the top: the team's journeymen would have to accept drastic wage cuts if a gross outlay of £1.5 million was to accommodate the arrival of world stars such as South African fly-half Henry Honiball.[69] On the other hand, cup-holders Wasps proved quite ruthless in their efforts to save £400,000, releasing recent or current internationals such as Canada captain Gareth Rees. Wasps were by no means unique in bidding farewell to the fans' favourites in order to appease the bank.

Clubs' treatment of individual players was too often demeaning, but this merely contributed to the appalling image professional rugby had acquired after four years of incessant squabbling and near universal malevolence. The game had a remarkable capacity for shooting itself in the foot, witness the Five Nations contriving to repeat the fiasco of 1996: early in 1999 England was again suspended from the tournament over its reluctance to begin transferring the approximate £30 million which over a five-year period would compensate Ireland, Scotland, and Wales for the RFU's separate deal with BSkyB. Twickenham was accused of ignoring the independent valuer, and not formally recognising the accord reached in September 1996. The RFU countered by arguing that they could not offer unconditional recognition, particularly as more needed to be known about France's position, and more crucially, how Italy stood to gain once the Six

Nations Championship commenced in 1999–2000. If it was tragic that England was thrown out of the Five Nations in July 1996 then it was truly farcical that history repeated itself in January 1999.

It was obvious that both sides would have to compromise given that the loss of revenue would be so enormous. The RFU stood to lose somewhere between £10 and £15 million if England's home games with Scotland and France were cancelled, while compensatory fixtures, with Italy replacing England, were unlikely to attract large crowds – and in the case of Wales, playing 'home' games at Wembley was likely to leave the WRU with a loss on the hire of the stadium. But what almost certainly brought both sides to their senses was the insistence by Lloyds TSB in its capacity as tournament sponsor that no England meant no money. Such a threat had even greater resonance given the bank's status as principal sponsor of the 1999 World Cup. With the WRU sweating over completion of the Millennium Stadium, and the Scottish Rugby Union wracked by internal feuds and a general malaise in the game that too often left Murrayfield half full, the Celtic nations were in no position to ignore the Lloyds TSB warning. Neither could England afford to antagonise BSkyB. A vague compromise was finally agreed, and England was readmitted to the competition, yet the RFU remained bullish in its insistence that the independent valuer would conclude no money need be paid into the common revenue pool that formed the heart of the Five Nations' accord.

The RFU expected to contribute nothing because it anticipated a loss in 1998–99 of around £2.3 million, having lost £10.3 million in the previous two years. It calculated that since the onset of professionalism in 1995 costs had risen by over 300 per cent. Twickenham's new chief executive officer, Francis Bacon, was scathing about the absence of even the most basic standard business practices.[70] The scale of the RFU's losses, and the complete absence of effective corporate management, confirmed the survival of amateurism of the very worst kind at the highest level of the English game. It placed the owners and executives of EFDR in a more flattering light, generating sympathy for their complaint that they had consistently had to battle with an unbusinesslike culture within the RFU.[71]

In many respects the 1999 Five Nations Championship reinforced the 'old guard' charge that change was occurring too fast and was not always necessary. Scotland's recovery from pre-Christmas mediocrity to win the tournament in style, France's disappointing performance,

173

and Wales's heroic defeat of England, demolished the argument that the Celtic nations were no longer adequate competition for the big two. True, the Celtic revival did augur well for the World Cup, particularly when Wales went on to beat the Springboks, but the quality of rugby was directly attributable to the infusion of coaching and playing talent from the south Pacific, and the unprecedented standards of fitness and technique that only a professional game can deliver (with, again, none fitter and more skilful than the former rugby league players). The technical support for each national squad was so large and sophisticated because of the lessons learnt from the southern hemisphere, especially New Zealand, plus the readiness to introduce ideas and expertise directly from rugby league. The England squad boasted an ex-Great Britain RL coach, but Clive Woodward's uneasy relationship with the clubs was highlighted by a renewed complaint that 'we're not playing on a level playing field':

> The southern hemisphere is totally different. Because the players are contracted to the Union everything is totally under control. They play less games yet play together more.[72]

Conclusion – The Brave New World

What is the future of rugby union in England as a professional sport? In early 1998 the general consensus among coaches, administrators, and commentators was that the game could only support a very small number of genuinely professional, commercially viable clubs, a view confirmed 12 months later.[73] EFDR knew that only an elite could generate sufficient income from attendance, merchandise, sponsorship and broadcasting to sustain commercial viability. Periodic cash injections might come via modest share flotations and the cautious investment of a second generation of corporate or individual proprietors. A crucial factor, at least in theory, would be sensible wages and realistic transfer fees. The EFDR salary ceiling indicated a belief that the top clubs just might secure a fragile stability if big salaries were reserved for the select few who were genuine crowd-pullers: players should earn what the market justified, and this required universal recognition that throughout the British Isles rugby union is not a mass spectator sport comparable to football, or to rugby league in the north of England. The summer of 1998 marked the beginning of the second phase of professionalism, with most Premiership Two – and a year later many Premiership One – club players retained and paid on a part-time basis. In future rugby's journeymen will complement their income from the game with related work elsewhere in the area of leisure and recreation, or through a wholly unrelated activity. In this respect their lifestyles will be comparable to that of a 'non-league' footballer, or ironically, a rugby league player outside the Super League.[74]

Even the wealthiest, most generous and most committed of benefactors will stop subsidising their clubs if forever faced with a deadly combination of high wages and low attendance. In Premiership Two the summer of 1998 saw a degree of reality return to rugby, albeit at a cost. The financial collapse of most second division clubs confirmed that unit costs had to be slashed, and that this meant the end of their two-year adventure as fully professional organisations. In Premiership One the winter of 1998 saw a haemorrhage of high profile proprietors. Newcastle and even Bedford secured new owners; yet Richmond's unhappy experience highlighted how much professional rugby risks future entrepreneurs eschewing low-return investments, and potential sponsors deterred by poor gates and static television audiences. The new big-spenders, Bristol and Worcester, wanted to buy their way into Premiership One because their multimillionaire owners recognised that it would soon be too late: EFDR will become a self-perpetuating elite, enjoying a near monopoly of major sponsorship and the bulk of TV revenue. EFDR already determines the rules for Premiership One, thereby ensuring the top clubs' exclusivity; it is again a major presence in European competition; and it enjoys a de facto veto on any future British League. Even within EFDR there is clearly a pecking order, with success on and off the pitch determining who will survive. The super-elite will no doubt keep a firm grip on domestic and even European trophies by virtue of their full-time players' superior fitness, skills and tactics, let alone the talent of their high-profile internationals.

Most clubs not able to buy – and sustain – success have climbed a steep learning curve since that first euphoric embrace of professionalism. Relaunched as fresh business organisations, clubs such as Sale have had to reconcile a company structure appropriate only to the professional elite with the old voluntarist committee-based system, albeit free of the worst facets of pre-1995 amateurism. Once-great clubs like Coventry need to forget past triumphs, swallow their pride, and accept exclusion from the highest echelons of English rugby. A permanent second division would include the old guard, but also those up and coming clubs that in recent years have provided the most sensible model for professional or semi-professional rugby, most notably Worcester.[75]

Middle ranking clubs like Coventry have had to downsize, restructure, and learn from younger clubs that have achieved recent success through a contribution of initiative, imagination and caution. Mergers are only possible within the same conurbation and then deep-rooted rivalry and suspicion have to be overcome, the antipathy between Bristol and Bath being an obvious example. The potential for cross-sport ground-sharing is limited in that the Saracens/Watford and Richmond/Reading initiatives do not seem to have triggered interest among other football or rugby league sides, not least because the Majedski Stadium experiment proved so disastrous.[76] Neither has any football team followed Chris Wright's QPR/Wasps experience and sought to take over a neighbouring, cash-strapped rugby club. Thus, Coventry City showed no interest in a minimal outlay to secure full control of Coventry RFC when it folded, with the idea of a rugby alternative at the planned multi-purpose Arena 2000.[77] In this case an alternative strategy was available: the ex-players consortium which rescued the Coventry club from bankruptcy entered into partnership with the local authority and FE college in modernising and adapting an obsolete athletics stadium. Any attempt to maximise stadium usage has to come from rugby union itself, and usually from EFDR clubs not distracted by the need to seek immediate as opposed to longer-term survival. Thus, while talk of a single code is usually speculated upon by business analysts ignorant of the fact that rugby league and rugby union have evolved since 1895 as two very different sports, the exchange of players since 1995 has hastened a remarkable change of attitude on both sides. Cardiff RFC's aggressive 1998 campaign to secure a Super League franchise, Harlequins' lease of their ground to London Broncos, and the much published crowd-pulling encounters between Bath and Wigan in May 1996, all signalled the commercial potential of collaboration – but with no hidden agenda to move towards fusion.

Despite evidence that senior sides may become more like US-style franchises, clubs still recognise the need to be firmly rooted in their local communities, especially outside London. Richmond's failure to sell rugby to Reading suggests Saracens' success in Watford is an exception to the rule. Not only does long association with a particular area guarantee a hard core of supporters and club members loyal through thick and thin, but it also ensures a ready supply of new talent from feeder schools and junior clubs. The influx of overseas players has, at the highest levels, ensured excitement and direct acquaintance with skills and flair rarely witnessed outside international fixtures. However, open rugby has also brought into the English game too many over-rated and over-paid overseas or ex-league players, with even the most successful sides making mistakes. The professional game can only survive if the majority of players are English and home-grown: the clubs benefit from bringing on young players who are reluctant to move on (particularly if the lure of big wages is no longer present), and the national side benefits from a much larger pool of English players experiencing regular first team rugby at the very highest level. The Mayfair Agreement and the removal of Cliff Brittle as chairman of the RFU Management Board went a long way to destroying the unreal proposition that 'Club England' could enhance the fortunes of the national team by isolating the senior clubs and dealing directly with the players. The forward-looking element within the RFU conceded that the greedy ploy of maximising the number of international fixtures, at home and on tour, had damaged all parties, not least the reputation of English rugby within the IB. At the same time the EFDR clubs for the moment conceded that unilateral action was unjustifiable if in the process it crippled England's preparations for the 1999 World Cup, and perhaps most crucially of all, it antagonised the clubs' principal paymaster, BSkyB.

If the price of a new tournament in Europe was to alienate the monopoly satellite broadcaster then naturally a more softly, softly approach was required. British or pan-European rugby is not a panacea but clearly top teams, especially those with multinational sponsors such as 'NEC Harlequins', need to be on television regularly in order to retain their credibility as marketable assets. (What applies to the clubs is equally relevant to the players themselves as they seek to compensate for reduced earnings on the field by becoming involved in promotional and PR activities where the traditional prosperous image of English rugby may prove an advantage over football or rugby league. Where Will Carling and Jeremy Guscott led the way from the late 1980s, the first generation of genuine professionals now follows.)[78]

It would not be an exaggeration to say that to study the impact of professionalism on rugby union is to trace the ever-changing relationship between Twickenham and television from that fateful decision in 1973 to install perimeter adverts which not even the most adroit *Grandstand* cameraman could avoid. The achievement of terrestrial television in retaining rights to the first three World Cups – and in consequence confirming the success of Carling's Grand Slam sides in significantly raising the profile of rugby union within the most densely populated parts of the UK – delayed the full, global impact of Rupert Murdoch on union as well as league. However, satellite television was already cultivating the senior clubs, rendering them more and more dependent on Sky Sports' largesse even while they were still technically amateur. The 1996 decision of the RFU's modernisers to sell sole rights to BSkyB destroyed forever the unique character of the Five Nations.[79] It also left the senior clubs even more dependent upon News Corporation goodwill. In this respect rugby union is no different from league, except that the latter's clubs earn a lot more and, for all the headline-grabbing transfers, and big new stadiums, spend less.[80]

It is a bizarre thought that the three million satellite subscribers to Sky Sports are contributing more financially to English rugby than the sum total of the game's supporters and club members up and down the country. BSkyB's £87.5 million, plus the array of sponsorship deals negotiated by the RFU, make Twickenham's operating losses in the late 1990s appear an even greater indictment of its former management structure than its inept handling of relations with just about every other rugby union from Cardiff to Cape Town. The danger is that the RFU, with huge interest payments and its stadium's equally huge operating costs, has become dangerously dependent on external revenue – and indifferent to the needs and concerns of a market which is large and loyal but which can not be taken for granted. Given that the number of people prepared to pay to go and watch rugby union is far smaller than the potential audience for league football, and shows few signs of significant growth, a cavalier approach to pricing could result in a significant drop in gate revenue. A dismal turnout for England playing the likes of Italy and Argentina, and poor attendance at the 1999 Tetley's Bitter Cup Final, signals a pricing policy based on greed and/or indifference rather than an astute judgement of what potential spectators are prepared to pay.[81] One sign of the RFU accepting that it has moved too far ahead of English rugby's core support was an admission in June 1999 that terrestrial television still has an important role to play, particularly if the BBC is prepared to regain lost ground, and ITV can capitalise upon retaining exclusive coverage of the fourth World Cup.[82] The grassroots – and the other home unions – could be appeased by the RFU sometime in 2000 negotiating a series of separate deals to succeed Sky's exclusive rights. Digital technology would facilitate a mixture of terrestrial, satellite and cable provision, with each competition open to auction. The logical outcome of such a scenario is BSkyB losing its monopoly, just as it needs to see off new rivals such as ONdigital and to consolidate its share of the pay-per-view market.[83] In both hemispheres in the mid-1990s News Corp/BSkyB was the motor of revolution, providing fresh momentum as rugby union crawled painfully towards an open game. Yet, at the dawn of a new century, it appears that in England at least, the governing body is trying to square the circle by appeasing the traditionalists, while at the same time exploiting the new technology so as to maximise TV revenue. Clearly Twickenham will feel no guilt in emerging out of the shadow of Rupert Murdoch.

Those who lament the passing of rugby union as a quintessentially amateur game no doubt regard television as a corrupting influence, particularly when the corrupter is Middle England's demon Antipodean. The interdependence of satellite television and senior rugby, and the no-holds-barred efforts of Cliff Brittle and his supporters in the shires to disrupt this delicate but nevertheless crucial relationship, undoubtedly did temper the enthusiasm, relief and optimism generated by the onset of open rugby and the demise of 'shamateurism'. However, concern that the RFU and all the other ruling bodies had sold their souls to Rupert Murdoch obscured the fact that well over 95 per cent of clubs in the British Isles remain wholly amateur. Rugby union is an *open* game and not a professional sport: so too, for that matter, is rugby league. An over-precious attitude to the impact of money in rugby union further obscured the fact that the standard of senior rugby in England improved dramatically, and that this impacted upon the national side, and most clearly of all upon the 1997 Lions. The latter were successful because of: the players enjoying a level of fitness built up over a season of full-time training with no distractions; an infusion of handling skills and attitude previously unique to rugby league (which the prodigal sons brought back with them); and a fluency, adventure and flexibility previously seen as the preserve of the southern hemisphere, France on a dry day in the Parc des Princes, and the 1973 Barbarians. Not every major club match in the 1996–97, the 1997–98, or even the 1998–99 season, displayed all, or even some of these qualities, but there was no doubt that standards were rising and attitudes changing. It was sad in 1998 to see Sky Sports schedules transforming the Barbarians' annual and much-loved New Year visit to Welford Road into a B-team fixture on a wet weekday evening in February, but is this a price worth paying when Leicester backs run in a succession of sparkling tries instead of relying on the pack to grind out another low-scoring result?[84] Reluctantly, the answer may be yes. Yet an acceptance that neither the top clubs nor the RFU could shy away from supping with the devil, however damaging the consequences in terms of internal harmony, must be tempered by acknowledgement that over-commercialisation can damage a sport fundamentally and irreversibly. In a sensitive and perceptive essay written on the eve of the game going open, Mark Bailey warned of the pursuit of success over-riding all other considerations. He feared a maldistribution of financial reward dividing the haves from the have-nots, and an excessive dependence upon sponsorship and broadcasting leaving the sport dangerously vulnerable to manipulation and repackaging. Bailey did not regret the arrival of professionalism, but he did fear that rugby might prove incapable of controlling rampant commercialism:

> Excessive commercialism knows the price of everything and the value of nothing, and will destroy rugby's special qualities. The danger for any sport comes when the influence of commercial forces reaches a critical mass, and rugby union is fast approaching that point.[85]

An older generation, deprived of their Barbarians New Year fixture and *Grandstand* at Twickenham, doubtless felt that rugby had already reached Bailey's point of critical mass. Younger enthusiasts, no doubt similarly battered and perhaps even embittered by England's four years of civil war, nevertheless still believed total surrender to the totems of global capitalism to be avoidable: that the benefits of a genuinely open sport more than outweighed the departure of traditions and practices forged in the late Victorian era, but ill-suited to the continued development of the modern game.

The Impact of Professionalism on Rugby Union, 1995–99

ACKNOWLEDGEMENTS

My thanks to Ian Malin (*The Guardian*) and Huw Richards (*Financial Times*) for their help, and indirectly to Donald McRae for writing a brilliant book on contemporary rugby.

NOTES

1. Ian Malin, *Mud, Blood and Money: English Rugby Union Goes Professional* (Edinburgh: Mainstream Publishing, 1997), pp.36–7. On the events described in this article, see Donald McRae, *Winter Colours: Changing Seasons in World Rugby* (Edinburgh: Mainstream Publishing, 1998), pp.62–3, 96–8, 326–37.

2. Martin Polley, *Moving the Goalposts: A History of Sport and Society Since 1945* (London: Routledge, 1998), p.69; Gareth Williams, 'Rugby Union', in Tony Mason (ed.), *Sport in Britain A Social History* (Cambridge: Cambridge University Press, 1989), p.333; Malin, *Mud, Blood and Money*, p.76. On sponsorship of the home-based 1991 World Cup, a key stage on the RFU's learning curve, see Derek Wyatt, *Rugby Disunion: The Making of the Three World Cups* (London: Victor Gollancz, 1995), pp.71–6.

3. Williams, 'Rugby Union', pp.333, 332.

4. Gareth (Edwards), JPR and JJ (Williams) were a marketing dream in being known (often beyond the normal rugby audience) in both hemispheres solely by their Christian name or initials.

5. Wyatt, *Rugby Disunion,* pp.73, 91.

6. The RFU, however, chose to ignore the remarkably generous terms on which British Gas employed Jeremy Guscott, and National Power Ben Clarke.

7. 'Thank God we weren't playing the whole of Samoa' – ex-player Gareth Davies at full-time. A *Business Age* survey in 1993 calculated Jonathan Davies's annual income at £240,000, although English rugby's best-known 'defector', Martin Offiah, was being paid £435,000 by Wigan, *the* dominant force in rugby league in the 1990s. Proportionately fewer English than Welsh players were recruited by rugby league scouts, as a common assumption (rooted in class?) was that they could not easily adjust to a radically different game. Thus the English RFU, with its much larger pool of senior players to draw upon, was more relaxed than its Welsh counterpart. Ironically, Offiah's immense talent was never recognised when he played union, an oversight some critics have linked to his being black. *Business Age* also calculated that the 'amateur' Will Carling was already worth £1.3 million via his Insight management training company. *Business Age* survey quoted in Geoffrey Moorhouse, *A People's Game: The Official History of Rugby League*, second edition (London: Hodder & Stoughton, 1996), p.338.

8. Scott Gibbs [left Swansea for St Helens] quoted in John Duncan and Ian Malin, 'Kicked into touch', *The Guardian*, 25 May 1995.

9. Will Carling quote, and estimate of England players' income from the second World Cup (in 1995 the RFU secured £6 million shirt sponsorship from Cell-net, of which up to £50,000 could go each year to a contracted England player), in Duncan and Malin, 'Kicked into touch'.

10. Malin, *Mud, Blood and Money*, pp.127–8.

11. Wyatt, *Rugby Disunion,* pp.106–9.

12. Wyatt, *Rugby Disunion,* pp.104–7.

13. Duncan and Malin, 'Kicked into touch'; Wyatt, *Rugby Disunion,* pp.110–11.

14. Moorhouse, *People's Game*, pp.345–6.

15. Moorhouse, *People's Game,* pp.345–6; Duncan and Malin, 'Kicked into touch'.

16. Statement of International Rugby Football Board, 27 Aug. 1995.

17. Hallett quoted in Robert Armstrong, 'Amateurism ditched in pay go-ahead', *The Guardian*, 28 Aug. 1995.

18. Dick Tugwell, *Champions in Conflict: The Bath Rugby Revolution* (London: Robson Books, 1998), p.16.

19. Garry Whannel quoted in Polley, *Moving the Goalposts*, p.67. Rupert Murdoch informed News Corp's 1996 AGM that sport 'absolutely overpowers' all other forms of entertainment in attracting satellite TV viewers, providing a 'battering ram and a lead offering in all our pay television operations'; quoted in Stuart Millar, 'Courtship ends as soccer and TV are united', *The Guardian*, 7 Sept.1998.

20. Wyatt, *Rugby Disunion,* pp.70–3, 128, 147–9. When Rob Andrew's last minute drop goal gave England a 25–22 quarter-final victory over Australia, ITV secured its best ever lunchtime viewing figure for a lunchtime sports fixture (8.3 million). Advertising rates were proportionately higher as the assumption is rugby union attracts a disproportionate number of ABC1 viewers; Wyatt, *Rugby Disunion,* p.148.

21. Wyatt, *Rugby Disunion,* pp.183–4. On history and impact of Super 12 (5 NZ, 4 SA, 3 Australian teams), see Garry Ferris, 'Super men lie in wait', *The Guardian*, 29 May 1998. For a comparison between English club rugby and the Super 12, see McRae, *Winter Colours*, pp.82–3, 326–9.

22. On *Rugby Special*, see Malin, *Mud, Blood and Money*, pp.107–9. Sky Sports audience levels for Saturday afternoon rugby rose from approximately 100,000 to 450,000 during the 1996–97 season, with a claim that in total nearly 5.5 million residential viewers (i.e. not in pubs and clubs) watched during 1997–98. Figures quoted in Malin, *Mud, Blood and Money*, p.111 and in Paul Morgan, 'Record rugby crowds', *Rugby World*, Aug. 1998, p.32.

23. Stuart Barnes, *Rugby's New Age Travellers* (Edinburgh: Mainstream Publishing, 1997), pp.1, 14; Malin, *Mud, Blood and Money*, pp.110–11. The BBC was expected to buy the right to broadcast England's home games 'as live' two hours after kick-off. In the event *Grandstand* continued to cover the other Five Nations matches and ITV recruited Will Carling to introduce what proved to be extended highlights.

24. The success in South Africa of the 1997 Lions silenced those insistent that tours were outmoded; and England's poor performance in the southern hemisphere a year later tempered the Tri-nations' enthusiasm for more frequent encounters with at least one of the two dominant sides in the Five Nations.

25. Carling was temporarily stripped of the England captaincy in May 1995 for describing the RFU as a 'bunch of old farts'. For a roguishly partisan insider's account of the dispute, see Barnes, *New Age Travellers*, pp.1–26.

26. Brittle quoted in Malin, *Mud, Blood and Money*, p.110; Barnes, *New Age Travellers*, pp.25–6. Brittle's complaint of being repeatedly sidelined was to some extent justified, as technically he was the most senior administrator within the RFU's management structure.

27. Brittle's most powerful allies inside and outside the RFU's labyrinthine management structure were the widely-respected 1980 Grand Slam captain and television personality Bill Beaumont, and the victorious 1997 Lions manager, Fran Cotton. By

1998 the pro-Brittle faction within the RFU was organised nationally as the Reform Group.

28. In 1997–98 England played an absurd 13 tests in 10 months, fuelling concern that the demands of the modern game will bring early 'burn out', notwithstanding the much higher fitness levels enjoyed by full-time professionals.

29. Malin, *Mud, Blood and Money*, p.34. Private information. Rugby attracted successful businessmen in other sports: Gloucester's Tom Watkinshaw (F1 motor racing – Arrows team owner), Bedford's Frank Warren (boxing promoter) and Wasps' Chris Wright (football – Queens Park Rangers chief shareholder).

30. Bath's adoption of a fresh corporate image and an aggressive marketing strategy while the team was failing to match its ambitious and impatient new owner's high expectations made compulsive viewing in a 6-part fly-on-the-wall BBC1 documentary series early in 1998. Bath desperately sought to remain a 'family club' while absorbing the managerialism of greetings card entrepreneur Andrew Brownsword. For an even more revealing account of Bath's 1996–97 travails, by the club's former fly-half, see Barnes, *New Age Travellers*, pp.59–100, and most especially Dick Tugwell's *Champions In Conflict*.

31. To ensure Wasps won the 1996–97 championship Dallaglio played every late-season fixture, and then toured with the Lions. A year later he courted controversy by refusing to captain England on tour in order to recover fully from injury in time for Wasps' first match of the 1997–98 season. Barnes, *New Age Travellers*, p.134; Ian Stafford, 'The Nightmare Is Over – Interview With Lawrence Dallaglio', *Rugby World*, Aug. 1998, pp.39–45. On the relationship between the professional player and his club see also Lawrence Dallaglio, *Dallaglio On Rugby* (London: Hodder & Stoughton, 1998).

32. Malin, *Mud, Blood and Money*, pp.29, 112. EPRUC's withdrawal of players from the North versus All Black Barbarians (i.e. New Zealand) was a mortal blow to divisional fixtures but a PR disaster for the top clubs.

33. In one month a seriously under-strength England lost all seven games in Australia, New Zealand, and South Africa, including four tests: 88 points were scored for and a staggering 328 against. On 6 June 1998 in Brisbane the Wallabies won 76–0, a defining moment in English rugby. The host nations protested over an absurdly tight schedule and the absence of RFU sanctions against the 15 non-touring current internationals. Thus the NZRU chief executive insisted that, 'We're talking about a world game, where the revenue driver is international-driven and not club rugby in England.'

34. English First Division Rugby Ltd., 'English Rugby Charter', in *Allied Dunbar Premiership Weekly Update*, I (14–15 Mar. 1998), p.17.

35. For Fran Cotton's increasingly unreal perception on the English game nearly a year later, see interview with David Irvine in Robert Kitson and Ian Malin, 'Sweating on the future of the game they love', *The Guardian*, 22 Mar. 1999.

36. The IB threatened to expel the RFU if it could not stop the clubs from complaining to the European Commission about the Board's rules, particularly relating to broadcasting rights. A limit of 37 club and international appearances in any one season was agreed, the next Lions tour postponed a year until 2001, and the Six Nations (Italy included from 2000) shifted to the end of the season. Club fixtures would henceforth be played on international weekends, creating possible future conflict. The latter was confirmed as early as November 1998 when Bath and other

championship contenders lost matches because their best players were involved in World Cup qualifying matches against Holland and Italy. Robert Armstrong, 'Clubs shut the door on Europe', *The Guardian*, 9 May 1998.

37. Baister beat Brittle by 520 to 345 votes. Ian Malin contrasted the euphoric atmosphere at the 1997 RFU AGM following the Lions' triumph over the Springboks with that of a year later when all four home unions had sent weakened sides to be comprehensively beaten in the southern hemisphere: in 1997 Brittle was easily re-elected, and in 1998 a clear majority knew he had to go. See Ian Malin, 'Clubs in a cash ruck', *The Guardian*, 23 July 1998. Blaister was no poodle, pointing out that 'The clubs are being assisted by the union to the tune of £1.5 million a year. Therefore, the sooner we recognise that they need to look after their own competitions, sponsorship, and the like, the sooner the money can be redirected to the grass roots.' Quoted in Chris Hewett, 'Baister ready to step into the line of fire', *The Independent*, 18 July 1998. In 1996–97 the then Courage Division One clubs had made a total operating loss of £15 million. Blaister signalled at the outset his willingness to join EFDR in creating a new, commercially viable European Competition. See Robert Kitson, 'Between a ruck and a hard place', *The Guardian*, 25 July 1998.

38. 'If they are losing you feel as if you are losing too. We [NEC] will monitor the relationship and re-evaluate if Quins continue to do badly,' Taka Furuhashi, NEC's Senior UK Promotions Executive, quoted in Paul Charles, 'The price of peace', *The Guardian*, 1 May 1998.

39. On Bath's financial problems and the need to expand or replace the Recreation Ground, see Tugwell, pp.129–30, 195–6, 263.

40. 'Attendance figures for Allied Dunbar matches 1997–98', *Rugby World*, Aug. 1998, p.32. Loftus Road's ground capacity is 19,000.

41. 'Attendance figures for Allied Dunbar matches 1997–98', p.32. Vicarage Road's capacity is 22,000. Saracens' home fixture with Newcastle attracted 19,764, over 1000 more than Nationwide Division 1 Watford's biggest attendance in 1997–98. Sunday rugby meant junior players could still see Saracens play. Ian Malin, 'Saracens winning their crusade', *The Guardian*, 9 May 1998; 'Pienaar', *Rugby World*, Sept.1997, pp.26–33.

42. For the wide range of marketing ploys used by other Premiership One clubs during the 1998–99 season, see Pete Nichols, 'Counter culture: your rugby club needs you', *The Guardian*, 7 Nov. 1998.

43. 'Attendance figures for Allied Dunbar matches 1997–98', p.32. Adult tickets were in the £14–20 price range, itself a disincentive given a traditional assumption that rugby union is cheaper to watch compared with professional football.

44. Malin, 'Clubs in a cash ruck'. Further pressure was placed on the Heineken European Cup's organisers when France's top nine clubs withdrew, rejecting the French Rugby federation's plans for an expanded national championship. They wanted to join EFDR in marketing a more lucrative pan-European competition.

45. Of the six players who had switched codes and in 1996–97 returned to rugby union in time to tour with the Lions the following summer, only three were playing for top clubs (and Wales) one year later. The mixed fortunes of rugby league stars playing rugby union for the first time (great ball skills, and often unstoppable in attack, but poor in cover defence) did not deter ambitious northern clubs such as Leeds.

46. Cardiff and Swansea originally sought entry to the Allied Dunbar Premiership, but their plans were thwarted by the Mayfair Agreement. Cardiff's outgoings of £2.5

million in 1997–98 gave an insight into the even greater costs incurred by comparable English clubs. The WRU concluded Llanelli was too great a totem of Welsh rugby to go bankrupt, but Neath was allowed to fold in July 1998.

47. Peter Bills, 'Players pay price as family silver sold off', *Sunday Times*, 15 Mar. 1998; Ian Malin, 'Moseley left on rugby's back burner', *The Guardian*, 14 Mar. 1998; 'Club Guide – Midlands', *Rugby World*, June 1997, p.92. Even Orrell, famous for preserving the amateur ethos and family image of club rugby in the shadow of rugby league's all-conquering Wigan Warriors – and for a decade of humbling fashionable clubs before relegation to Premiership 2 in 1997 – found itself in deep trouble 12 months later. For a profile of Orrell, the 'lay-by off the M6' (one defeated Harlequins captain's description), see Malin, *Mud, Blood and Money*, pp.166–7.

48. See Adrian Smith, 'An Oval Ball and a Broken City: Coventry, Its People and its Rugby Team, Part 2, 1995–98', *International Journal of the History of Sport*, Vol.16, No.3 (1999) pp.155–68.

49. 'The decline and fall of once ship-shape Bristol is a sorry saga of arrogance, self-delusion and unerring foot-shooting'. Frank Keating, 'From local gods to downright clods', *The Guardian*, 23 May 1998.

50. Businessman Paul Mackings' decision to invest in Newcastle was at the expense of previous support for West Hartlepool, ever the poor relation. See Michael Prestage, 'Andrew on hand for the next assault', *The Guardian*, 13 Mar. 1999. The small crowd for the 1999 cup final was also attributable to the high price of the tickets.

51. IT millionaire and new club chairman, David Thompson, quoted in Robert Kitson and Michael Prestage, 'Ragged Richmond axe 34 staff', *The Guardian*, 12 Mar. 1999.

52. Ian Malin, 'Levett cuts his losses, as club left in turmoil', *The Guardian*, 5 Mar. 1999.

53. Ironically, Newcastle was the only EFDR club to vote against Richmond's extinction. For a sympathetic profile of a beleaguered post-Levett Richmond, see Donald McRae, 'Dreading the blow of a final whistle', *The Guardian*, 19 May 1999. For sympathetic profiles of Walkinshaw, see Robert Kitson, 'Glos boss puts his foot down', *The Guardian*, 30 June 1999, and Stuart Barnes, 'Saint or Sinner', *Rugby World*, Aug. 1999, pp.53–6. Walkinshaw's ruthlessness was matched by Northampton's Keith Barwell's view that 'There are only so many rations in the lifeboat, and the weak have to be pushed out so the majority can survive,' quoted in Tim Glover, 'Clarke leads fight to survive', *The Independent*, 10 May 1999.

54. In fact reverberations continued throughout the summer of 1998, exposing deep divisions within EFDR. At the same time promotion runners-up Rotherham sought a High Court ruling as to whether the Mayfair Agreement gave the EFDR legal authority to reduce the size of Premiership One. London Irish's success lay in their ability to retain their identity, their generous sponsor (Guinness), and their ultra-loyal following among the capital's first and second or third generation Irish middle-class, while in a single season transforming the first XV into a successful team of southern hemisphere veterans and the odd home-grown star. Unable to redevelop a ground deep in the heart of suburban Sunbury, the new club hoped to fill the Stoop's 8,000 capacity, and crucially its 23 corporate hospitality boxes (unlike London Scottish with its gates of fewer than 1,500). The name London Irish remained, with no concession to the new 'partners' other than shirts that incorporated all three clubs' colours; Ian Malin, 'Dry eyes at Sunbury', *The Guardian*, 27 Apr. 1999. A fresh emphasis on corporate branding meant that a few weeks later Wasps became 'London Wasps'.

55. EFDR also decided, in February 1999, that the following season there would be no

automatic relegation, but a playoff with the Premiership Two champions – just in case a big club had a bad season. It was becoming ever more difficult to break into the ultra-elite league.

56. Ian Malin, 'Worcester in move to trade places' and 'Worcester's Sale scheme blocked', *The Guardian*, 18 June and 3 July 1999. For details re Worcester RFC, see the club's very glossy 1999 publicity material, *Gold 'n' Blues*.

57. For a profile of Welsh rugby on the eve of the national team's spectacular resurgence under New Zealander Graham Henry, and the critical financial state of both the clubs and the WRU in the autumn of 1998, see Owen Slot, 'Wales hit crisis point as World Cup looms', *Sunday Telegraph*, 4 Oct. 1998.

58. Paul Rees, 'Pugh's exit hits Welsh peace plan', *The Guardian*, 5 May 1999.

59. Stephen Baines, IB chief executive, quoted in Robert Armstrong, 'England get fine and warning as International Board gets tough', *The Guardian*, 4 Feb. 1998.

60. Armstrong, 'England get fine and warning'. The Tri-nations pointed to the weakness of the England Sevens squad (only one full international) at the 1998 Commonwealth Games as further evidence that English clubs were too powerful and not placing the interest of the world game first: the likes of Dallaglio were unavailable because the Mayfair Agreement gave the RFU only eight weekends on which players were obliged to put international duty ahead of their club commitments.

61. 'We [Premier League] want more representation for the professional game. We have to do away with this complicated [FA] committee structure which delays the decision making process.' Quoted in Vivek Chaundhary, 'Analysis: who runs football?', *The Guardian*, 15 Jan. 1999. In July 1999 the Restrictive Practices Court unexpectedly ruled against the OFT and in favour of the Premier League, BSkyB and the BBC.

62. The RFU accepted almost immediately the fait accompli of the EFDR reneging on the Mayfair Agreement by still looking to a future British League.

63. Stephen Jones, 'Stuff this turkey at birth', *Sunday Times*, 13 Dec. 1998.

64. A major review commissioned by the SRU reported in July 1999 that the presence of the two superclubs in Wales's Premier Division from 1999–2000 could only be a stopgap measure, and that a British League was the best means of raising the standard of Scottish rugby.

65. Even Leicester, with its 11,000 members and 15,000 spectators, was open to a charge of commercial naiveté: investors, put off by safeguards to members' interests, bought only one-third of the 4.4 million shares available when the club was publicly floated. The £1.8 million raised was barely enough to cover the 1998–99 wage bill; Robert Armstrong, 'First time beano for Deano', *The Guardian*, 24 Apr. 1999. For a portrait of Leicester as a 'family club' *and* an ultra-professional set-up, see Michael Tanner, *Tigers: A Season in Stripes* (Edinburgh: Mainstream, 1998).

66. If England repeated the experience of 1998 and sent an under-strength party to Australia then they would again face disciplinary action from the IB, but the host nation now had the power to call off the tour – a right demanded by the irate Tri-nations at the October 1998 meeting of the IB. The same meeting rejected the view increasingly voiced by EFDR that the British Lions should tour every six instead of every four years, by setting out a 15-year programme and defying the English clubs to challenge it. In a global arena the latter were as yet powerless to do so. See Robert Armstrong, 'Board act to stamp out weak tours', *The Guardian*, 3 Oct. 1998.

67. Data derived from Deloite and Touche 1999 report on Premier League finances, quoted in Julia Finch, 'Chelsea fuel wage explosion', *The Guardian*, 30 Apr. 1999; Pete

Nichols (ed.), *Radio 5 Live Sports Yearbook* (London: Oddball Publishing, 1999);
'What the major players can expect to earn this year', *The Guardian*, 4 Jan. 1999.

68. Ian Malin, 'Players may go to law over rugby wage cap', *The Guardian*, 27 Mar. 1999.

69. Similarly, in Wales Cardiff was insistent that the free market should determine players' long-term loyalties – and the long-term survival of Premier Division rivals. Thus, Cardiff courted Neil Jenkins, Wales's talisman at fly-half and a one-club man at Pontypridd. A further squeeze on ordinary club players was that the WRU facilitated the recruitment of southern hemisphere talent if through descent they could qualify for Wales. This – very successful – ploy by all the Celtic nations prompted accusations of poaching, and a major row between Australia and Wales in July 1999.

70. Francis Bacon's press briefing reported in Robert Armstrong, 'England stir fresh money row with Celts', *The Guardian*, 24 Feb. 1999. One of Bacon's first acts was to sack 191 personnel, suggesting 'Headquarters' was grossly over-staffed.

71. Not that EFDR always gave the impression of being an efficient monolith, witness the split between the clubs with the most current internationals and the others over the idea of playing Premiership One fixtures before and during the World Cup, but with less points for match wins in September and October – a further example of how clubs could rewrite their own league rules without any outside monitoring.

72. Clive Woodward quoted in Robert Kitson, 'Wary Clive plays it safe', *The Guardian*, 5 Oct. 1998.

73. Les Cusworth (Leicester), Ian McGeechan (Northampton) and Geoff Cooke (Bedford) interviewed in 'The Millennium File', *Rugby World*, Feb. 1998, pp.80–83, and Tony Hallett (Richmond), Dean Ryan (Bristol), and Chris Wright (Wasps), interviewed by Kitson and Malin in 'Sweating on the future of the game they love'.

74. For a guide to constructing a championship-winning side in the new financial climate, see Michael Lynagh, 'Building a club to storm the country', *The Times*, 1 May 1999.

75. For profiles of Worcester and Newbury as 'rugby's new middle classes', see Malin, *Mud, Blood and Money*, pp.121–5, and for Worcester's own publicity see *Gold 'n' Blues*.

76. Orrell's 1996 experiment of playing at Wigan's Central Park was a disaster, and, despite talk of a similar experiment in Leeds, simply confirmed that, where the two codes are actually played side by side, it would take time for a century of mutual loathing to abate.

77. Chairman Bryan Richardson did not reply to the author's inquiry in July 1998 as to why Coventry City FC's board did not consider a takeover. In 1998–99 Wright found that neither a cup-winning Wasps (average gate 6,500) nor a poorly performing QPR could attract large crowds to Loftus Road, and admitted he would sell if a wealthier investor made him an offer. See Kitson and Malin, 'Sweating on the future of the game'.

78. Polley rightly anticipates a 'professional elite of rugby union players emerging, with economic and cultural advantages over footballers and rugby league players to allow them more quickly to exploit their situations'. See Polley, *Moving the Goalposts*, p.125. Jeremy Guscott is clearly the crucial figure in bridging the old and the new, and a role model for ambitious and talented young professionals. Will Carling's rapid fall from grace in the autumn of 1998, and the drug allegations against Dallaglio ten months later, confirmed that top rugby players risk media exposure and disgrace just like any other high profile entertainers.

79. The RFU could claim vindication of their decision when Sky Sports won the 1998 BAFTA award for 'best live-event coverage' of over 50 club games and England's home internationals in the 1997–98 season, plus the Lions in South Africa the previous summer. RFU dependence upon BSkyB is not solely financial: every week the England coach receives from Sky Sports a video-based 'players index' that logs 16 different match actions by each player in every Premiership One fixture and in all internationals worldwide.

80. Rugby league clubs had over a century to learn cost-effectiveness. Each of the 12 Super League sides earned in 1998 from BSkyB £900,000, while the First and Second Division Clubs' Association received a total of £27 million compensation for the decision not to continue the very occasional broadcast of their games after 1999. See Andy Wilson, 'Clubs agree to Sky deal', *The Guardian*, 16 July 1998. 'We've learnt nothing from rugby league. It has taken league 100 years to get into such a mess while it has taken us literally 100 days.' Orrell's chairman, Ron Pimblett to Cliff Brittle, 1997 'Listening to the Game' tour.

81. Nor is such complacency and dependence on television income unique to the RFU, witness the absurd arrangements for acquiring World Cup tickets: on the one hand, professionalism run rampant in that seats could be secured via licensed hospitality packages, and on the other, *plus ça change* amateurism, in that the remainder were largely available through clubs affiliated to the Five Nations. Any tickets not sold via official channels, notwithstanding those available via unlicensed hospitality packages (a polite phrase for upmarket ticket touts), would belatedly be made available to the general public.

82. RFU growing concern over the absence of an alternative to BSkyB was fuelled by Channel Five dropping a sponsor-less *Rugby Express* after one season; and a MORI poll suggesting that the retention rate of teenage players dropped by 12 per cent 1996–98, and that not being able to watch the game on terrestrial TV was a key factor. See 'Sidelines – Express in the Slow Lane, *Rugby World*, Dec. 1998, pp.14–15.

83. Robert Armstrong and Chris Barrie, 'Sky set to lose TV rugby rights', *The Guardian*, 24 Jun. 1999. Murdoch saw sport, with rugby second only to football, as crucial to ensuring his companies retained a dominant position worldwide as digital television spawned a multitude of channels, including club-based channels, hence BSkyB's £575 million bid for Manchester United in September 1998, vetoed by the Monopolies and Mergers Commission in April 1999. The MMC feared that if the takeover was sanctioned the subscription to Sky Sports would rise by up to 10 per cent. Information from Nicholas Finney, ex-MMC member, at conference on football and finance, Birkbeck College, 8 July 1999.

84. For the impact of professionalism on Leicester's current British Lion three-quarter Will Greenwood, as an example of how performance was dramatically improved, see his remarks in Malin, *Blood, Mud and Money*, pp.148–51. In fact, the Barbarians' New Year fixture was restored in 1998–99, and ironically, Leicester reverted to forward-dominated play in winning the 1998–99 championship.

85. Mark Bailey, "For Neither Love Nor Money': Modern Rugby Union and the Victorian Concept of Amateurism' in Stuart Barnes and Mike Seabrook (eds.), *Nice Tries: A Collection of New Rugby Writing* (London: Victor Gollancz, 1995), pp.163–4.

Notes on Contributors

Richard Holt is Research Professor at the Centre for Sports History and Culture at De Montfort University, Leicester. His previous publications include *Sport and Society in Modern France* (1981) and *Sport and the British: A Modern History* (1989). He is currently completing a book on post-war British sport with Tony Mason and is co-writing the centenary history of the Professional Golfers Association.

Ray Physick is a PhD student at De Montfort University, Leicester, where he is researching the social and economic history of the professional golfer, c.1890–1975. His publications include several contributions to the *Encyclopaedia of British Sport* and the *Encyclopaedia of British Football*.

Martin Polley is Senior Lecturer in History at King Alfred's College, Winchester. He has published a number of articles on sports history as well as diplomacy; his books include *Moving the Goalposts: A History of Sport and Society since 1945* (1998) and *A–Z of Modern Europe, 1789–1999* (forthcoming 2000).

Dilwyn Porter is Reader in History at University College Worcester and also a Visiting Research Fellow at the Business History Unit, London School of Economics. He has made recent contributions to *Media History, The International Journal of Retail, Distribution and Consumer Research* and *The International Journal of the History of Sport*.

Adrian Smith is Senior Lecturer in Historical Studies at the University of Southampton New College. His previous publications include *The New Statesman: Portrait of a Political Weekly 1913–1931* (1996) and *Mick Mannock: Fighter Pilot* (2000).

Stephen Wagg is Senior Lecturer in the School of Sport, Exercise and Leisure at the University of Surrey, Roehampton. He has written extensively on football, as well as on comedy and childhood. He is currently preparing a book on the politics of English cricket since 1945.

Wray Vamplew is Professor of Sports History and Director of the International Centre for Sports History and Culture at De Montfort University, Leicester. He is a member of the RAE Panel for Sports-Related Subjects, and is currently working on a history of the relationship between sport and alcohol.

Index

191

Index

Index

Index

197